# CHRISTIANS AND POLITICS BEYOND THE CULTURE WARS

# CHRISTIANS AND POLITICS BEYOND THE CULTURE WARS

## an agenda for engagement

EDITED BY

DAVID P. GUSHEE

A Division of Baker Book House Co
Grand Rapids, Michigan 49516

Published by Baker Books
a division of Baker Book House Company
P.O. Box 6287, Grand Rapids, MI 49516-6287

Printed in the United States of America

**Library of Congress Cataloging-in-Publication Data**

Christians and politics beyond the culture wars : an agenda for engagement /
edited by David P. Gushee.
    p.      cm.
Papers presented at a conference held in Oct. 1998 at Union University.
Includes bibliographical references (p.  ) and index.
ISBN 0-8010-2231-2 (pbk.)
    1. Christianity and politics—Congresses. 2. Christianity and politics—United
States—Congresses. I. Gushee, David P., 1962–    .
BR115.P7 C38163      2000
261.7'0973—dc21                                                    00-021685

For information about academic books, resources for Christian leaders, and all new releases
available from Baker Book House, visit our web site:
                    http://www.bakerbooks.com

To my children—Holly, David, Marie, and Madeleine

# CONTENTS

# PREFACE

The editor of a book about Christian engagement in politics published in the year 2000 is tempted to make grand millennial claims. A title or subtitle along the lines of "Christian Politics for the New Millennium" is almost too tasty to resist. It might even sell a few extra books. But a review of books on this subject written over the last thirty years or so is highly instructive. Whether written in 1970, 1980, 1990, or 2000, books about Christian engagement with politics tend to have a remarkably short shelf life. Their claims that this or that (often long-forgotten) moment, election, or issue is pivotal for the future of the nation generally reveal themselves as painfully overstated. Issues, politicians, and pivotal moments come and go. This is of the essence of politics, a this-worldly enterprise that must nonetheless remain a matter of abiding significance for Christians.

Thus I do not claim that this work will settle all (or even any) outstanding questions about the issues that arise at the intersection of Christian faith and American public life. Instead, it is intended as a contribution tied to this particular moment in American political history and to Christian engagement with politics in this moment. In broader view, it is part of an ongoing conversation about the role of Christian faith in American public life. That conversation has gone on since the earliest days of our nation's history and will continue—we dare to hope—as long as there is a United States of America. It will be interesting to see how the snapshot we offer here, in this Y2K Christianity and politics volume, will look even five years from now.

What are the characteristics of the particular moment in which this book has been constructed? The papers gathered here were originally prepared for delivery at an October 1998 conference on Christian faith and public policy hosted by Union University. At the national level, American politics was at the time fixated on the impeachment process related to President Clinton's involvement with Monica Lewinsky and his subsequent cover-up. The president had at the time admitted his affair and lying about it, but the dramatic events of impeachment and then acquittal were still to come.

As this preface is being written, the last months of the Clinton presidency are upon us, as is the 2000 campaign. George W. Bush enjoys a lead in the nomination battle on the Republican side—though John McCain poses a threat—while Democrats Al Gore and Bill Bradley circle each other warily in their increasingly fierce *mano a mano* contest. The economy is hugely prosperous, Hillary Clinton is running for New York's open Senate seat, and government budget forecasters are predicting enormous surpluses for fifteen years or more.

I am aware that these political realities may change at any time. That, ironically, is part of the significance of this volume. For while each of the chapters here is written against the backdrop of the politics of the moment, the issues they consider are not ephemeral—nor is the task of thoughtful Christian engagement with politics.

This work is divided into two parts, the first focusing on a variety of historical, theological, and theoretical issues related to Christian engagement with politics, the second considering several current moral and political problems.

Several key themes emerge in part 1. Michael Cromartie sets the stage for the rest of the work in chapter 1 by offering a recent history of evangelical political engagement. He traces the story back to the turn of the twentieth century, considering arguments first about *whether* evangelicals should be involved in political and social action and later the ideological and political divisions that emerged among those who *were* thus engaged. He reminds us that Christian political engagement in the twentieth century was contested in terms of nearly every dimension one can think of: whether it should happen, what issues should be addressed, what tone should be employed, what strategies should be pursued, how Christians should relate to political parties, ideologies, and leaders, and how political engagement fits in with other aspects of the church's mission. There is no evidence that the contesting of such issues is going to abate anytime soon.

Indeed, this contest is carried forward in the rest of the book. The essays by Harry L. Poe and me (chapters 7 and 2, respectively) in different ways both argue for a throttling back of Christian political efforts in the context of our losing battle for the soul of the American people and the values of American culture—thus the title, *Christians and Politics beyond the Culture Wars*. At the turn of the millennium Christians engage a culture that is far more pluralistic, and at key points hostile to Christianity, than could have been imagined one hundred years ago. The issue to be considered is the place of political strategies for Christians in the context of this kind of culture—not *whether* political engagement is a part of our "arsenal" of kingdom efforts, but *what kind* of politics we should engage in and what level of priority our politics should receive vis-à-vis other dimensions of the church's world-transforming mission.

In such a bewildering cultural moment it is helpful to turn to traditions of Christian political thought that can shed some light on the path ahead. The essays by James Skillen (chapter 3) and John Carr (chapter 4) offer insights from the Reformed and Roman Catholic traditions. Both traditions contain highly disciplined patterns of thought rooted in solid biblical exposition, theological reflection, and centuries of actual experience in relation to government. The inclusion of a Roman Catholic voice intentionally signals and affirms another key aspect of our particular moment: the increasingly intense intra- and interreligious conversation and coalition-building on issues of common moral concern. Older sectarian differences are these days giving way to a practical recognition among Christians and others of our need for each other and for the insights of each other's traditions. Ronald Sider (chapter 6) seeks to synthesize many of the key principles emerging from Scripture and these various traditions, principles that can govern Christian political engagement and perhaps can serve as a basis for a common Christian political vision.

The chapters by Jean Bethke Elshtain (chapter 5) and Paul Freston (chapter 8) offer fascinating glimpses into the religion-and-politics question in particularly American and particularly third world perspectives. Elshtain considers the insights of Alexis de Tocqueville and others to argue for the great value of an "institutionally robust" American Christianity for the vitality of American civil society. She reminds us of the genius of our founders, nearly all of whom recognized the essential role of religion in upholding and transmitting the social mores without which our experiment in democracy would be deeply impoverished if not impossible. While many of the rest of the chapters focus on what Christians need and want from American politics, hers reminds us of what American politics needs from Christians. Freston's chapter takes us on a remarkable and hugely informative tour of evangelical Christian political engagement in several third world nations. Readers may draw many particular lessons from this chapter, but I was struck by the devastating "rookie mistakes" made by newly empowered evangelical Christian politicians in the third world—authoritarianism, corruption, triumphalism, cronyism, ecclesial self-interestedness—and am convinced that many American evangelicals would make the same kinds of mistakes if the structure of our nation's political system did not hinder us from doing so.

Part 2 of the work considers issues of education, family, poverty, refugees, church and state, abortion, and peacemaking. Taken as a whole, these chapters remind us that we do not live in any kind of utopia and certainly do not yet experience the kingdom in its fullness. Far from it. We live in a nation with a troubled educational system (chapter 9), collapsing families (chapter 10), established secularism (chapter 13), millions of poor people (chapter 11), and millions of abortions and unwanted pregnancies (chapter 14). Internationally, we are the most powerful nation on earth but are not nearly as hospitable to the refugee (chapter 12) or as skilled in our peacemaking (chapter 15) as we could be. Many other issues could have been addressed. But these seven are particularly important to consider because each is seemingly intractable and yet on each Christians can make a difference.

My thanks are extended to each contributor. They bear witness to the growing quality of Christian political reflection. Their presence on the Union University campus was deeply appreciated, and it is good to see their work reach a broader audience through this volume. All of them, of course, are widely published in their own right, and it is a privilege to be their editor for this volume.

I also would like to thank Cindy Meredith of Union University for her invaluable assistance in preparing this manuscript for publication.

# PART I

# CHRISTIAN POLITICAL ENGAGEMENT

*Retrospect and Prospect*

# I

# THE EVANGELICAL KALEIDOSCOPE

*A Survey of Recent Evangelical Political Engagement*

## MICHAEL L. CROMARTIE

In a cover story in the influential literary magazine *The Atlantic Monthly,* liberal theologian Harvey Cox shares his observations on having been a visiting lecturer at Pat Robertson's Regent University in Virginia. Professor Cox was surprised to find that the conservative Christians at Regent University were not monolithic in their political views. He found that while fundamentalists, evangelicals, and charismatics were often lumped together in the press, they in fact "represent distinct tendencies that are frequently at odds with one another."[1]

Harvey Cox is not unlike many observers outside of the evangelical movement who are often surprised when they discover just how diverse evangelical intellectual opinions are on political and social issues. The late historian Timothy Smith described evangelicalism as being like a large "kaleidoscope"[2] that includes not only a diversity of denominations but also Christians from the political right, left, and center. Evangelicals are by

Michael L. Cromartie (M.A., American University) is a Senior Fellow in Protestant Studies and the Director of the Evangelical Studies Project at the Ethics and Public Policy Center.

no means monolithic in their political views. While they have largely maintained an alliance with political conservatism, they do have moderate and liberal contingents that have had an important influence.

There are still many political pundits and observers who believe Christian conservatives represent a mass movement of cultural dinosaurs with religious views akin to what the journalist H. L. Mencken called a "childish theology" for "halfwits," "yokels," the "anthropoid rabble," or the "gaping primates of the upland valleys."[3] The *Washington Post,* while not as colorful as Mencken, more recently said they were "poor, uneducated, and easy to command."[4]

Well, to the bewilderment of many, the poor, uneducated, and easy to command gaping primates from the upland valleys are still very much with us, and they have become a very large voting bloc.[5] Mencken said this in 1924: "Heave an egg out a Pullman train window and you will hit a Fundamentalist almost anywhere in the United States today."[6] If Mencken were living today, he might put a different spin on it: "Heave an egg out a window anywhere on Capitol Hill today and you will likely hit an evangelical political activist." And while that activist is most likely to be politically conservative, he or she may be just as mad at the Republican party as at the Democratic party.[7]

There was a time when political involvement by evangelicals was seen as a worldly, or even sinful, activity. Now, political celibacy, if you will, is considered a dereliction of Christian responsibility. The change has resulted in American evangelicals creating a lively debate among themselves about social justice and the nature and extent of political involvement. My task in this essay will be to give an overview as to how these issues have developed and to highlight the diversity that resides within the conservative Protestant community on political and social questions. I will conclude with a few personal concerns about the public rhetoric of conservative Christians involved in the public arena.

For several years in the twentieth century, from roughly 1925 until the end of World War II, a large sector of conservative Protestant social thought was influenced by a pessimistic form of dispensational eschatology and a pietistic individualism that looked with disdain on efforts to improve social conditions and political structures. Conservative Christians believed that the process of secularization was simply irreversible, and this pessimism was reinforced by their premillennial theology.[8] But this had not always been the case.

Historian Winthrop Hudson wrote that as late as 1900 "few would have disputed the contention that the United States was a Protestant nation, so self-evident was the fact that its life and its culture had been shaped by three centuries of Protestant witness and influence."[9] Up until the Scopes trial in Dayton, Tennessee, in 1925 (where a biology teacher, John

Scopes, challenged a Tennessee law that banned the teaching of Dar-
winism), conservative Protestants had aggressively addressed almost
every major social and political question in American public life. At the
Scopes trial, William Jennings Bryan defended the Tennessee law and
won, but his performance against ACLU lawyer Clarence Darrow was so
embarrassing that it was ridiculed in the press and he—and fundamentalism—lost in the court of public opinion. As George Marsden has
pointed out, this made it increasingly difficult to take conservative Protestantism seriously, and it caused evangelical and fundamentalist Christians to retreat from society and politics. Marsden points out that

> within the span of one generation, between the 1890s and the 1930s, the
> extraordinary influence of evangelicalism in the public sphere of American
> culture collapsed. Not only did the cultural opinion makers desert evan-
> gelicalism, even many leaders of major Protestant denominations attempted
> to tone down the offenses to modern sensibilities of a Bible filled with mir-
> acles and a gospel that proclaimed human salvation from eternal damna-
> tion only through Christ's atoning work on the cross.[10]

The preeminence of conservative Protestant Christianity was challenged from all sides. Theological liberalism was growing in influence as
it attempted to accommodate modern scientific thought. The fundamentalist-modernist controversy led to radically different understandings of salvation, evangelism, and the authority of Scripture. These dis-
putes led to opposing views concerning the proper Christian response
to social action and political activity. As theological modernists began to
interpret the entire Christian message in terms of its social implications,
evangelicals and fundamentalists began to grow suspicious of social
activism. The fundamentalist leader William Bell Riley labeled liberal
understandings of the gospel a form of "social service Christianity."[11]

In theological circles there was a controversial debate surrounding the
redefinition of the Christian message led by leading liberal Protestant
thinker Walter Rauschenbusch. His influential book *A Theology for the
Social Gospel* (1917) challenged conservative Protestants for having an
individualistic approach to personal salvation that neglected social reform.
His concept of the social gospel was an attempt to enlarge and intensify
the older message of salvation. He said: "The individualistic gospel has
taught us to see the sinfulness of every human heart and has inspired us
with faith in the willingness and power of God to save every human soul
that comes to him. But it has not given us an adequate understanding of
the sinfulness of the social order and its share in the sins of all individuals within it."[12] Rauschenbusch redefined sin to mean anything that was
selfish in its essence,[13] and he argued that the essential concerns of the

gospel "lie on earth, within the social relations of the life that now is."[14] His strong critique of capitalism led him to believe that to renounce it in favor of socialism was to "step out of the Kingdom of Evil into the Kingdom of God."[15] His influence was far-reaching and his redefinition of the Christian meaning of salvation can still be seen in many of our mainline Protestant churches today.

The reaction of conservative Protestants to the influence of Rauschenbusch might be summed up by looking at two very different responses to the challenges of the social gospel. In an essay in the book *The Fundamentals* (1914), Princeton theologian Charles Erdman expressed his deep concern about the social gospel movement. He emphatically stated that it was dangerous to identify the Christian message with any political or economic system, being especially concerned with the attempts by many to identify socialism with Christianity. He cautioned that socialism could become a substitute religion that was hostile to Christianity, and warned that while "the strength of socialism consists largely in its protest against existing social wrongs to which the Church is likewise opposed," these wrongs can be "finally righted only by the universal rule of Christ."[16] Erdman was critical of socialism, but he was emphatic that the Christian gospel should never be ultimately linked to any political or economic system.

But another outspoken fundamentalist critic was less nuanced. A more strident response to the growing social gospel movement was constructed by the Presbyterian fundamentalist Carl McIntire in his book *The Rise of the Tyrant: Controlled Economy vs. Private Enterprise* (1945). McIntire argued that capitalism, free enterprise, and individual liberty were "grounded in the moral nature of God." The Bible, he said, "teaches private enterprise and the capitalistic system, not as a by-product or as some sideline, but as the very foundation of society itself in which men are to live and render an account of themselves to God."[17] McIntire even insisted that many, if not most, of the major figures of biblical history, including Abraham and Moses, had been capitalists.

We should note here, then, the diversity of evangelical and fundamentalist opinions concerning politics and economics, and their varied responses to the challenge of the social gospel movement. It is clear, says Craig Gay of Regent College (in Canada), that "somewhere in between Charles Erdman and Carl McIntire a theological line had been crossed. While Erdman had maintained the impossibility of identifying Christ with any particular political-economic system, McIntire had all but equated modern industrial capitalism with the will of God in the world."[18] This form of theological reductionism is ironic because it collapses economic and political concerns to a this-worldly level in an attempt to make the Christian faith relevant to the economic debate—the very charge leveled at leaders of the social gospel movement in its promotion of socialism.

In the early 1940s there were a number of more moderate fundamentalists who began to question the militant and confrontational style of fundamentalists like McIntire. In 1947 Carl Henry published *The Uneasy Conscience of Modern Fundamentalism*. Its impact was significant. It was a clarion call for evangelicals to confront the modern world with a Christian apologetic that was intellectually respectable and socially responsible. According to Henry, the theological separatism of fundamentalism had led to a separation from cultural and social responsibilities, and to a mistaken disengagement from the important issues of the day. This backlash reaction to the social gospel movement had created an almost complete avoidance of social programs and politics for fear of resembling the social gospel. This divorce between Christian proclamation and Christian compassion, Henry argued, was an abandonment of the clear mandates given by Scripture and church history. Henry condemned this tragic development in the strongest terms. He noted that "against Protestant fundamentalism the non-evangelicals level the charge that it has no social program calling for a practical attack on acknowledged world evils. . . . On this evaluation, fundamentalism is the modern priest and Levite, bypassing suffering humanity."[19] He agreed that although capitalism was a superior economic system, there was no excuse for neglecting the clear biblical teachings regarding the duty and obligations of evangelicals toward social and political problems. He pointed out that "fundamentalism in revolting against the Social Gospel seemed also to revolt against the Christian social imperative."[20] Further, he complained that fundamentalism "is a stranger, in its predominant spirit, to the vigorous social interest of its ideological forbears. Modern Fundamentalism does not explicitly sketch the social implications of its message for the non-Christian world; it does not challenge the injustices of the totalitarianisms, the secularisms of modern education, the evils of racial hatred, the wrongs of current labor-management relations, the inadequate bases of international dealings. It has ceased to challenge Caesar and Rome. . . . The apostolic Gospel stands divorced from a passion to right the world. The Christian social imperative is today in the hands of those who understand it in sub-Christian terms."[21]

Parenthetically, on the fortieth anniversary of the founding of Fuller Seminary and the fortieth anniversary of the publication of his *Uneasy Conscience*, Henry gave a lecture at Fuller where he remarked that, looking back on his book, two things surprised him: how little he had said, and how boldly he had said it! But in that same lecture he admitted that one of the weaknesses of his book was that he "failed to focus sharply on the indispensable role of government in preserving justice in a fallen society. Essential as regenerative forces are to transform the human will, civil government remains nonetheless a necessary instrument to constrain human beings—whatever their religious predilections—to act justly, whether they desire to do so or not."[22]

Making connections between faith and politics was quite novel and, at the time, controversial among evangelicals. Neoevangelical leaders like Henry, E. J. Carnell, and Harold Ockenga had their persistent critics among separatist fundamentalists on their right. But critics began to form on their left as well. The many issues and questions raised by the political activism and social turbulence of the 1960s caused a further reexamination of evangelicalism's often cozy link to the establishment status quo.

A new, younger generation of "radical evangelicals" felt that Henry and the neoevangelicals had not gone far enough in their critique of capitalism and social injustices in American society. They accused the mainstream evangelical establishment of being "ideologically captive" to a "decadent American capitalist culture."[23]

The founding of the magazines *The Other Side* in 1965 and *Post American* in 1971 (renamed *Sojourners* in 1974) created forums for an ongoing critique of what the editors saw as a "truncated gospel" that neglected to attend to the abundance of biblical passages exhorting believers to seek justice for the oppressed and care for the poor. Jim Wallis, the editor of the radical evangelical magazine *Sojourners,* said in the first issue of that publication (when it was called *Post American*):

> We have become disillusioned, alienated, and angered by an American system that we regard as oppressive; a society whose values are corrupt and destructive. We have unmasked the American Dream by exposing the American Nightmare. . . . Our ethical revolt against systemic injustice, militarism, and the imperialism of a "power elite" is accompanied by our protest of a technocratic society and a materialistic profit-culture where human values are out of place. . . . Money is a measure of status and worth in a society of created needs and garbage heaps of wasted abundance in the midst of want; a society in which things are valued more than people. . . . The ulcerating drive for air-conditioned affluence has not given satisfaction or fulfillment, but has instead produced lives that are hollow, plastic, and superficial; characterized by economic surplus and spiritual starvation.[24]

Such pleas for compassion to the poor and the oppressed corrected a prior imbalance in evangelicalism's history. However, some of these calls for social justice on behalf of the poor and oppressed almost always looked for statist solutions to these intractable problems without any consideration that the state might make matters worse. I want to emphasize that within the evangelical academic community (and the larger religious community as well) there are some strong differences regarding just what social justice is, and to what extent and degree the state is ultimately responsible for maintaining it.

The early impact of the radical evangelicals was significant, as these magazines further pricked evangelicals' "uneasy conscience" on issues such as racism, sexism, and poverty. And their writers and editors played a vital role in the drafting of a landmark statement in 1973.

"Some day," wrote a reporter for the *Chicago Sun-Times* in December 1973, "American church historians may write that the most significant church-related event of 1973 took place last week at the YMCA Hotel on South Wabash."[25] It was there that some fifty evangelical leaders gathered for a two-day workshop that culminated in what became known as the "Chicago Declaration of Evangelical Social Concern." This significant statement on evangelical social responsibility was drafted and signed by evangelicals as diverse as Carl Henry, Frank Gaebelein, Vernon Grounds, Bernard Ramm, and younger self-styled "radical evangelicals" such as Ronald Sider (who had convened the meeting) and Jim Wallis. "We affirm," the statement said, "that God lays total claim upon the lives of his people. We cannot, therefore, separate our lives in Christ from the situation in which God has placed us in the United States and the world. We confess that we have not acknowledged the complete claims of God on our lives."[26] The statement further emphasized that God requires his people to be loving, just, and abounding in mercy, but "we have not demonstrated the love of God to those suffering social abuses" and "have not proclaimed or demonstrated his justice to an unjust American society."[27] The declaration acknowledged the need for repentance from the racism, sexism, materialism, and militarism that afflicted the attitudes of the church and the nation.

The "Chicago Declaration" set the tone and themes for much that was to be written about evangelical social concern. It (along with the publication of *Rich Christians in an Age of Hunger* by Ronald Sider[28]) put on the table for vigorous discussion the need for evangelicals to take just as seriously the admonitions in the books of Amos and Jeremiah as they do concerns for fulfilling the Great Commission. It also helped initiate a lively interaction of different Christian approaches to social ethics, and sparked a healthy debate among, for instance, Anabaptist social ethicists and Reformed political philosophers.[29] And with the growth of the "health and wealth" gospel preached by many televangelists, radical evangelical writers sharpened dull consciences by calling their fellow Christians to simpler lifestyles, wiser stewardship, and compassion for the victims of poverty, racism, and other forms of social and political injustice. While statistically small in numbers, the influence of the radical evangelicals has been far greater than they are often given credit for. Their books and magazines provided an invaluable service in keeping evangelical leaders aware of the need to be compassionate toward the poor and the hungry.

This new interest in finding the proper balance between evangelism and social responsibility had effects in the larger worldwide evangelical movement as well. The International Congress on World Evangelization, held in Lausanne, Switzerland, in July 1974, produced the significant document "The Lausanne Covenant." *Time* magazine called the Lausanne Congress "possibly the widest ranging meeting of Christians ever held."[30] Over 2,700 participants attended, representing 150 nations and the whole spectrum of evangelical Protestant denominations. It was an international forum on world evangelization, but the issue of Christian social and political involvement was vigorously debated. The drafting of section 5 on "Christian Social Responsibility" sparked vigorous discussion among the international leaders at the Congress. The debate continued all day and night and was not settled until the early morning hours. The final version affirmed that "although reconciliation with man is not reconciliation with God, nor is social action evangelism, nor is political liberation salvation, nevertheless we affirm that evangelism and socio-political involvement are both part of our Christian duty. For both are necessary expressions of our doctrines of God and man, our love of neighbor and our obedience to Jesus Christ."[31]

But the biggest growth of evangelical political activity did not come as a result of reading passionate proclamations from statements drawn up at international congresses or declarations from Chicago. Edward Dobson, a former assistant to the Reverend Jerry Falwell, has said that Reverend Falwell realized how much potential there was to influence the political process in 1976, when, on his national television program, he criticized then presidential candidate Jimmy Carter for giving an interview to *Playboy* magazine. Much to his surprise, Falwell soon received a call from Carter's special assistant Jody Powell, asking that he refrain from making such comments. "Back off," Powell said to him. Falwell was startled to find that what he said had caused Carter such concern. He came to perceive this incident as his "initial baptism" into the world of politics.[32]

Many members of the evangelical right had similar triggering experiences, on a personal level, that left them obliged to become politically involved, something they had not been inclined to do previously, largely for theological reasons. Their emergence on the political scene in the late 1970s caught many journalists and public policy experts by surprise.

A standard sociological theory used to explain new social movements is what has been called the status defense theory. This view was developed in the 1950s by theorists such as Daniel Bell, Seymour Martin Lipset, and Richard Hofstadter to explain the rise of McCarthyism and radical right groups like the John Birch Society. It argues that it is the loss of economic and social status that causes many people on the right to become involved in social and political movements. Daniel Bell made this observation in 1962: "What the right as a whole fears is the erosion of its own social position, the collapse of its power, the increasing incomprehensibility of a world—now overwhelmingly technical and complex—that has changed so drastically within a lifetime."[33] Similarly, social scientist Joseph Gusfield has argued in his study of the American temperance movement that moral reform campaigns were the result of a cultural group engaging in political action as a clear form of "status defense." He argued that a moral reform movement can acquire public affirmation of its own status if it can persuade the state to affirm and endorse its values.[34]

Over against status defense theories for the origins of social movements, I want to argue that it was their conservative Protestant subculture, rather than their social and economic status, that many in the new Christian right felt to be in danger and caused them to organize politically.

The original priority of religiously conservative leaders was not so much to persuade others of their views as it was to sensitize other evangelicals, fundamentalists, and charismatics to become involved in public issues that concerned them. It was not an easy task, since many had been taught for decades that such activity was irrelevant and, in fact, unbiblical.

But increasing pressures from a number of factors caused these evangelical leaders to feel, as sociologist Steve Bruce says in *The Rise and Fall of the New Christian Right,* that "they were not getting their due and their due could be got[ten] if they organized to claim it."[35] And organize they did. Their effective use of television and direct mail, the declining membership of liberal denominations, and the increasing numbers within evangelical churches and denominations gave them confidence and combined to make political involvement appear to be a promising and worthwhile endeavor.

What stirred them most was a sense that various Supreme Court decisions were giving increasing power to the opponents of traditional Christian values. They became engaged in what Harvard professor Nathan Glazer has called a "defensive offensive"[36] against what they saw as an aggressive imposition of secular views on American society, including their own private communities of faith.

In due course, religious conservatives began to be accused of "imposing their views" and "forcing their beliefs" on the larger community. But was this really the case? Gary Bauer, former director of the Family Research Council, has made this observation: "Our opponents will often picture us attempting to exert our values on the rest of society. I think the people we work with see . . . what has happened in the last ten years as being more of a reaction of self *defense* than as an effort to violate American pluralism."[37] Nathan Glazer made a similar observation over fifteen years ago:

> Abortion was not a national issue until the Supreme Court, in 1973, set national standards for state laws. It did *not* become an issue because evangelicals and fundamentalists wanted to *strengthen* prohibitions against abortion, but because liberals wanted to abolish them. . . . Pornography in the 1980's did *not* become an issue because evangelicals and fundamentalists wanted to *ban* D. H. Lawrence, James Joyce, or even Henry Miller, but because in the 1960's and 1970's under-the-table pornography moved to the top of the newsstands. Prayer in the schools did *not* become an issue because evangelicals and fundamentalists wanted to introduce new prayers or sectarian prayers—but because the Supreme Court ruled against *all* prayers. Freedom for religious schools became an issue *not* because of any legal effort to expand their scope—but because the IRS and various state authorities tried to impose restrictions on them that private schools had not faced before.[38]

This imposition of a liberal ethos by what many social scientists have called the "new class elites" (made up of newspaper journalists, television producers and commentators, and the "knowledge class" from the universities) is what aroused many previously apolitical and socially indifferent evangelicals to action. While many evangelicals have always found plenty to complain about in the wider culture, the rapid changes in American society during the 1960s and 1970s sent shock waves through their community. Sociologist Steve Bruce has pointed out that "conservative Protestants of the 1950s were offended by girls smoking in public." But by the late 1960s, "girls were to be seen on newsfilm dancing naked at open-air rock concerts."[39] In short, the era of Eisenhower's America was far different than the America of the 1960s and 1970s.[40]

Moreover, Bruce points out that "by the 1950s and the 1960s . . . the Supreme Court and the Congress were imposing cosmopolitan values on the South. . . . In 1976, there were 77 federal regulatory bodies and 50 of them had been created since 1960. . . . At the same time the distinctiveness of regional culture had been threatened by the growth of national corporations, population movements caused by four wars, and the gradual concentration of the media. Putting it simply, the 'Bible Belt' was penetrated by cosmopolitan culture."[41] Or as political analyst Kevin Phillips has put it, "The world of Manhattan, Harvard, and Beverly Hills was being exported to Calhoun County, Alabama, and Calhoun County did not like it."[42]

This concern about the secularized views of reality being promoted by cosmopolitan and elite culture was not the concern of religious conservatives only. The late social democrat Christopher Lasch made the following observation in the last book he wrote, *The Revolt of the Elites and the Betrayal of Democracy:*

> Our public life is thoroughly secularized. The separation of church and state, nowadays interpreted as prohibiting any public recognition of religion at all, is more deeply entrenched in America than anywhere else. . . . Among elites [religion] is held in low esteem—something useful for weddings and funerals but otherwise dispensable. A skeptic, iconoclastic state of mind is one of the distinguishing characteristics of the knowledge classes. Their commitment to the culture of criticism is understood to rule out religious commitments. The elites' attitude to religion ranges from indifference to active hostility.[43]

If Lasch's description is correct, then it would help explain why so many conservative Christians feel that they live in an environment totally devoid of, and actively hostile toward, their most fundamental Christian beliefs. As a result, they have formed and developed what William Kristol calls a "parallel culture"[44] that has been totally foreign to those who attend cocktail parties in New York and Washington. But that foreign parallel culture has become an avid curiosity for our national media, as evidenced by frequent cover stories in our major newsmagazines.[45] In a cover story in an October 1998 issue of *The New Republic,* Peter Beinart argues that those involved in the politics of the Christian right feel they are living in an alien environment that is radically different from the world in which they grew up. They feel that the "cultural liberalization" and "cultural pluralism" of American society are undermining their schools and their homes.[46] "Time and again," writes Beinart, "Christian conservatives . . . described the same epiphany: the day they realized that the schools were not teaching with them but against them. Sometimes the epiphany was not about the schools but about some other arm of the government, . . . but the epiphany always involved an undermining of the home."[47]

It is hard to predict what the future holds for Christian conservatives involved in politics. It is clear that at some point, barring a revival and a reformation of the culture, they will have to face the fact that America will not soon become, as Irving Kristol has observed, "a 21st century version of 'Our Town.'"[48] In the meantime, they will need to develop what sociologist John Murray Cuddihy calls an "esthetic for the interim" that encourages patience and "puts a ban on all ostentation and triumphalism *for the time being*"[49] while working for what are often very lofty goals that seem unreachable. As I have suggested, Christian conservatives' involvement in politics has been reactive and not proactive. They see themselves as defendants, and not the aggressors, in the culture war. As a result, they become involved in politics for cultural reasons without seeking theological justification for that involvement until after the fact.

One gets the impression that the underlying public philosophy for such activism is constantly evolving and is still being framed from election to election and issue by issue.

Arguably, this may explain why the political rhetoric of some religious conservatives reminds one of the careless and reactive language of fundamentalists from earlier in this century. Unfortunately, some evangelical leaders have at times been divisive and have used unnecessarily strident language toward their opponents—and even toward some of their natural allies. Taking positions for righteousness in the public arena without being seen as self-righteous requires spiritual discipline and enormous effort. But it is an effort that must be made. Richard Mouw reminds us why: "The antithesis between godliness and ungodliness is very real; but it is discernible not only in the larger patterns of culture, but also in the inner battlegrounds of our own souls. How we speak and act faithfully in the larger public realm while working out our own salvation with the requisite fear and trembling—this challenge is of supreme importance for evangelicals as we think about the proper rhythms of the life of discipleship."[50]

Some leaders have expressed similar concerns about the public witness of Christian activists. Ralph Reed, in his book *Active Faith,* dwells at length on the need for Christian activists to remember that they will be judged by God "not according to political victories . . . but by whether our words and our deeds reflect His love."[51] Whether the advice of Reed will be heeded remains to be seen, but clearly, all Christian activists should display more epistemological humility, public modesty, and charity toward even their most virulent opponents. Mark Noll challenges evangelical activists to never forget "that they are not God."[52] He further warns: "A Christian politics that forgets the cross, a Christian politics that neglects the realities of redemption, a Christian politics that assumes a godlike stance toward the world, is a Christian politics that has abandoned Christ."[53]

It is strange that twentieth-century evangelical Christians would have ever needed to be convinced that they have a duty to be concerned about social problems. Their spiritual forebears always had been. The compassion and fervor of William Wilberforce and Lord Shaftesbury animated the campaigns against the slave trade and child labor in England. Such faith in action was the basis of many reform initiatives of the early nineteenth century.[54] According to American religious historian Grant Wacker, "Evangelicals, seeking to be the moral custodians of the culture, have always known how to play political hardball when the prayer meeting let out."[55]

The intermingling of Christian faith with social and political concerns was always a part of our country's history. In his classic book *Democracy in America,* Alexis de Tocqueville said: "In the Middle Ages the clergy spoke of nothing but a future state. . . . But the American preachers are constantly referring to the earth, and it is only with great difficulty that they can divert their attention from it."[56] The claim that the faith of American Christians should always be only an intensely private affair between the individual and God would have been surprising news to such diverse persons as John Winthrop, Jonathan Edwards, Abraham Lincoln, the abolitionists of slavery, fifteen generations of the black church, civil rights leaders, and antiwar activists.

For this reason, religious values have always been a part of the American public debate. The argument should never have been whether evangelicals ought to be involved in social and political issues. Rather, the issue should be: On what matters should we be most concerned, and what are the most prudent ways to express such convictions? It is our duty to be concerned citizens, to indeed strive, as Richard John Neuhaus has said, "to build a world in which the strong are just, and power is tempered by mercy, in which the weak are nurtured and the marginal embraced, and those at the entrance gates and those at the exit gates of life are protected both by law and love."[57]

Working for social and political change often requires the patience of Job because politics is, as Max Weber once said, "a strong and slow boring of hard boards."[58] Many evangelicals have learned that politics frequently requires prudent and principled compromise and that it is the art of the possible and not the reign of the saints. Some have come to realize that even the most prudent Christian has to sometime make choices in the political realm between "relative goods" and "lesser evils." And some have even learned through the hard knocks of battles fought, victories won, and disappointments beyond measure that politics is, because of the effects of the fall, "the method of finding proximate solutions to insoluble problems," as Reinhold Niebuhr put it.[59]

Evangelicals of every perspective no longer need convincing that political and social concern is an important part of Christian discipleship. It is a settled issue that "the least of these" among us must be treated with both charity *and* justice. The debates center now on prudential questions regarding which policies are in fact the most effective in meeting the normative standards of justice. Many times these are empirical questions that need honest and rigorous exploration.

While the problems of the modern world will not soon disappear, it is the existence of those very problems that will keep evangelicals engaged in social and political activism. But it is worth noting that just as conservative Christians have gathered momentum to have influence in the political arena, many of the seemingly intractable problems facing American society are cultural in nature and not easily affected by political solutions.

Evangelicals and fundamentalists are quick to remind us that this age, like all ages, is "standing in the need of prayer." The ravages brought on our culture by social and political injustice, by the corroding effects of secularization, and by the debilitating ethos of rampant moral relativism are sobering. But, as evangelicals have always insisted, miracles still happen and grace has always been amazing. And for the love of Christ and the duties of charity entailed by following him, they will continue to be engaged, not only with the world, but also, because of their own diversity, with each other.

# 2

# FROM DESPAIR TO MISSION

## Toward a Christian Public Theology
for the New Millennium

### DAVID P. GUSHEE

Every scholar is also a person—a person shaped by experiences of various types that have fundamentally shaped his or her presuppositions, perspectives, and identity. Sometimes we reveal a bit of this as we lecture and write. Usually we do not. But as I address the issue of Christian faith as it relates to public life, I must take you back to the Gushee family dinner table in Vienna, Virginia, a bedroom community about fifteen miles from our nation's capital.

At that dinner table, holding forth most nights was David E. Gushee, my father, an environmental and energy policy analyst for the Congressional Research Service of the Library of Congress. As the four Gushee kids crowded around the kitchen table fought over who would get the roast beef first, Dad would usually begin to tell us about some scintillating policy issue such as chlorofluorocarbon emissions, atmosphere alteration, fleet gas mileage standards, and the comparative benefits of solar, coal, wind, oil, natural gas, and nuclear power. As you can imagine, I was

David P. Gushee (Ph.D., Union Theological Seminary, New York) is Graves Professor of Moral Philosophy and Senior Fellow of the Center for Christian Leadership at Union University.

much more interested at the time in girls and sports. But over time, as both girls and sports did me wrong, I began to tune in much more carefully to what my father was saying.

My father was excited about the convergence of what he liked to categorize as *facts, values,* and *interests* in the policy-making process of our American democracy. As a policy analyst, Dad's job was to provide to the Congress the most impartial and objective rendering of the facts relevant to an environmental or energy issue that he could offer. He made it clear how very difficult this was to do because policy "facts" are extremely difficult to disentangle from the values (normative beliefs about right and wrong) and interests (outcomes that would most benefit the power or pocketbook of each actor in a policy dispute) that also are an inevitable part of the policy-making process. He argued that each policy decision involves vigorous debate about both facts and values, all of which occurs in the context of self-interest and power quite ruthlessly wielded to determine desired outcomes.

He knew there were times that the government, especially under the impact of self-interested lobbying and power politics, made bad policies. But after many years of close involvement in the process, he evinced an abiding faith both in the structure of our governmental system and in the goodwill of those who serve the nation in government either as civil servants or elected officials. He communicated to me that government service in this country is an honorable and even exciting profession, and that we ought to count ourselves uniquely fortunate to live in the United States of America.

## Christian Faith and Politics: The Current Moment

These are some of the presuppositions and commitments that I bring to a discussion of how to conceive of the relationship between Christian faith and politics at the dawn of a new millennium. I think it is fair to say that, at the current moment, they are not widely shared either in the culture or in the church. Let us briefly focus our attention on the church's reading of our current political/cultural moment as well as on the shape of contemporary Christian political activism.

Christian individuals, denominations, parachurch organizations, and lobbying groups are more involved in political action and engagement as of 2000 than at any time in living memory. If one considers the landscape of American religious life, and segments off just the indisputably Christian slice of it, one can roughly categorize what we find into the following major groups: Roman Catholics, Eastern Orthodox, white evangelical Protestants, mainline Protestants, and the historic black churches. Of those groups, only the Eastern Orthodox are not currently notable for vigorous political engagement in the American context. All of the other groups are deeply involved—through a variety of structures—in political analysis, advocacy, and action. Of course, that involvement is a messy mix of the profound and the superficial, of culture and Scripture, and of political ideologies of all types. In no sense does the contemporary church speak with one voice when it speaks to policymakers; the sound is more like a cacophony of voices. But the church *is* speaking. The sound cannot be missed.

Yet even as Christians make themselves heard as they perhaps never have before, it is hard to miss the growing note of despair in all those voices. The historic black churches despair over the existence of a seemingly permanent black underclass, over the disastrous conditions of our inner cities, over the continuing problem of racism in America, and over what appears to be near-absolute governmental indifference to these problems at every level.

The Roman Catholic Church despairs over the entrenchment of what Pope John Paul II has decried as "a culture of death"[1] in Western societies, especially the assaults on life that go by the names of abortion and euthanasia—but also including other assaults on human dignity such as hunger and genocide. Yet it is abortion that continues to be the Catholic church's capstone issue. Well entrenched and seemingly irreversible in itself, abortion on demand now appears to have laid the intellectual and legal foundation for assisted suicide on demand, which has its foot in the door in Oregon and is being advocated in several other states.

The mainline churches despair over many of the concerns already mentioned but also over such issues as the environment, the plight of the working poor, the continuing threat of nuclear war and the possible use of other weapons of mass destruction, justice for women and for homosexuals, and what mainliners perceive as the ominous rise of Christian fundamentalism on the American right.

Meanwhile on the right, the mood of conservative evangelicals turned especially bitter in the wake of the acquittal of President Clinton despite what this slice of the spectrum saw as overwhelming evidence of his guilt for a wide range of moral and legal offenses. As Clinton the man transmuted into Clinton the symbol of Christian cultural despair, Christian conservatives began to float the despairing idea that American culture really is (perhaps irretrievably) neopagan and that Christians are much more a "moral minority" than we ever knew.[2] Politically active conservative evangelicals, in general, hate Clinton, have nothing but contempt for the Democratic party, think most Republican leaders are spineless jellyfish, and consider the New York/Washington/Los Angeles media the redoubt of the enemy.

Now consider the contrast of this "Christian politics of despair" with the values I learned around the dinner table. The faith in the sturdiness and reliability of our governing institutions is by now taking severe hits from every side. The confidence that values will be significantly considered in American policy-making is in radical decline. The idea that government is an honorable profession and that we can generally count on the character and goodwill of our leaders is nearly dead. The concept that life in these United States is perhaps the best available anywhere on this globe is no longer such a sure thing. And perhaps most frightening is the growing fear among Christians that the people of this nation, with whom we share our lives, no longer share our values. Many Christians feel like strangers in a strange land. We do not know what lies ahead or what to do next.

I want to suggest that God has not left Christians without a witness as we wrestle with the issues of our time. We need not flounder around in despair as people without hope, without understanding, and without resources for crafting a public theology for our current moment.

Indeed, the Word of God, especially as we find it in the New Testament, has rarely been more directly relevant to the situation of the Western church than it is today. For seventeen centuries—ever since the conversion of Constantine and the Christianization of the Roman Empire and the Western world—Western Christians have read the witness of the New Testament concerning the Christian's relation to politics through the lens of the marriage of church and state. During most of that history, in most Western nations, that marriage was an official one. In the United States, Christianity was legally disestablished with the First Amendment. But despite this constitutional arrangement, the eighteenth-century observer Alexis de Tocqueville had it right when he said of our nation, "Christianity reigns without obstacles, by universal consent."[3] The fact is that it is really only in the last thirty years or so that the essentials of the Christian worldview and way of life have begun to be *culturally* disestablished in this nation. That cultural disestablishment has proceeded unevenly—it is much further along in, say, San Francisco than it is in my adopted hometown of Jackson, Tennessee. But the evidence of this turn of events is unmistakable in every corner of our land. It is a fact: Christianity has been dethroned as the worldview that dominates American public life.

There are a number of reasons for this dethronement. One can trace it in broad historical perspective to the slow but seemingly inevitable impact of the Enlightenment and the secularization of the Western world. Those of an economic turn of mind would be sure to remind us of the culturally and intellectually corrosive impact of laissez-faire capitalism—and then of its even more materialistic rival, communism—on the historic beliefs and practices of every society touched by these ways of organizing economic life. Or one could note the significance of developments in the twentieth century (two world wars, Holocaust and genocide, weapons of mass destruction) and the way in which they have disenchanted and disillusioned Western civilization and thus contributed to the decline of the Christian worldview. Nowadays it would be relevant to speak of postmodernism in at least some of its forms as an advanced and accelerated expression of intellectual trends unleashed during the Enlightenment era. Another factor particularly relevant in the American setting has been the influx of immigrants from every land, carrying their religious beliefs along with them, and the increasingly undeniable philosophical and religious fragmentation created by these and other trends. Then, of course, one would have to name the explicit rejection of Christian beliefs and norms during the social revolution of the 1960s, a revolution that essentially has become an entrenched feature of American life, and to which we will return later.

These realities make it all the more important to recover a biblical theology of the state and of public and political engagement. As we take a fresh look at the Scriptures, we discover that the situation facing the U.S. church today is much more similar to that of the New Testament churches than at any time in the last 1,700 years. Perhaps because that is the case, we can gain fresh insights for our current situation through a careful appropriation of God's self-revelation in the New Testament.

**Recovering a Biblical Theology of Public Life**

Jesus and his followers in the early church lived in contexts in which despair about public life was eminently possible—indeed, eminently *reasonable.* The Promised Land, *Eretz Israel,* was under the occupation of pagan Rome. Roman soldiers patrolled the streets, Roman money served as the official currency, Roman governors enforced imperial dictates with ruthless severity, Roman immorality was openly practiced, and Roman gods were freely worshiped. Jewish religious leaders struggled with the immense challenge of maintaining the integrity of Torah observance while trying to prevent a turn either toward assimilation into Roman ways or toward a fruitless and bloody revolution—the latter of which, in fact, finally did occur in the mid-60s, with catastrophic results. The whole situation was a far cry from the original public theocracy envisaged in the earliest Old Testament documents or the Yahwistic monarchy later attempted under David and his successors. Nor was there any longer an opportunity for the exercise of the prophetic vocation, which had been so important in calling Israel again and again to covenant fidelity in public life and in private. Imperial regimes are not much interested in pro-phetic voices, as John the Baptist discovered (Matt. 14:1–12).

As did Jesus of Nazareth, who entered this tense political scene as he began his public ministry. There can be no doubt that Jesus' message carried political implications: the proclamation of the eschatological king-dom (or reign) of God over all of life (Matt. 4:17), inaugurated in his own person and mission, is more and other than political. Yet it is, irreducibly, political in that it has to do with the ordering of every dimension of human affairs and the submission of those affairs to the God who is rightfully sovereign over them. Jesus meant to initiate the most fundamental change imaginable in human life, beginning with the household of Israel but finally extending into all the world—that is, the reclaiming of creation and all of its creatures by the one through whom creation was established (John 1; Col. 1), in order that the will of God would ultimately "be done on earth as it is in heaven" (Matt. 6:10, NIV).[4]

Yet in relation to the political authorities of his own context Jesus was wary and distant. According to Matthew, Jesus' early years were spent as a fugitive from Herod the Great, who murdered a whole community's baby boys in the vain quest to do him in (Matt. 2:13–18). Herod's son Herod Antipas, who reigned over Galilee during Jesus' ministry, had John the Baptist murdered as a reprisal for John's prophetic critique of his immoral behavior, but was apparently fascinated with Jesus. He tried to see Jesus (Luke 9:9), but Jesus did not give him that opportunity until forced to meet the king during his trial, at which time he did not bother to answer Herod's inquiries—much to Herod's murderous frustration (Luke 23:8–9; cf. Luke 13:32). Jesus' approach to Pontius Pilate was sim-ilar—Jesus neither sought him out nor responded very cooperatively when before him for trial. The one who earlier had told his followers to "give to Caesar what is Caesar's, and to God what is God's" (Matt. 22:21, NIV) simply did not bother to give any political authority much attention.

The clue as to why this is the case can be discovered in Jesus' answer when under questioning by Pilate. When asked about the issue of his king-ship, Jesus affirmed his kingly identity but immediately declared it to be different in kind than earthly kingships: "My kingdom is not of this world. If it were, my servants would have fought to keep me from being deliv-ered to the Jews. . . . But as it is, my kingdom is not from here" (John 18:36, author's translation). Any Jesus-centered Christian public theology must come to terms with the paradox embedded in these words: Jesus is a king, and his kingship has everything to do with the affairs of this world, but his kingship is not exercised in the manner of this world. He will reign, and his reign must not be construed as a gnosticized "spiritual" reality that cares nothing for concrete human living. But he will not govern con-crete human living in the way that earthly kings exercise their rule.

Then Jesus went to the cross. There he died, punished as a common criminal under the sentence imposed by Rome with the collaboration of some of his own people's most influential religiopolitical leaders. Under normal circumstances, claims to kingship do not long outlive those who make them. But Jesus was raised from the dead. A gracious power far transcending that which any human sovereign can exercise was unleashed in the tomb now emptied of its inhabitant. Having appeared a few times to his followers, Jesus soon ascended to his Father in heaven—but not before commissioning these men and women with the following mandate: "All authority in heaven and on earth has been given to me. Therefore go and make disciples of all nations, baptizing them in the name of the Father and of the Son and of the Holy Spirit, and teaching them to obey everything I have commanded you" (Matt. 28:18–20a, NIV). Now that God had confirmed Jesus' identity, ratified his ministry, released resurrection power on his body, and transferred *all* earthly authority into his keeping, Jesus responded not by initiating an apostolic lobbying campaign or running for office but instead by commissioning his followers to engage in an international evangelistic and disciple-making ministry and then leaving them to their task.

Following the anointing of the disciples by the Holy Spirit at Pentecost, that is precisely what his followers began to do. The exciting story of their efforts is recounted in narrative and letter throughout the rest of the New Testament. Notice that in relation to government and its leaders the basic pattern is the same. Commissioned by the greatest authority in the universe to make disciples of all nations, the early church went about doing so with relentless energy and determination. As they undertook the task of "turning the world upside down" (Acts 17:6, NRSV), they did not do so through courtesy calls in congressional offices. That was neither their strategy nor their agenda. They dealt respectfully with government officials when those officials required an audience. On every such occasion they offered clear and courageous testimony to their faith in Jesus Christ, carrying out their evangelistic mandate even under trial (cf. Acts 26:28). They were surely grateful for times in which government officials prevented mob violence against them (cf. Acts 19:35–41), and they counseled Christians to submit to government authority and treat its leaders with respect (Rom. 13:1–7; 1 Pet. 2:13–17)—a norm that applied except when the authorities commanded their disobedience to Christ as Lord, especially any silencing of their proclamation about him (Acts 5:28–29). Yet even when they could not obey unjust government leaders and decrees, they sought above all to do nothing that could compromise their witness to Jesus and his Way (cf. 1 Pet. 3:13–17). They were prepared to die—and never to kill—as a part of what bearing witness to Christ meant in their context. And death at the hands of government is precisely what most of the earliest Christians experienced, what tens of thousands of Christians suffered in the first three centuries of the church's history, and what some face even today.

Let me sum up the biblical claims that I am making in the following way. The message of the kingdom of God has profound this-worldly consequences. No area of human life is unaffected, for God means to exercise sovereignty on earth as he does in heaven. The time of human rebellion is to come to an end; Jesus inaugurates the reclaiming of what Abraham Kuyper called "every square inch" of creation, every human institution, every government, every human life. And yet the consistent evidence of both the teachings and the practice of the early church is that this world-retaking strategy was focused primarily on evangelism and disciple making, that is, on leading people to accept Christ's claims on them and then to reconfigure every aspect of their lives in accordance with his explicit teachings about how this life is to be lived. Given an almost infinite range of options for making world transformation happen, God in Christ chose salvation by grace, the establishment of a disciplined covenant community we call the church, and the mobilization of this band for relentless evangelistic and disciple-making efforts. While both Jesus and the early church recognized the existence, task, and authority of human governments, neither paid much attention to them. Governments were viewed as God-ordained and useful in accomplishing a limited range of tasks within their particular sphere of responsibility under God's sovereignty, such as securing public order and justice, deterring evil, and ensuring the unhindered proclamation of the Gospel.[5] On the other hand, when governments transgress the boundaries of their God-given authority or otherwise violate their mandate, the church's commission to bear witness to Christ changes not a bit. In such times, the task for Christians may become more difficult and the level of suffering may increase even to the point of martyrdom, but the work of the church goes on. There is a place for Christian engagement with government and its policies, as I will argue later and others argue in this volume, yet it is a matter of putting first things first to note that Jesus established evangelism and disciple making as the primary means for the accomplishment of the church's task until he returns. In undertaking its evangelistic and discipling work, the church has every reason for hope and none for despair.

**Despair: How We Got Here**

How, then, did we get to the place in American Christianity in which despair is the dominant mood? I contend that this has happened as the natural and perhaps inevitable outcome of our losing sight of New Testament principles related to the church's public mission—an outcome that has come about in the context of the radical social changes that have occurred in American life over the last four decades.

I would narrate this turn of events in the following way. The social revolution that occurred (or should we say culminated?) in the U.S. in the 1960s and early 1970s came as a terrific shock to Christians, and rightly so. On nearly every front, Christian convictions faced direct challenge. Consider the transformation of cultural values and practices in such areas as sexual morality, the nature and permanence of marriage, the shape of family life, the values communicated by the media, birth control and abortion, patriotism and national pride, drugs and alcohol, the role of women, religious pluralism, and so much more. It is possible to trace tremendous changes in every one of these areas, especially in the period running from 1960 to 1975.

Meanwhile, during this same period, a religiously inspired social and political revolution in the area of race was also occurring. The civil rights movement, which brought such tremendous and important social changes to our nation, was headquartered in the black churches and led by black church leaders, most notably Dr. Martin Luther King Jr. Tragically and inexcusably, many in the white churches resisted this movement, and some of them articulated this resistance in spurious religious terms. But the movement succeeded in accomplishing at least its basic legal goals, and the model of religiously based political action was (once again) established as a significant factor in American public and ecclesial life. In the aftermath of the civil rights movement, many on the religious and political left allowed the proclamation of the gospel message to be left behind and permanently established political and social activism as their primary public mission.

These events were not ignored by conservative evangelicals. As they witnessed the church losing its cultural hegemony and moral decay of all types setting in, conservative Christians either drifted or rushed headlong in the direction of addressing these problems through a political strategy. Beginning in the mid-1970s, first the Moral Majority and then the entire movement that came to be called the Christian right made political organization, rhetoric, and engagement with the purpose of defending their values and promoting them in society their *modus operandi*. But here is where the problem lies. Both as a practical matter and as a matter of New Testament principle, it turns out to have been a serious mistake to attempt to address the dethronement of Christian values in American culture primarily through a political strategy.

At the practical level, political organizing involves the mobilization of a grassroots base of people sharing similar values and interests with the purpose of enhancing the political clout of that group in order that its will might come to prevail. There can be no denying that groups such as the Moral Majority and later the Christian Coalition, Focus on the Family, the Family Research Council, the Eagle Forum, and so on have organized their grassroots base effectively. The problem is that this base is a definite minority of the population—and, as Hal Poe argues in this volume (see chapter 7), a shrinking minority at that. There are enough conservative evangelical Christians at this time to be culturally visible and to be a burr in the saddle of the Republican party, but not enough to control the Republican party and certainly not enough to set the political course of the nation. There simply are not enough people with this particular value set to accomplish the movement's goals, and these days it is possible to watch the political power of this group ebb before our eyes. Those numbers—and that power—are destined to decline more and more unless the leaders of conservative evangelical churches prove to be more effective than they currently are at the church's fundamental mission: evangelism and disciple making.

The Catholic church has run into the same problem in a somewhat different form. In terms of sheer numbers of church members, the Catholic voice would appear to be one to which politicians must seriously attend. To a certain extent, they do. However, politicians know that not every Catholic, by any means, shares the values articulated by the church's leaders. In other words, non-Catholic cultural norms have crept into the Catholic church at the grassroots level in such a way that the church's leaders cannot accurately claim to speak for a voting bloc united by shared Catholic values. Thus any power that might be generated by Catholic political activism is seriously diminished. The regularly unsuccessful effort of the church's hierarchy to discipline or restrain pro-choice Catholic politicians such as Mario Cuomo or Ted Kennedy is a good indicator of the problems the church faces here.

Jesus knew what he was doing when he exercised his cosmic authority to establish the church and instituted evangelism and disciple making as the primary Christian strategy for transforming the world. Let us think about why he did so for a moment. When a human being accepts the claims of Christ upon her life, she begins a lifetime of relating personally and intimately to the loving Savior of the world and the Lord of human life. When she is taught to obey everything Christ commanded his disciples, she similarly embarks on a lifetime of retraining her habit patterns, lifestyle, and moral values in every corner of her life in order that she might be found obedient and faithful. When she then joins with dozens, hundreds, or thousands of others in communities of faith committed to introducing others to Jesus and his Way, the multiplied impact of these lives begins to permeate the institutions, communities, and nations in which they are found. A particular set of values is communicated effortlessly and naturally, and both through its inherent appeal and also through its wide distribution those values begin to have significant cultural impact. Inevitably, a dimension of this cultural impact will be political, for politics—at least in a democratic society, but not only there— is an expression of culture and its regnant values. There is no values-free politics, for values are embedded in legislation and most aspects of the activities of government. Thus from communities widely characterized by Christian values political leaders will emerge who share and represent those values and bring them to bear on the values dimension of policy-making as best they are able. If they fail to do so faithfully and effectively, they will be replaced by others who *will* do better.

My argument is that Jesus chose to establish evangelism and disciple making as the fundamental task of the church—even as its fundamental political (or, if you will, prepolitical) task—because he knew how human character and human societies operate. Changed people bring changed values into public life. If there are enough changed people, they have the potential to make a transformative impact on culture and on its political expression, though one should never expect public life to reflect Christian values perfectly or without remainder, and it is very important not to forget the structural dimension of sin in public life. The corollary of this analysis is that it will, perhaps paradoxically, prove impossible for Christians to have a significant impact on politics through a disproportionate focus on politics itself. Political change will emerge primarily from the bottom up rather than the top down: through a renewed zeal for Jesus Christ, the reform and creation of faith communities of theological and moral integrity and discipline, genuine and unforced evangelistic passion, and thoughtful training in the way of Jesus for those who become his followers.

## Elements of a Renewed Christian Public Witness

So, where do we go from here? How should we think about the church's public witness? Let me close this chapter with elements of a public theology and practice for the early days of the new millennium.

### Evangelism and Mission

In obedience to Christ's command, the church must recover its vision of America as a mission field and its energy for the evangelization of our nation. I have already addressed this issue at length and thus will simply reaffirm this claim here and argue that it is now and always the first priority for a Christian public theology. There is no branch, denomination, or wing of the church that is exempt from the Great Commission or that does not need desperately to invest itself in the (re)evangelization of American culture—beginning with the unregenerate who might happen to occupy a seat in our pews. We must learn anew to test all other aspects of our public witness against their impact on evangelism. *If possible, we will do nothing to drive even a single unbeliever away from Jesus Christ—* this commitment should be written on our hearts. Evangelism is ultimate; everything else, penultimate.

### Disciple Making

Our loss of the culture—and I am claiming that we have in fact lost the culture—reveals the sad state of disciple making in our churches. Given church membership statistics and public opinion polls concerning belief in God and the experience of being "born again," we ought to have far more cultural impact and thus political influence than we actually now do. The reason for the gap is that we have done much better in filling our pews than in discipling those who occupy those seats. We have not successfully taught them to "obey everything I have commanded you," to use the Great Commission's language once again. There are many reasons for this, including theological errors, misplaced priorities, ecclesial structures and traditions, lack of ministerial courage, and the overall accommodation of the churches to an increasingly pagan culture. But the plain fact of the matter is that Jesus' world-transformation strategy simply does not work if believers, so-called, are not also made into obedient disciples of his Way (cf. Matt. 7:21–23). When that does not occur, churchgoers never acquire—or never fully acquire—Christ's values and practices. Thus they cannot bring those values into public life at any level, including politics. They are also most unlikely to be involved actively in reproducing themselves in any setting (home, school, work, community, church) through their own evangelism and disciple-making efforts.

### The Church as Countercommunity[6]

It has always been the case that the church constitutes its own *polis*— its own political community. We are a people, and everything about our way of life as a people publicly communicates something about our understanding and practice of the Way of Jesus. In times when the church has been a minority struggling to keep a foothold in a hostile culture, the only public witness available to us often has been this one—our shared ecclesial experience. Whether or not the president or the Speaker of the House or the justices on the Supreme Court listen to us, the church always speaks through its corporate way of life and at this level cannot be silenced. Now more than at any time in recent American history, the church in this country needs to recover an understanding of the centrality of the witness that comes from just being who we are.

Christians believe that Jesus knew how to live this human life better than anyone who ever lived. We believe—and he taught—that if we live as he said and did, we will experience an abundant and joyful life beyond what most people can imagine possible (John 10:10). And as we do this together, in congregations, we will be noticed. When we are racially inclusive without having to be told to be, abstain from sex outside of marriage, stay married for life and are glad to do so, relate respectfully to each other as male and female, do not resort to abortion as a form of birth control, support those in crisis pregnancies, care for our aged with respect, honor, and concrete help, feed the hungry and house the homeless and empower the poor, communicate in loving truthfulness, and offer grace to the broken and despairing and abandoned, we offer a radiant public witness that carries political implications and creates political opportunities. As the free church tradition and its current advocates have long argued, "Let the church be the church." This may be the source of our greatest influence—only if, though, the church is characterized by obedient and joyful following of the Way of Jesus Christ.

### Public Engagement for the Common Good

Certainly one aspect of the church's public witness must continue to be public engagement, including politics. But much hinges on the manner, tone, and shape of that engagement. I want to conclude by proposing that the whole church, including especially my Southern Baptist and evangelical brothers and sisters, needs to consider the witness offered by Catholic social teaching and social practice as one aspect of a way forward.

It has been most interesting to watch the evolution of the Catholic public witness. For centuries the Catholic church exercised cultural and even political hegemony over Western European nations. During the medieval period, Catholic leaders grew accustomed to directing the course of political events. Indeed, they became habituated to significant political power, sometimes with spiritually and morally disastrous consequences.

As the Catholic church lost hegemony over Europe—through the Protestant Reformation, the Enlightenment, and many other historical developments—it struggled for a long time with, one might say, keeping the frustration out of its public voice. There was the same sense of aggrievement concerning privileges lost that one now hears from voices on the Christian right. But by the twentieth century the Catholic church had found a new tone. It would continue to express concern for public affairs, for the governance of nations and the international community. But it would do so by offering thoughtful and constructive public reflection with an eye to the common human good under the sovereignty of God the Creator. It would also do so by offering itself sacrificially in service to those in need. The name of one important Catholic encyclical, *Mater et Magistra* (1961), illustrates these crucial points quite nicely. *Mater et Magistra* is a Latin phrase translated into English as "Mother and Teacher." And that is precisely the tone taken by this document as well as by the whole body of contemporary Catholic social teachings. The church is concerned not mainly about its own power or interests but in a motherly way about the whole of the world and all who dwell therein. She will serve the world with all of her love and all of her energy. Consider this representative excerpt from *Rerum Novarum* (1891), the first of the papal social encyclicals, which captures both the "mother" image and the already existing commitment to sacrificial service, in this case service to the poor:

> Acting as the mother of the rich owners of the means of production and of the poor alike and drawing upon the great fount of love which she every-where creates, the Church has founded congregations of religious and many other useful institutions which have done their work so well that there is hardly any kind of need for which help is not provided.[7]

What does a mother do? She pours herself out for the total well-being of her children. She loves, she nurtures, she cares, and she sacrifices on behalf of her children, and all of her teaching and instruction are offered in the context of this loving service. She wants always what is best for her children and never fails to act on their behalf. She leads through service and loving instruction.

This is the official Catholic approach today (as John Carr demonstrates in his essay—see chapter 4), and it is at times amazingly fruitful. Can we learn something from it? Here is the model: a church that cares for the well-being of the society regardless of whether the society is appreciative or not. A church that offers sophisticated Christian moral instruction in a respectful public language to communicate its values in a way people can understand. A church that focuses its activism not on its own narrow interests but on the well-being of the whole society, in particular those trampled on by the current cultural and political order. A church that retains its independence and refuses to align itself with any particular politician, party, or regime, so that it might serve the whole. A church that does not fight culture wars to the bitter end, does not hate, does not seek to destroy enemies, but instead lays down its life for its society, like a mother for her children.

Adherents of biblical Christianity constitute a minority of the population of late twentieth-century America. As such it is unfortunate but to be expected that our values have lost much of their sway with the American public as a whole. It is not the first time Christians have constituted a cultural minority, and it won't be the last. Indeed, it was where we began some two thousand years ago. We can choose to respond to that reality with an angry and hateful despair. Or we can reclaim the church's public mission in all of its richness: evangelism and mission, disciple making, the formation of disciplined communities of faith, sacrificial service, and loving political involvement grounded in a commitment to the common good under the sovereignty of God. I am convinced that our nation will respond to this kind of public witness with surprising openness. Let's move from despair to mission, and look forward with joyful anticipation to what God will do in our land.

# 3

# CHRISTIAN FAITH
# AND PUBLIC POLICY

## A Reformed Perspective

## JAMES W. SKILLEN

The person, work, and authority of Jesus Christ, according to the biblical testimony, relate to everyone and everything in all creation. Consequently, Jesus Christ has everything to do with government and public policy, just as he has everything to do with families and parenting, with education and teaching, with science, art, and everything else that is part of human experience. The question is not whether Christian faith is connected with public policy but how it is connected.

The history of Christianity offers a wide variety of answers to this question, and many of those answers continue to be affirmed by different streams of the Christian tradition. I have been asked to offer a Reformed perspective on this matter, which means working from the perspective of those who trace their roots back to John Calvin, and from Calvin back through Augustine to biblical revelation. Given limited space, I will not be able to outline this history. Moreover, there are many streams within the Reformed tradition, particularly with respect to politics. So I simply

James W. Skillen (Ph.D., Duke University) is the Executive Director of the Center for Public Justice and Editor of the Center's Public Justice Report.

ask you to think through what I have to say and to evaluate it carefully on biblical grounds.

## The Vine and the Branches

Let's begin with the Bible, specifically with a passage in John's Gospel that may at first glance appear to have nothing to do with politics. The apostle records Jesus' words about the vine and the branches in chapter 15. The followers of Jesus, like branches, are supposed to bear fruit as evidence of the new life they have been given in the vine, which is Jesus. One cannot be alive in the vine and not bear fruit; dead branches will be pruned away. Then follows this radical statement: "Apart from me you can do nothing" (15:5, NIV). Jesus does not say, "Apart from me you cannot get to heaven," or "Apart from me you cannot be a good evangelist." No, he says, "Apart from me you can do nothing."

This passage is not about politics in particular, but neither is it about family life or church life or evangelism in particular. It is about everything. It is all-or-nothing language about the Christian life, about discipleship. Believers either live entirely in the vine and bear Christlike fruit in all of life, or they become dead branches. Life is whole, of one piece. We who claim to believe in Jesus Christ should be bearing fruit in all areas of our lives in keeping with the life of the vine, or we should expect to be cut off. For apart from him we can do nothing. Not only was everything created in and through the Son of God, but Jesus Christ, the living vine in God's vineyard, came to redeem and restore the creation God loves so much.

This simple, metaphorical passage of Scripture opens up several primary biblical themes emphasized in the Reformed tradition. The first is God's sovereignty over all of life. Jesus is the vine and his Father is the vineyard keeper. There is no life or territory outside the vineyard, outside God's life-and-death authority. Therefore, God's judging and redeeming purposes in Christ cannot be separated from a so-called secular world that has nothing to do with Christ's kingship and the full coming of God's kingdom. Political life belongs to human beings and it thereby falls under the authority of the King of Kings. The final revelation of Christ's glory, when every knee bows before him and every tongue confesses that he is Lord (Phil. 2:10–11; 1 Cor. 15:24–28), will culminate all of God's purposes, including the political ones, on earth.

The second biblical theme emphasized in the Reformed tradition is the doctrine of creation, and particularly, I would stress, the truth that the entire creation was established and is upheld by the Son of God, the Word of God (John 1; Col. 1; Heb. 1) who became flesh in Jesus Christ.

Jesus is not a visitor to, or intruder into, a strange land. He is the world's Savior, to be sure. But first of all, the Son of God is the Word through whom all things were created and in whom all things hang together. He is the Alpha as well as the Omega of creation. This world, including human political responsibility, belonged to God through the Son even before the Son's incarnation.

The third theme concerns human responsibility. Biblically speaking, those who hold offices, such as government officials, church officials, parents, teachers, and others, bear genuine, God-given responsibility. They are never independent of God, but neither are they mere automatons. Their created nature, their calling before God, is to act and bear fruit, to steward creation as servants of God. They hold their offices with accountability before God. They bear real responsibility for one another and other creatures.

## Meeting Together

At this point I want to draw in another passage in Scripture, Hebrews 10:19–25. The author of the Letter to the Hebrews urges Christians to keep on meeting together in order to "spur one another on toward love and good deeds" (v. 24, NIV). The admonition not to give up regular meetings is a plea for more than regular Sunday church attendance. The plea is for believers to encourage one another, to build up one another in every way, so they can pursue love and good deeds. As with the John passage, there is no specified limit to the range of love and good deeds here. The admonition touches all of life and its implications hold for Christians in the civic arena. If what it takes to stir one another to excellent political good deeds is the organization of an association and the hiring of full-time staff, then that is what Christian citizens should do in order to fulfill the apostolic admonition. The emphasis here falls especially on the community character of the Christian life, namely, that Christians bear responsibility together, in community, not as isolated individuals. We cannot do what God has called us to do in Christ without doing it together. We are a *body* of believers, a *community* in Christ.

If we connect this passage with the one in John, we can see some of the important *political* themes the Reformed tradition stresses. The first of these is the importance of institutions and their responsibilities. Public policy and various aspects of political life, including elections and lobbying, can be properly understood only in the context of the political system or institution of the state as a whole. Politics is not just about single issues and moral stances on issues; it is about the exercise of governmental authority in a state for the good of the body politic as a whole.

Christians often focus on particular political issues or individual personalities without examining carefully enough the obligation of government to do justice for the well-being of the entire political community over time. Government is not simply a means to various human-chosen ends and causes. It is a God-ordained authority obligated to do justice to all citizens in order to establish and uphold a just political community.

A second theme is that Christian civic responsibility represents more than an obligation for each individual. Christians participate as citizens in a political community—the body politic—which has its own distinctive communal character and in which they need to work together in a political way to understand and exercise the common responsibility they bear in it as *Christian citizens*. This means developing a biblically oriented public philosophy with which to sort through and organize diverse public issues. It means working and arguing together to build agreement on the many dimensions of justice—distributive, retributive, and proportional justice, for example—from a Christian point of view.

Altogether these themes call for a Christian approach to public policy that rejects the dualism of sacred versus secular, of Christ against creation. I am recommending an approach, in other words, that refuses to play the game of interest-group politics, that takes a holistic approach to political life, treating it as a community of citizens under a government responsible to God, and that looks to the culmination of God's kingdom not as the dismantling or dismissal of politics but as the fulfillment of political order in Christ's justice and *shalom*.

This does not mean giving in to utopian expectations about human achievements on earth through politics. Reformed Christians emphasize the thorough penetration of sin in all aspects of created life. Human politics will continue to exhibit corruption and injustice just as every other institution—including the church—does, because we are sinners. It is not by human political effort that God's kingdom will come in its fullness. Nevertheless, the work of God in Christ by the power of the Holy Spirit is to reconcile all things to God, and "all things" include human political life. Therefore, in our politics as in every other sphere of life, we should be giving evidence of Christ at work in us, doing his good will (Phil. 2:13).

Set in this biblical context, what are the parameters of a Christian public philosophy? We have already stressed that political life is an arena of human responsibility. We bear it not as a foreign substance but as something belonging to our service to God and our neighbors. Yet it is also something corrupted by sin and facing God's judgment, as is every other arena of human responsibility. Moreover, even though Christ claims kingly authority over all the earth now, his kingdom has not yet come in its fullness. How should we behave politically in this time between Christ's first and second comings?

## Confessional and Structural Pluralism

There are at least two answers I want to offer to these questions about the parameters of Christian political responsibility between the two comings of Christ. The answers point to two important principles of pluralism that Christians should uphold as a matter of justice, as a matter of obedience to Christ.

The first answer flows from the admonition of Christ to his followers that they should be like their Father in heaven, who sends rain and sunshine on the just and unjust alike (Matt. 5:43–48). It has its roots in the parable of the wheat and the tares (Matt. 13:24–30, 36–43), which explains why God is withholding final judgment and allowing both wheat and tares to grow up together in the field of the world. The principle is that believers and unbelievers should enjoy the same common grace of God, the same rights, the same protection of the law, the same standing as citizens in the political community. And since all people live by faith—faith either in the true God or in false gods—they should all enjoy the same religious freedom. Public justice requires equal treatment of all citizens, regardless of their faith. This is an expression of the way Christ is exercising his kingship now, through patience and long-suffering, making room and giving time for all to come to repentance.

This principle, which I refer to with the shorthand phrase "confessional pluralism," requires that government respect people as religious creatures. From a Christian point of view, government is not the highest authority in human life, and thus it may not predefine the meaning of the ultimate commitments people make. Neither government nor a constitution should ever be allowed to confine religion to the private realm since that is to prejudge religion as a private matter that can be isolated from public life. Such a prejudgment presupposes that government is above religion and responsible for public life without reference to God. But religion is a whole-life matter, a public matter. Thus, public laws will be just only when they treat equally all religious communities and other communities of conviction in public as well as in private life.

The second pluralist principle I want to affirm is what might be called "structural pluralism." By this I mean the public-legal recognition that human beings exercise a variety of different responsibilities and authorities in God's creation, most of which do not fall under the direct authority of government. The limits of government, therefore, are not merely procedural, grounded in regular elections and constitutional safeguards. Government's limits are determined as well by the nongovernmental responsibilities God gives human beings.

All citizens, to be sure, share the same public laws that bind them together in a political community. This is the political *unum,* the civic unity that all citizens hold in common. However, a political constitution or government does not possess omnicompetent or totalitarian authority over people. A community of citizens under government can flourish only where justice is done to the other social institutions and human responsibilities—the *pluribus*—which belong to the same people. The political principle of structural pluralism is grounded in the very order of creation, where God holds humans directly accountable for many different kinds of tasks and gives different ones authority for those tasks. And since the creation was made by and holds together in the Word of God, it is a matter of Christian principle that we ought to be good stewards of creation's diversity, seeking recognition and protection of that diversity in public law itself.

Bringing these lines of argument together, I hope you can see that I am making a strong moral argument for a just political order; I am not giving a rationalization for Christians to accommodate themselves to relativism. Every political/legal system necessarily imposes an order that excludes alternative political systems. A truly pluralist society cannot exist side by side in the same territory with a nonpluralist order. Just as the disestablishment of the church three hundred years ago meant the partial displacement of one type of political order by another, so the establishment of true pluralism in areas such as education and welfare services, for example, will mean the partial displacement of our present political system by another. There is nothing neutral about the kind of political order I am recommending. My argument is simply that the full establishment of the principles of structural and confessional pluralism satisfies the norm of public justice in a way that no other political order can match, because it does justice to religious diversity and to the diverse range of social institutions.

There is more to a just political order than structural and confessional pluralism, of course. Many of government's tasks require uniformity across the board. There can be no pluralism when it comes to highway safety rules, for example. Everyone has to drive on either the left or the right side of the highway. Military decisions and tax codes need to be uniform. Determination of what constitutes a criminal offense will have to be the same for all citizens. Yet even in these cases we must go back to the basics of what is right and just for the creatures God has made—for the good creation order. And we must consider government's responsibility within the framework of its own structural limitations and calling to do public justice in this time of God's patience between the first and second comings of Christ.

To extend the argument for public justice further, therefore, let me conclude by looking briefly at three matters of great importance for the

United States today: racial justice, environmental justice, and the just use of force.

## Racial Justice

One of the especially reprehensible facts of American history has been the treatment of African American and Native American peoples. The beginning of the injustice to African peoples was to reduce them to the identity of property to be bought and sold for slavery, stealing from them the right to function as human beings in all areas of a structurally diverse society. Even their families were not protected. Human beings may not justly be classified according to a single all-encompassing category such as skin color or gender or income level. And they certainly may not be reduced to disposable property. To speak of black people as a group classified by skin color is to ignore and violate their full humanity.

Human beings have been created in the image of God with a diverse range of characteristics, capabilities, and social/institutional roles to play. From this standpoint, there is no such thing as an undifferentiated "group" in our society. Humans belong to different kinds of organizations, relationships, and communities. Citizenship means membership in one kind of institution; marriage means participation in another kind; employment in one industry or another means yet another kind of group membership. Black as well as white Americans function in all of these kinds of communities and institutions simultaneously. Wholesale, legalized discrimination against black or "red" people was a fundamental injustice.

The challenge today is to find ways to redress the grievances of the past 350 years of racism without continuing to treat African Americans or other minorities primarily as undifferentiated groups based on skin color. Only so much can be done by strict legal means, however, because the positive encouragement and inclusion of people in society requires a very different approach than the ending of legalized racial discrimination that excluded an entire range of people from basic civil rights because of their skin color. Public justice demands that no one be excluded from citizenship and equal civil rights, but it also demands freedom of association, freedom to marry and have children, freedom to choose schools and learn employments, and much, much more. Government can protect against arbitrary, racist exclusion; it cannot make people love one another or intermarry or attend interracial churches. The challenge, then, is so to reform basic social, educational, and economic laws as to make it increasingly possible for people of all races both to have equal opportunities and to be free to choose and develop those opportunities.

## Environmental Justice

With respect to the environment, another principle of justice comes to the fore. God has placed land, water, animals, and other nonhuman resources and creatures under human stewardship. Our human calling is to care for these creatures both for their sake and for our own. From a Christian perspective, humans are not the ultimate owners of anything. We are stewards under God's ownership. Thus, even our private properties are stewardship properties, not things that belong to us absolutely and without limits.

Since many of the earth's resources, such as air and water, should be held and protected for the common good, public laws that can distinguish between different kinds of stewardship or use are essential. This does not mean that the public—or government—should own everything. Much of what is needed by all of us can be developed by different persons, corporations, and communities. But the laws will need to specify the stewardship rights that belong to these different entities so that justice can be done to all. Zoning in a town is like this. My wife and I own our home; the city does not own it and our neighbors do not hold part ownership in it. But our home is not ours to do anything we want with; it is ours as citizens and residents of our town to use within certain parameters. We are obligated by certain stewardship rights. We may not use the property for commercial or industrial purposes; we may not sell it to anyone other than another resident; we must keep the walks shoveled when it snows; we must not let garbage accumulate on it; and so forth.

Think of stewardship rights this way. Land and water are among the earth's most precious resources. They have an identity not dependent in the first place on human ownership. They do not exist only or primarily as economic commodities whose value is defined by market exchanges. Good public law should recognize the full value of land and water and not allow them to be treated as having only the value given them by buyers and sellers who want to exploit them for one use or another. Since land and water have multiple values and characteristics, human beings should be stewards of them as servants of the Creator and of one another for the long term. It is entirely legitimate, then, for public law to qualify private ownership or exploitation by stipulating the stewardship responsibilities that go with that ownership or exploitation.

If we also keep in mind that human beings have been created by God for generational continuation, then our responsibility to one another must take into account future generations, as most parents do when raising their children. This means that we should think in terms of environmental sustainability. This is not entirely a governmental responsibility, but various public laws are necessary to define the terms of sustainable care of the environment within which individuals and corporations can live and work.

Some types of land, for example, can support high-quality production of food and fiber, while others cannot. Wetlands are extremely important for the interdependence of fish, fowl, animals, and humans and should not be drained. In a world where more and more people depend on one another and on precious land and water for their existence, it is essential that distinct types of land be preserved for their best use. The principle here is basic justice for the interdependence of all creatures. Environmental laws are, in this sense, like basic constitutional rights for human beings. The protection of individual rights may be costly and time consuming, requiring adjudication, enforcement, and limitations on legislators and employers alike. But they are essential preconditions for a just society. The same must be said for the basic resources and other creatures on which humans are dependent for life and for which God has called humans to be good stewards.

## The Just Use of Force

Finally, let us look briefly at the matter of justice in the use of force. From the beginning of the Christian era, Christians such as Augustine have faced questions about government's responsibility to use force. On the one hand, as Paul points out in Romans 13, many Old Testament principles continue in force in the Christian era. Government has the responsibility to use the power of the sword to enforce justice. On the other hand, since Christ is the Lord over all governments, and since Christians are supposed to be patient and merciful, not using force either to gain their own ends or to bring final judgment on unbelievers, it seems clear that the use of force should be limited. What, then, are those limits in this time between the two comings of Christ?

The so-called just war doctrine emerged from these concerns and considerations, beginning with Augustine and developing up to our own time. Not all Christians have agreed with the principles and conclusions of this doctrine. Many pacifists, for example, believe that Christians themselves should never use force and therefore should never hold a governmental office that might be responsible for using force. Yet even most pacifists have argued that governments should limit the use of force for purposes of justice. Two dimensions of just war teaching try to weigh in the balance of justice the decision to enter into war *(jus ad bellum)* and decisions about how to conduct warfare *(jus in bello)*. In other words, there are conditions in which it can be judged unjust to go to war just as there are conditions in which entrance into war can be justified. Likewise, there are ways to conduct war that may be considered unjust and ways that may be considered just. None of this teaching suggests that war is a good thing or that a so-called just war would be one in which no injustice is done.

This is not the place to try to trace the development of the just war doctrine or even to outline all of its dimensions. By mentioning some of the general principles, however, we can see how the norm of justice has shaped thinking about how a government should act. One principle is that only a public authority, not private individuals, may make the decision to go to war. Here we recognize the way that institutional responsibility and offices of accountability enter the picture. Government acts may not be expressions of mere vengeance taking or of self-aggrandizement. They must be deliberate attempts to do justice or to limit injustice. In that sense, the decision to enter war or to prosecute it is like police activity, which should always aim to keep the peace and uphold justice.

A second principle is that entrance into war can never be justified unless a government has first tried to reach a negotiated settlement of any dispute. Every other means of settling a dispute must have been tried and exhausted before declaring war.

A third condition for *jus ad bellum* is that the cause of going to war must be just. In other words, the reason must be defense against aggression, protection of the innocent, or maintaining peace. Initiation of aggression against a nonthreatening country can never be just. And even if every condition of justice seems to be met for a government to enter war justly, entrance will still be unjustified if there is not a strong possibility of success. If a government judges, for example, that in going to war to defend innocent citizens from the aggression of an enemy the enemy will probably win anyway, then to declare war rather than to treat for peace right away would only be to guarantee that many more people would die fighting in a losing cause. That would not be just.

A principle that holds for both going to war and conducting war is the one that says harm caused by fighting should never be greater than the offense that the government is trying to correct. It would obviously be unjust for a country to respond to an enemy that had captured one of its naval vessels at sea by launching a full-scale nuclear attack on that enemy's territory.

Closely related to this principle is the principle of proportionality in the conduct of war. Proportional justice in conducting a defensive war means that the costs of warfare should not exceed the good that is intended. The means of warfare should be consistent with the end in view.

One of the most familiar elements of just war doctrine is that in conducting war, military actions should not harm noncombatants. In this day of missiles and highly destructive bombs, the principle of noncombatant immunity from warfare may often be difficult to observe. Nevertheless, it may not be ignored or else many other principles of justice will also fall.

Finally, I should mention the principle that a country should always make clear to its enemy the terms on which it may have peace. The aims of warfare should be declared, and when they have been accomplished, or when the enemy has weighed its own disadvantage against those aims and asks for a negotiated settlement, the war should end. Total war aiming for complete destruction of another country or for unconditional surrender is unjust.

## Conclusion

The constant search for justice whereby citizens and governments measure public policies and government decisions in its light is central to a Christian approach to politics. The attempt to clarify government's responsibility for protecting everything from innocent life to religious freedom, from precious resources to the rights of families, is something that should compel Christians everywhere and at all times. The reason is that this is part of our Christian service, part of the way we acknowledge Christ our Lord and seek to love and serve him. This is one of the ways in which we act as disciples of Jesus and love both our enemies and our friends. Loving Christ above all and in all that we do means taking all of creation seriously, taking sin seriously, and taking God's judgment and redemption seriously.

# 4

# A CATHOLIC PERSPECTIVE ON CHRISTIAN FAITH AND PUBLIC LIFE

## JOHN L. CARR

I am pleased to contribute to this impressive collection of essays. The contributors comprise a remarkable roster of Christian leaders to reflect on where we go from here on Christian faith and public policy. Several of these leaders are both allies and friends of mine, promoting a growing evangelical-Catholic dialogue on the public demands of our common faith.

Among all these distinguished analysts and commentators, I believe I have two distinctions. First, I have the most pompous title. How would you like to be in charge of "Social Development and World Peace for the U.S. Catholic Bishops"? It's a great job but a lousy title—a remarkable combination of Washington arrogance and ecclesial pomp.

When I was in Chicago in 1997 for the bishops' meeting and was anxious to leave, I got on the elevator with a couple who seemed to take an interest in my obvious Bishops' Conference name tag. "You're not a bishop," the gentleman declared. I don't know if it was the way I was

John L. Carr is Secretary of the Department of Social Development and World Peace for the U.S. Catholic Bishops.

dressed or my wedding ring that gave me away. Anyway, I explained that I worked for the bishops. He looked at my badge and said, "He's in charge of social development and world peace." His wife looked at me underwhelmed and said, "Judging by the morning paper, you need to do a better job." Judging by today's paper, that's still the case.

Second, I am the only Catholic to contribute an essay. While I'm happy to be a part of this impressive effort, in some sense I am an outsider as Protestant and evangelical leaders dialogue about where your community goes from here.

Nonetheless, I am happy to offer a Catholic perspective on this timely and important topic. I emphasize that mine is *a* Catholic perspective. I serve a large and diverse church. While you may see us as a rather hierarchical and centralized ecclesial structure, the reality is more complex and diverse. A community that includes Pat Buchanan and Jerry Brown, Henry Hyde and David Bonior, Al Haig and Daniel Berrigan is not a monolith or a voting bloc to be delivered.

I learned at an early age that Catholics can act on their faith in different ways in public life. I am a product of a mixed marriage. Both my parents are Minnesota Catholics, but my dad is from Minneapolis and my mom is from St. Paul. Of more relevance today is the fact that my dad is a die-hard Democrat and my mom is a committed Republican. In my youth, they each served as precinct chair of their own party in my neighborhood.

My own family history and the challenges of the upcoming election lead us to focus today on a stark question. What does it mean to be both a believer and a citizen at this moment? As Christians, we are heirs of a long tradition of thought and action on questions of human life and human dignity, justice and peace. We are also participants in the most powerful democracy on earth, blessed with the freedom to help choose the leaders and policies that will guide our state and nation. This dual heritage of faith and citizenship takes on special meaning in these times.

My reflections will focus on four questions:

1. What is the mission and message of the Christian community in public life?
2. What is the political and social context for our efforts? What are we up against?
3. What are the assets and agenda of the Christian community? What do we bring to the public square?
4. What are some directions and dangers for the Christian community? Where do we go from here?

## Mission and Message

We have to be clear about our mission and message. What brings us together is not some political program or ideological agenda but religious faith, the Word of God. We are not the Democratic party at prayer or the religious caucus of the Republican party but leaders of communities of faith, called to "renew the earth," to be "leaven" in the larger society, to "hunger and thirst for justice."

As religious leaders, our contract is not a campaign document; our covenant is not a throwaway line in the State of the Union message. Our mission is found in the Scriptures, expressed in our worship and lived out in the experience of our congregations and charitable efforts.

The best mission statement I have ever read was not some management text or church document; the best inaugural address I've ever heard was not on the steps of the Capitol. It is found in St. Luke's Gospel (Luke 4:18–19). As he began his public life in his hometown synagogue of Nazareth, Jesus read those familiar words from Isaiah 61: "The spirit of the Lord is upon me, because he has anointed me to bring good news to the poor. He has sent me to proclaim release to the captives and recovery of sight to the blind, to let the oppressed go free" (NRSV).

What does it mean to bring "good news to the poor" when 25 percent of our preschoolers grow up poor in the richest nation on earth, in a world where thirty-five thousand children die every day from hunger and its consequences?

What does it mean to bring "release to the captives" when so many sisters and brothers are enslaved by discrimination and addiction? In a world where people of Bosnia, Kosovo, China, or Rwanda are still denied their lives or their rights because of their religion, their race, their tribe, or their gender?

What does it mean to bring "sight to the blind" in a society where materialism, prejudices, and excessive thirst for power and pleasure can blind us to the dignity of millions?

How can we "let the oppressed go free" when many family farmers can't sustain a way of life, in a society where joblessness, disinvestment, and self-destructive behavior leave whole neighborhoods and rural communities without a real sense of hope? These questions are at the heart of our public mission and personal lives.

The mission calls us to engagement and to genuine citizenship. We are not sects fleeing the world. We believe citizenship is a virtue, participation in public life is an obligation. Politics is a worthy vocation. The religious community is called to participate in the political process not to impose some sectarian doctrine but to speak for those who cannot speak for themselves, to share our experiences in serving the poor and the powerless, to stand up for human life and human dignity, justice and peace. What our nation needs is not religious interest groups but communities of conscience within the larger society, testing public life on the basis of the central values of human life and human dignity, justice and peace.

Now this kind of talk makes some people nervous. They believe the active involvement of religious groups and believers in politics represents a danger for the nation and for religious communities. I believe these critics misunderstand both our Constitution and our religious calling. They seem to invoke the principles of separation of church and state in an attempt to silence the religious community or weaken its voice. This turns the Bill of Rights upside down. The First Amendment ensures that the state has no right to establish a religion or impose religious beliefs or practices on its citizens. That same amendment protects the rights of religious bodies to speak out without governmental interference, endorsement, or sanction. Religious groups should expect neither favoritism nor discrimination in their public roles.

Society is strengthened—not undermined—when groups motivated by basic values, including religious values, join with others of every faith and no faith in seeking the best laws, policies, and leadership to direct our nation and communities. If public life is not about basic values, then it may be simply a playground for personal egos, organized special interests, and partisan power groups.

In a contemporary dialogue about religion and politics, there is both good and bad news. The good news is that there is a growing rediscovery of moral values and religious commitments in American life. Not long ago, many commentators proclaimed that religion was on its way to the fringes of America. It is now increasingly recognized that most important issues have clear moral consequences and religious dimensions. From abortion to apartheid, the budget to Bosnia, health care to human rights, environment to euthanasia, welfare to warfare, there are clear ethical principles and religious values at stake, and religious communities are increasingly active in the public arena.

The bad news is that stronger links between religion and politics can diminish both religion and politics if we are not careful. These moral dimensions can serve simply as a way to repackage the old agendas of right and left. Sometimes the biblical message gets lost in the political and ideological temptations of our time.

The key question is: Does our faith shape our politics, or is it the other way around? Speaking personally, I sometimes find the religious right more right than religious, acting like a powerful faction of the Republican party, acting as apologist of some candidates and opponent of others. I wonder, where do "the least of these" fit in their agenda?

Likewise, I worry about some "politically correct" Christians on the left who seem to find no significant differences with secular liberals or the Democratic party. They will protect the eggs of endangered species but not the lives of unborn children. Why does it sometimes seem that smoking is the only sin left in some segments of elite America?

All of us are tempted to be selective in our witness. One example is the family values debate. Some religious leaders focus with considerable passion and clarity on the moral and cultural forces that undermine family life but lose their urgency and voices when it comes to the economic forces and discrimination that destroy families. Others stand against joblessness, homelessness, and economic injustice, which hurt families, but are simply not comfortable addressing the moral and spiritual crisis in our society and its profound implications for children.

The rediscovery of religious values can often be superficial, selective, and partisan. We should be very wary of religious leaders using their authority to lay hands on Bill Clinton or any of his possible successors.

## Social Context

We take up the public mission in a very difficult cultural and political context. I recently went white-water rafting, and I found in that exciting experience a metaphor for our tasks in public life. We are being pushed along by powerful social, moral, and economic currents, and there are many rocks along the way, only some of which are visible. What are the currents and rocks that shape our journey? What are the signs of our times?

### A Society in Moral Disarray

You know the data. Families are increasingly broken by widespread divorce; destroyed by violence, especially against women and children; undermined by a wide variety of behaviors and trends (e.g., substance abuse, absence of fathers, racial discrimination); and weakened by major institutions—business, media, and government—that ignore family roles and responsibilities.

### An Economy Pulling Us Apart

We live in an economy of paradoxes. Profits and productivity grow while many workers' income and sense of security decline. Parents wonder whether their children will live as well as they themselves do. The power and productivity of the United States economy is leading not to one nation but to three nations living side by side.

In one nation people are moving ahead—coping with the challenges of the global economy and information age, growing more powerful and productive. They surf the Web, manage their growing investment port-folios, and wonder if the stock market will keep rising.

In the second nation people are falling behind, left out of economic growth, the families often without fathers, jobs, or living income. Hunger, homelessness, and hopelessness are the symptoms of an economy that leaves millions behind. They wonder whether they can pay the rent or afford food at the end of the month.

In the third nation people are being squeezed by declining real incomes, scared by downsizing and fearful about keeping their jobs and health care. They wonder whether they can afford a good education for their kids and a decent retirement for themselves.

Children pay the greatest price for this "every person for oneself" eco-nomic ethic. The poorest persons in America are our children—as men-tioned earlier, one-quarter of our preschoolers are growing up poor in the richest nation on earth. These forces are exacerbated by continuing racism and other forms of discrimination.

### A Nation Turning Inward

Just a word about international concerns. The world has changed—walls have fallen, communism has collapsed. Lech Walesa, Václav Havel, and Nelson Mandela went from prisoners to presidents. But we still face a world of too much violence and not enough development. Sadly, our nation seems to be turning inward, hostile to immigrants, indifferent to global responsibility, ambivalent about troubled nations. There is a lot for us to do. Among industrial nations, the U.S. is first in arms sales and last in development assistance to poor nations.

### A Culture of Violence

No nation on earth has as much violent behavior as we do—in our homes, on our televisions and in our streets. Tragically, our society looks to violent measures to deal with some of our most difficult social prob-lems: millions of abortions to address problem pregnancies, advocacy of euthanasia and assisted suicide to cope with burdens of age and illness, and increased reliance on the death penalty to deal with crime. A nation that destroys its children, abandons its elderly, and relies on vengeance is in serious moral trouble.

We know something is wrong when

- Two men and two women in Wyoming hang a young man on a fence because he is gay.
- A high-school senior gives birth to her baby in a bathroom stall, throws the baby in a trash can, and returns to the prom.
- Children shoot their classmates and teachers.
- People blow up federal buildings and day-care centers and mail bombs to people to make political points.
- So-called pro-lifers kill for the cause.
- The state says we will kill those who kill others to teach that killing is wrong.

### Political Signs of the Times

The context of public life is dominated by scandal, cynicism, and special interest power. The only thing that many candidates seem to really believe in is the urgency of their own election.

Politics is a big part of the problem—public life seems to be becoming a long-running soap opera.

A broader sign of the times is the current lack of meaning and morality in public life. The cynicism and soap operas that pervade public life are eating away at our national fabric and our capacity to act.

The best (or worst) example was the spectacle involving the president and the intern, allegations of sexual misconduct and cover-up, perjury and obstruction of justice. Reckless behavior in the White House was matched by reckless reporting in the media and reckless tactics by both prosecutors and defense attorneys. All this left the country appalled and titillated, confused and fascinated, and perhaps in need of a long national shower.

But just as ominous is the way national choices are being distorted by powerful political money and determined by short-term political considerations. Is there any doubt that Clinton's decision on the 1996 welfare bill was dictated more by Dick Morris's polls and focus groups than by policy considerations? Is there any doubt that policy toward human rights in China and tobacco was decisively influenced by the investments of millions of dollars?

Equally significant, major challenges are simply ignored in the search for short-term fixes and sound-bite solutions. We have politics by bumper sticker—three strikes and you're out; two years and you're off; one more child and we'll cut your benefits. When did you last hear our leaders talk about the jobs that will really help families overcome poverty, or address the debt that is literally killing sisters and brothers in the poorest nations, or take on the policies that hinder prospects for peace in the Middle East?

We are watching the "demoralization" of politics in the multiple meanings of that word—in the reckless conduct of our leaders, the way political money dictates outcomes, and the neglect of the "least of these" in national dialogue.

Too many know every aspect of Princess Diana's life and death, every detail of our president's conduct, every failing of the Kennedys but not the names of their neighbor's children, who their representatives are, or where Kosovo is on the map.

## Christian Assets and Agenda

The common good is not advanced by politicians who posture and polarize for their own partisan advantage. It is easy to get discouraged. There is a terrible temptation to retreat or withdraw. This would be a huge mistake.

We need to be clear about what we bring to this challenge. We are leaders of communities of faith, not political interest groups. We don't play the game the way the NRA or AMA play, and we don't have PACs. We don't endorse candidates. We bring a different set of assets.

The Scriptures insist, "Without a vision the people perish." We have quite a vision. We have a consistent moral framework, which begins with the life and dignity of the human person, priority for the poor, and the dignity of work. In the Catholic community we have a formal body of social teaching that is anchored in the Scriptures and articulated in centuries of encyclicals and pastoral letters and other ecclesial documents.

The basic message is quite simple—our faith is profoundly social. Believers are called to "choose life," to care for "the least of these," to "hunger and thirst for justice," to be "peacemakers." Followers of Jesus are called to be the "salt of the earth" and the "light of the world." More specifically, my church has developed and articulated a series of principles and themes to guide believers in their public and personal choices. Permit me to offer a brief version of some of the central themes of the Catholic public witness.

Our tradition is complex and nuanced. It affirms the free market and recognizes its limits. It teaches that government is neither the solution nor the enemy. We affirm the importance of the family and mediating institutions but insist they cannot substitute for just public policy.

Along with these strong convictions, we bring broad experience to the public square. Think about it. Who feeds the hungry? Who shelters the homeless? Who educates the young? Who cares for the sick? Who welcomes the stranger?

The religious community offers the largest nongovernmental commitment to education, health care, and human services. The poor and vulnerable are not abstract issues for us. They have names and faces. They are in our parishes and schools, our shelters and soup kitchens. We are the community institutions the politicians pontificate about. My sense on Capitol Hill is that national leaders listen to us not because of what we believe but because of what we do every day.

We have an institutional presence, an organizational structure, and a set of global relationships. A Protestant friend of mine once said, "You Catholics are terrific; you divide up the world and call it yours." It is true of all of us.

At the neighborhood and community level, we have tens of thousands of parishes, congregations, and schools, more numerous than post offices. At the city and state level we have dioceses, school systems, charitable agencies, colleges, and universities. We have national institutions and structures. And at the global level we have the powerful presence and voice of the Holy Father.

Pope John Paul II, after more than two decades of service, is a model of consistency and integration. He played a decisive role in bringing down communism and may be the most serious and constructive current critic of Western capitalism.

We are a community of people—60 million people in my denomination. We are at the center and the fringes of American life—CEOs and migrant farm workers, senators and homeless children, the powerful and the powerless. We are Democrats and Republicans, liberals and conservatives and everything in between. We are a remarkably diverse community, but if we could come together around the core principles of human life and human dignity, we could make a real difference. While it remains true that without a vision the people perish, without people the vision is invisible.

We also have an agenda that begins with respect for life, emphasizes the priority of the poor, and extends to the pursuit of peace and justice at home and around the world. We are not politically correct by the standards of either right or left. We believe we must protect children's lives before and after birth. We're for family leave in employment and family choice in education. We oppose the violence of abortion and the vengeance of capital punishment. We support trade unions not just in Poland but also in America. We oppose condoms in schools and assault weapons in our communities. The agenda may be countercultural but it reflects a consistent concern for human life. Neither party is going to invite us to spend a night in the Lincoln bedroom.

Religious faith can test the political process; public life can test the religious community. We are called to be political but not partisan. The religious community cannot be the chaplain for any political party or cheerleader for any candidate. We are called to test each party and every candidate by how they address the life and dignity of the human person. We don't need more religious leaders telling believers how to vote. We need pastors and preachers, parishes and congregations that challenge believers to assess the moral and human dimensions of issues, to become active and informed citizens, and to vote their consciences, not their narrow self-interest.

We are called to be principled but not ideological. Our faith offers a moral framework for public life. We cannot compromise our moral principles or lower our voice in the face of controversy or conflict. We simply cannot abandon unborn children because they might be politically incorrect. We cannot become indifferent to poor children because they are not politically powerful. We cannot turn our backs on immigrants and refugees because they don't vote. We must keep faith with moral principles, as we are open to new ways to apply them.

The religious community is called to be civil but not soft. We must stand up for what we believe with conviction and persistence, but we must also maintain civility. Churches that speak for justice and charity must reflect these principles in the political arena. We can't come across as just another interest group, only a little more righteous.

The church should be engaged but not used. I suspect that both parties, many politicians, and some interest groups seek our support without really sharing our vision or dealing with our values. Political photo ops are not substitutes for policies that protect human life, place a priority on the poor, support the family, or advance justice at home or peace abroad.

## Where Do We Go from Here?

In the weeks and months ahead we need to chart our own course, not champion any particular party, challenging all candidates to stand up for human life and dignity, to work for greater justice and peace.

Let me talk about my family—not my kids but my parents. As I said, my dad is a die-hard Democrat who has been appalled by Clinton's personal behavior in the White House and disconcerted by the weakness of his policy agenda—the abandonment of a safety net for poor children, his failure to stand up for workers in signing the NAFTA treaty, and more than anything else, his veto of the ban on partial-birth abortion. He believes Democrats should stand up for the weak—and these new Democrats seem to be driven more by polls and PAC contributions. How did Democrats end up more committed to the abortion agenda than the labor movement, more opposed to school choice than tax breaks for the rich?

My mother is a long-time Republican. Her brother served in the Minnesota Senate and chaired the Republican party at the local level. But she runs a pro-life pregnancy center in my hometown. She knows that Medicaid, AFDC, and food stamps are not the source of all evil but lifelines for women and children without options. She wonders how the party of Lincoln, her party, became the driving force in ending a national safety net and reducing help for the vulnerable.

My parents are not alone. Many of us are politically homeless. Neither party and few politicians reflect our values. Some say we should head for the hills, retreat into social isolation, separating ourselves from a culture and politics that deny our values. Others insist that now is the time for participation and engagement, sharing our values and offering an alternative vision.

The challenge for us as Christians is not just whether we can get the words right but instead whether we can build a community that puts the gospel to work. We need believers who seek to shape the culture, not surrender to it.

At this point I fear that our central moral norm—the consistent ethic of life—is good theology and bad politics. It offers a map but not a movement. Consistent-ethic Catholics and even evangelicals are politically homeless in a world where Democrats embrace capital punishment more than entitlements for the poor and Republicans talk more about cutting taxes than protecting the unborn.

We cannot retreat, but we must be realistic. The status quo dominated by the money of the rich, the political correctness of the elites, and the get-along/go-along culture of Washington could not be more challenging.

So, what should we do? We need to change the culture, reshape the debate, and challenge the political status quo. We need a new politics that focuses on moral principles, not the latest polls; on the needs of the weak, not the contributions of the strong. We need evangelicals and Catholics working together for a pro-life, pro-family, pro-poor agenda, as Ronald Sider has suggested.

I believe Catholics and evangelicals can and should be allies in this new approach to public life. I believe we share some fundamental values—we seek a country that is pro-life at every stage and condition, pro-family in believing the family is our best bulwark against poverty, moral decline, and social disarray, and pro-poor in believing that the measure of our society is how the weak are faring.

## Conclusion

Where do we go from here? The ultimate answer is heaven or hell. But as a Catholic, I find us in "political purgatory," where neither party cares much for the unborn, the poor, and the vulnerable.

Our task is what Jesus gave us two thousand years ago—go and make disciples. Increasingly our work is focused not in Washington but in local communities of faith, trying to help believers integrate and not isolate our social mission, trying to weave the biblical call to care for the least of these, to hunger and thirst for justice, and to be peacemakers into every aspect of Christian life.

The measure of public life is not how the rich and powerful are doing but how the poor and powerless are faring. Every election we are asked the wrong question. It's not "Am I better off than I was four years ago?" It is "Are *we* better off?" Are the "least of these" better off? Our voices must be heard, our votes must be cast, or this question will probably go unasked.

The challenge is to look beyond the bumper stickers, the attack ads, and sample ballots to see the names and faces of those whose lives are touched by the choices we make.

I was in upstate New York, where I gave a talk about economic justice, focusing on the poor. I thought it was well received, but the president of the group was unhappy. "I'm sick and tired of all this talk about the poor and social justice. What about the hardworking middle-class people who keep this church and society going?" I asked him what he does for a living. He said, "I am a managing partner in a law firm." I said, "I bet you work hard, stay late lots of nights." "You bet," he said. I then asked him if he had met the woman who cleans his office and if he knew how much she earned. He responded, "I've seen her. She probably earns minimum wage." "Do her kids have health-care coverage?" I asked. "I don't know, probably not. What are you getting at?" he asked. I said, "This is not really about politics but about people. This is not about Newt Gingrich or Bill Clinton, the Chamber of Commerce or the AFL-CIO; this is about the woman who cleans your office."

We all need to see the faces and the families behind the numbers and theories. This is about the people who pick our strawberries, the folks who pick up our trash and make our kids' sneakers. It is not about numbers but about brothers and sisters, children of God—businesspeople being downsized and poor women on welfare looking for work who can't find it.

Christians are members of communities of faith, not interest groups. Our task is to help bring good news, liberty, new sight, and freedom by how we use our voices and votes in this democracy.

# 5

# RELIGION AND THE AMERICAN DEMOCRACY

## Jean Bethke Elshtain

Alexis de Tocqueville didn't miss much during his tour of America, a mission that yielded his nineteenth-century masterwork, *Democracy in America*. Although he failed to pick up the often extraordinary energies of American evangelism—his reaction to what he considered such frenzy being the following: "From time to time strange sects arise which endeavor to strike out extraordinary paths to eternal happiness. Religious insanity is very common in the United States"—he *did* see how thoroughly religion and politics were saturated with one another. American democracy from the beginning was premised on the enactment of projects that were a complex intermingling of religious and political imperatives. The majority of Americans were religious seekers and believers who saw in communal liberty the freedom to *be* religious rather than freedom *from* religion. It is, therefore, not surprising that such a huge chunk of American juridical life has been devoted to sorting out the often inaptly named

Jean Bethke Elshtain (Ph.D., Brandeis University) is the Laura Spelman Rockefeller Professor of Social and Political Ethics at the University of Chicago Divinity School.

church-state debate. In a less churched society this would be a far less salient issue.

But what does our profession of belief—some 95 percent of Americans claim belief in God, and fully 70 percent are members in a church, synagogue, or mosque—really mean? How does it play itself out on the ground, so to speak? Here a bit of backdrop is helpful in order that we might better situate and explore the vagaries of the present moment.

The West is perhaps unique in this regard, namely, that it has never been hospitable to theocracy, a fusion of, or nondistinction between, the political and the religious. Religion is not only established in theocracies; it dominates politics as in contemporary fundamentalist Islamic states in which mullahs also run the government. There were often close alliances in the history of the West between throne and altar, to be sure. But this isn't the same thing. In other words, a differentiation between politics and religion was sown in Western culture from very early on, quite pointedly so with the coming of Christianity. Christians asked: What has Christ to do with Caesar? The answers varied widely. Furthermore, the church, and the synagogue before it and ongoingly, embodied an alternative politics, having its own understanding of community membership, authority, rule, and the nature of the kingdom. The central distinction marked in medieval papal doctrine was that between *regnum* and *sacerdotium,* roughly marking the sword of earthly kingdoms and the spiritual kingdom respectively. The two got all tangled up with one another, to be sure, but they were nonetheless distinct. The spiritual sword was held to be superior because it gestured beyond the immediate realm to the eternal, but the secular sword had its own dignity, its own autonomy and purposes. It could, however, be called to account by the sacred realm, by those who wielded the spiritual sword in behalf of the city of God on earthly pilgrimage. The nations were under judgment and not wholly autonomous in all things.

The postmedieval history of the West is a story of various comings-together and, finally, definitively, teasing apart of church and state. But religion and politics are something else. These simply cannot be separated. Too much of the same territory is claimed by each. Consider the American democracy, then. We begin from the beginning with no establishment of religion but with the free exercise of religion. Bear in mind as well that the views of a few of the great founders of this republic were somewhat anomalous. Jefferson, first and foremost of these, famously claimed that it mattered not whether his neighbor believed in no God or twenty gods: it neither picked his pocket nor broke his leg. The vast majority of Americans, then and now, were not nearly so agnostic about their neighbor's beliefs.

It is utterly unsurprising, then, that when Tocqueville toured America in the Jacksonian era, he wrote of the ways in which religion in the United States (by which he primarily meant Christianity in its various incarnations, including Catholicism) both generated and made use of democratic instincts; religion helped to shape the mores, the habits of the heart. Tocqueville further observed that settled beliefs about God and human nature were indispensable in the conduct of daily life—you simply could not function if you woke up every morning and had to determine what truths would guide you over the next twenty-four hours—and that, in general, when a people's religion is destroyed, it enervates them and prepares them not for liberation but for bondage.

This is, of course, an extraordinarily complex story and an often bewildering one, especially for foreign observers. So let's add a few more Tocquevillian bits. Remember that, for Tocqueville, America embodied a coming age of democracy and equality. One could not understand the great movement toward equality without understanding the Christian insistence that all are equal in the eyes of God. This equality, enacted politically, brings great benefits, but it also opens the door to certain dangerous tendencies. Democratic egalitarianism tends to isolate people from one another as we all, as competing individuals, go in quest of the same thing. We become strivers and isolate ourselves one from the other. Here religion is vital as a chastening influence as it inspires contrary urges by drawing people into community and away from narrow materialism. Religion, in Tocqueville's words, helps to "purify, control, and restrain that excessive and exclusive taste for well-being human beings acquire in an age of equality."

Religion contributes to the maintenance of a democratic republic by directing the mores and helping, thereby, to regulate political life. Tocqueville insisted that the ideas of Christianity and liberty are so completely intermingled that if you tried to sever religion from democracy in America, you would wind up destroying democracy. Democracy needs the sort of transcendent justification that religion helps to provide; thus, the eighteenth-century philosophers were wrong about the weakening of religion. "It is tiresome," notes Tocqueville ironically, "that the facts do not fit their theory at all." For, surprisingly, the separation of church and state in America had led to an astonishingly religious atmosphere. By diminishing the *official* power of religion, Americans had enhanced its social strength. Perhaps, deep down, Americans understood that religion feeds hope and is thus attached to a constitutive principle of human nature. Amidst the flux and tumult of rambunctious democratic politics, religion shaped and mediated the passions. Were the day to come when those passions got unleashed upon the world unrestrained, then we would arrive at an unhappy moment indeed, a dreary world of democratic despotism.

For there were at least two great dangers threatening the existence of religion (and indirectly, democracy) according to Tocqueville, namely, schism and indifference. Schism pits us against one another in suspicion and enmity; indifference invites us not to care about one another at all. Were Tocqueville around today, I believe he would point to both and he would worry that we are in danger of losing that generous concern for others that religion, in institutionally robust forms, not "spirituality" in vaporous individualist forms, promotes. In addition, operating from some common moral basis that does not require doctrinal leveling but does demand searching for certain core norms we share, helps people learn how to compromise because they agree on so many important things.

If we slide into a world of schism, a world in which differences become the occasion for isolation, we lose authentic pluralism, which requires institutional bases from which to operate. It is pluralism that gives us the space to be both American and Protestant, Catholic, Jew, Muslim, and on and on. Absent robust and vibrant faith and civic institutions, we are thrown back on our own devices; we lose the strength that membership provides; we forget that we can know a good in common that we cannot know alone. Should we arrive at this Tocquevillian impasse, we would find that individuals, striving to stand upright in the winds blowing from centers of governmental or economic power now operating minus that chastening influence from other vital sources, would soon be flattened. People would grow apart and become strangers one to another. We might still have kin, but we would no longer have a country in the sense of a polity of which we were essential parts.

This is where a form of dogmatic skepticism, corrosive of all belief, enters. Tocqueville knew that people would always question and challenge. But what happens if there is nothing but skepticism of a dogmatic sort that is unable to sustain any beliefs? Don't you think Tocqueville would see that we Americans at the turn of this century might be in this danger zone as well? In our desire to be sophisticated, in our determination to be nobody's fools, we may well and truly be undermining our ability to believe and to affirm anything at all save the ephemeral ground of our own subjective experience.

So where are we at this point? What do we see when we look around? First, we see a smorgasbord religiosity whose primary aim seems to be to make us feel good about God, but God forbid that this should place any demands on us. Second, as a corollary, we see what might be called a hollowing out or deinstitutionalization of religion in many quarters, a loss of institutional robustness. This creates a real problem as faith absent strong institutions cannot be sustained over time. Religious life becomes all fission and fragment without framing rules and doctrines and under-lying beliefs: here *we* stand.

A deinstitutionalized, feel-good religiosity cannot carry out the tasks of formation Tocqueville found so central in forging a sturdy, decent, self-governing American character. If religion is just another voluntary asso-ciation, it isn't religion anymore in a strong sense. This puts us in danger of losing the connection between freedom and truth. For freedom isn't just me maximizing my preferences, as some who favor market models hold, but is tethered to truth as a part of our very being, our inner con-stitution. Freedom, rightly understood, which is always a chastened notion of freedom, frees us *for* solidarity with others. An authentic view of freedom—understood in and through the prism of relationality, of brotherhood and sisterhood—must challenge misguided views that undermine authentic freedom. But without certain formative institutions we cannot sustain freedom in the authentic sense. We enter a danger zone in which our differences, which should be great blessings, as Francis Car-dinal George has argued, become instead destructive divisions. Our great religious traditions offer hope and solace, the promise of a community of the faithful. One's Internet chat room isn't quite the same thing.

I want to be careful here because I would not want to leave the impres-sion that I believe religion performs certain useful functions and that is its ultimate and most defensible aim and purpose. No, instead the aim of religion is to bear us toward the truth; to direct our very beings toward a conformity with true freedom as relationality, as communion, grounded always in the dignity of persons. Religion opens us to the God in whose likeness we were created. In the words of the great St. Augustine, "Thou hast made us to thyself and our hearts are restless till they rest in Thee." And this restlessness—"Everybody's got a hungry heart," sings Bruce Springsteen—channeled and made ever fresh through religious belief, helps us to face and to try to make whole a wounded world. But this mis-sion of religion may be blocked nowadays, oddly enough, in the name of religious freedom or tolerance.

Let me explain what I mean. In a recent book by the distinguished soci-ologist Alan Wolfe, *One Nation after All,* Wolfe describes what he calls modern religious tolerance in a discussion entitled "Morality Writ Small." Wolfe's middle-class respondents—and the vast majority of Americans are middle-class and understand themselves through this lens—see reli-gion as a private matter to be discussed only reluctantly. This departs in quite dramatic ways from a deeper, richer understanding of what toler-ance is or what it requires, for one thing, and for another, it suggests that many of our fellow citizens have come to believe that to endorse a prop-erly secular state, which has no established ties to any religious institu-tion, means one is obliged to support a secularized society in which religion is reduced to a purely private role. Not so. Yet this is precisely what so many of the respondents in this important book seem to be saying they want. So much for William Lloyd Garrison, Dorothy Day, Martin Luther King, and a small army of other great citizens who didn't embrace this nicety!

Professor Wolfe sees his respondents as trying to be welcoming to all faiths. His Mrs. Tompkins—one of the people interviewed in the book— thinks that one way to ease the rough edges off religious conviction is to refuse to accept any particular "dogma whole" as if the doctrines or teachings of various faith communities were arbitrary impositions rather than worked-out and complex teachings that took shape over centuries. Instead, she continues, one should just "live with the concept of God as you perceive it."[1] Is this not a form of terminal subjectivism? If it's all up to you, a community of belief is lost and we slide into indifference.

But something even more troubling seems to be going on. There is a deep undercurrent of fearfulness running just beneath the surface of the words of so many of the middle-class Americans in Professor Wolfe's book. They seem to have struck a tacit bargain with themselves that goes like this: If I am quiet about what I believe and everybody else is quiet about what they believe, then nobody will interfere with the rights of anybody else. But this is precisely what real believers, whether political or religious or both, cannot do: keep quiet—whether believers in Martin Luther King's beloved community or in ending the war in Vietnam on justice grounds derived from religious conviction or in opposing the current abortion regime for similar reasons. To tell political and religious believers to shut up for they will interfere with my rights by definition, simply by speaking out, is an intolerant idea. It is, in effect, to tell folks that they cannot really believe what they believe or be who they are. Don't ask; don't tell.

What fears underwrite this attitude? One, surely, is of religious intolerance, even religious warfare, though, of course, if you were to do a body count, the murderous antireligious ideologies of the twentieth century would win that prize hands down. But the fear now seems to extend to public expression itself. Wolfe notes that his respondents are disturbed when religion is taken out of the private realm. But a private religion is no religion at all. One must have the public expression of faith for it to be faith. And public expression isn't forcing anything on anybody. But to those interviewed for *One Nation after All*, that in and of itself—public expression—seems to cross a line because you are supposed to keep quiet about what you believe most strongly. If you do not, it may require of me that I actually enter into an act of discernment—what do I think about what you are claiming?—and many Americans do not want to do that.

There are, of course, certain virtues here embedded: don't rush to judgment; live and let live. But I want to focus on the vices. Although Wolfe describes the demand for privatization as a tolerant one flowing from a desire to be "inclusive" and "nonabsolutist," I wonder. Many of his respondents do seem quite absolutist—about everybody shutting up. Consider the remarks of Jody Fields: "If you are a Hindu and you grew up being a Hindu, keep it to yourself. Don't impose your religion, and don't make me feel bad because I do this and you do this."[2] Surely this isn't tolerance at all but extraordinary intolerance of religious pluralism: if one changes Hindu to Jew in the comment, that becomes stunningly clear. So when we are told that "keep it to yourself" presages a "period of increasingly religious pluralism," I would say, "Hardly." Telling a Hindu to hide being a Hindu is scarcely a picture of robust pluralism.

Now some respondents in *One Nation after All* do seem to be authentic religious pluralists, more generous in their attitudes. Here, for example, is Cathy Ryan, perturbed because Christmas carols can't be sung anymore in the public schools of her town at Christmastime because Muslims may get upset. Her response: "Well, excuse me, but let's teach Muslim songs too—don't wipe out all culture, add to it. Do Hanukkah songs. Let's find out what a dreidel represents. Let's find out what Muslims do."[3] This is real tolerance, I would submit, of a sort that encourages the public expression and representation of differences with the view that we are all enriched through the process. As Pope John Paul II always tells us: "Be not afraid!" Cathy Ryan is open to robust pluralism. And one might argue that it is in America that such forms of transnationality, as Randolph Bourne called it, have found and continue to find multiple forms of relatively benign expression.

Legal scholar Michael McConnell, in an unpublished paper on "Believers as Equal Citizens," reminds us of several different historical versions of Jewish emancipation. One expected Jews to disappear as a distinctive group once they were given their civil rights. Under the terms of Jewish emancipation in France, for example, Jews were expected to give up civil aspects of Talmudic law, to disavow any political implications of their faith, to abandon altogether the use of Yiddish, and to relinquish their semiautonomous communal institutions. This by contrast to American pluralism. Writes McConnell:

> The great public feast given in 1789 in Philadelphia, then the nation's capital, to celebrate ratification of the Constitution included a fitting symbol of this new pluralistic philosophy: the feast included a special table where the food conformed to Jewish dietary laws. This was a fitting symbol because it included Jewish Americans in the celebration without requiring that they sacrifice their distinctiveness as Jews. By contrast, in France Napoleon sum-

moned the leaders of the Jewish community to a "Great Sanhedrin," where he insisted that the Jewish law be modified to enable the Jewish people to be integrated into the French nation. In a gesture no less revealing than the kosher table in Philadelphia, Napoleon's Minister of the Interior scheduled the first session to be held on Saturday. Here we see three alternatives. Under the *ancien regime,* Jews would be excluded from the celebration, for they could not be citizens. Under the secular state, Jews would be welcome to attend, but they would be expected to eat the same food that other citizens eat. If they want to keep kosher, they should do it at home, in private, at their own expense. Under the pluralist vision, multiple tables are provided to ensure that for Protestants, it is a Protestant country, for Catholics a Catholic country, [for Muslims, a Muslim country], and the Jew, if he [or she] pleases, may establish in it his [or her] New Jerusalem.

So let us not worry so much about conflict or difference that we deny pluralism its forms of public expression, for this is the only way, really, that we have of learning about the gifts others have to offer. There is a difference between "keep it to yourself" and tolerance. In the words of Stephen Carter: "Tolerance is not simply a willingness to listen to what others have to say. It is also a resistance to the quick use of state power . . . to force dissenters and the different to conform."[4] If we don't allow religious dissenters to display their beliefs as public moral critics, in their own voices, then it is we who are intolerant.

Now let us draw politics and religion together one more time. Political commentator E. J. Dionne has written that Americans are fed up with politics and many among us just want politics to go away.[5] The majority of middle-class Americans in *One Nation after All* also seem to want real religious conviction to go away, too, especially in light of their distrust of "organized religion," as if there was any other kind. I want to suggest that contemporary distrust of organized politics and distrust of organized religion go hand in hand. Both involve public expression, collectivities of persons involved in a shared enterprise, rules and convictions, and sometimes hard-hitting encounters. That we seem not to have the stomach for either suggests our capacity for democracy itself is growing ever more anemic. A distaste for conflict is a distaste for politics. The great Frederick Douglass once remarked that you cannot have rain without occasional thunder and lightning. Yet that is what so many of us seem to want: spring showers, lovely gardens, but no thunderstorms. Need I note that life doesn't work like that and that no complex democratic politics can survive if we go underground with what we care about most deeply?

To me this suggests that we are not doing a very good job of social and political and, yes, religious formation: preparing people for a world in which there are disagreements and there are decisions to be made and one cannot always tell the Hindus to keep it to themselves.

This draws us, at last, to certain basic questions. Who are we anyhow? In what does the good of human beings consist? How can we come to recognize, to honor, and to cultivate that good in wisdom and in truth? In two of the American director John Ford's great films, a shocked outsider asks fundamental questions. Consider *My Darling Clementine* when Henry Fonda as Wyatt Earp, who has given up his badge and left Dodge City with his brothers to try to create a new life, enters a town for a shave and finds people fleeing in horror and screaming as a drunk shooter lays waste to the place and law enforcement officials flinch and throw down their badges because they aren't getting paid enough for such really dangerous duty. "What kind of a town is this?" queries Fonda in amazement.

In the opening of *The Man Who Shot Liberty Valance,* Jimmy Stewart, as lawyer Rance Stoddard, is riding in a coach into Shinbone to start a new life in the West when the stagecoach is robbed. The local villain, Liberty Valance—who takes all sorts of liberties until those who struggle to create a settled civil society, to build churches and schools and political institutions, triumph—steals a brooch off a lady's garment although she pleads, "Please take everything else, but not that; it was a gift from my late husband!" Stewart, who doesn't carry a gun and is surrounded by armed desperadoes, cries out: "What kind of a man are you?"

An aim of religion is to help us, with God's help, to ask and struggle to answer those questions: What kind of a place is this? What kind of people are we?

6

# TOWARD AN EVANGELICAL POLITICAL PHILOSOPHY

## RONALD J. SIDER

In the last few years, evangelicals have had more political influence in the U.S. than at any time in this century. But we are not certain what to do with it. Unless we find out, we will squander a historic opportunity to nudge this society toward moral renewal and justice for all.

To be sure, there are many evangelical voices loudly promoting political agendas. But the voices are often confused, contradictory, and superficial. Evangelicals lack anything remotely similar to Catholicism's papal encyclicals and episcopal pronouncements on social and political issues, which have provided Roman Catholics with a careful, integrated framework for approaching each concrete political decision. (This deficiency, as Mark Noll points out, is one important aspect of the "scandal of the evangelical mind.")[1] On the other hand, when evangelicals have acted politically, we have usually jumped into the political fray without doing our theoretical, theological homework. That our confused, superficial activity has had little lasting impact should not surprise us.

Ronald J. Sider (Ph.D., Yale University) is Professor of Theology and Culture at Eastern Baptist Theological Seminary and is President of Evangelicals for Social Action.

If that is to change, we urgently need to develop a careful, systematic political philosophy to guide and sustain our activism. That, of course, is a task requiring years, indeed decades, of communal work. Here, I want first to illustrate some problems that arise because we lack an evangelical political philosophy; second, to outline how I try to move from a biblical normative framework and careful societal analysis to a political philosophy; and third, to point to a few ways to move forward.

Some may object to my assertion that we lack an evangelical political philosophy by pointing to the fact that Reformed, Lutheran, and to a lesser extent, Anabaptist evangelicals all have developed systematic reflection on politics. One thinks, for example, of the marvelous Kuyperian tradition of political philosophy that James Skillen articulates so well (see chapter 3).[2]

Careful political reflection within each of these evangelical traditions is very helpful for our work. But I do not think it is adequate to guide evangelical political engagement today and tomorrow. Why? There are a large number of evangelicals in this country and in many countries around the world who represent a vast array of different theological and ecclesiastical traditions. Pentecostals, Wesleyans, and African Americans, to name a few, are not about to fully embrace a Reformed political philosophy, even though they are glad to learn from Abraham Kuyper. But all these evangelicals from a vast array of traditions have some common sense of identity as evangelicals and to some extent want to work together on many things, including politics, in spite of their theological differences. In order to do that effectively, they need to embrace at least a common set of principles for a political philosophy.

## Present Confusion

It is not hard to illustrate the way the absence of a foundational political philosophy leads evangelical political activists to rush off madly in all directions. (In the early years of the Moral Majority, according to Ed Dobson, it was often "ready, fire, aim.")

Take the area of moral decay. Virtually all Christians, and certainly all evangelicals, agree that serious moral decay threatens this society, that religious communities are the only place to look for that radical spiritual conversion that transforms persons, and that such communities are the primary moral teachers of the virtues that decent societies require. Some evangelicals think the solution is a constitutional amendment to restore prayer in the schools. Others want constitutional, or at least legislative, action to guarantee equal benefits to adherents of all religious views. And other evangelicals think both of the previous proposals would violate the First Amendment and destroy both church and state.

Or consider evangelical pronouncements on the role of government. Sometimes, when attacking government programs they dislike, evangelical voices adopt libertarian arguments that would preclude almost all government activity to promote economic justice ("Helping the poor is a task for individuals and churches, not the government"). Then, when the issues change to abortion, family, euthanasia, and pornography, the same people loudly demand vigorous government action. There might be a good case to be made for private programs in the first case and legislation in the second, but if people use arguments in one area that run counter to their agenda in another, they appear confused and superficial.

The absence of a consistent ethic of life leads to absurd inconsistency. Some evangelical political voices make the sanctity of human life (up to birth and just before death) the overriding issue and neglect the way poverty and smoking destroy millions. Other evangelicals point out that racism, poverty, and environmental decay all kill, and yet they seem little concerned with millions of abortions each year.[3]

Some of our superficiality and confusion results from the fact that we have seldom taken the time to work out carefully the specific policy implications of biblical faith. Too often we just assume that traditional American values or the Republican (or, less often, the Democratic) party's platform are right. Former Christian Coalition director Ralph Reed, for example, says that when he became a committed Christian and started attending an evangelical church, "My religious beliefs never changed my views on the [political] issues to any great degree because my political philosophy was already well developed."[4] Without testing political agendas on the basis of biblical norms, Christians often uncritically endorse left-wing or (more often) right-wing ideological agendas.

I need not go on illustrating this basic point. Evangelical political impact today is weakened because our voices are confused, contradictory, and superficial. We contradict each other. Our agendas are shaped more by secular ideologies than divine revelation. We have no systematic framework for careful dialogue about our specific policy differences or even for successful repudiation of extremists. And the secular media love to publicize the worst examples, such as intolerant attacks on the civil rights of gay Americans or the murder of doctors who perform abortions.

Evangelicals urgently need some commonly agreed upon principles of a political philosophy. It would not solve all our political problems, but it would help.

## Methodology

Here I want to sketch the methodology I use in approaching political questions.

### *Jesus Is Lord*

The centerpiece of all genuinely Christian politics is the lordship of Jesus Christ. Christians believe that the Galilean champion of the poor and marginalized is the Creator of the galaxies, the Sovereign of the universe. Therefore, all who believe in him seek to submit every realm of life—whether family, economics, or politics—unconditionally to Christ the Lord.

Christians therefore reject the uncritical embrace of any and every secular ideology—whether right, left, "green," libertarian, or communitarian. The Christian's starting point must be the Word of God, which is revealed partially in creation, more fully in the Bible, and most completely in Jesus Christ, the eternal Word become flesh. Founding political engagement on ideologies of left or right rather than Christ is fundamentally un-Christian.

### *Four Components*

Starting with the lordship of Christ, however, does not instantly provide detailed political guidance on specific policy issues. Nor does citing specific biblical texts instantly solve complex political questions. Serious Christian political engagement must recognize the complexity and ambiguity of political decisions. Every political judgment rests finally on a normative framework on the one hand and careful study of society and the world on the other. It is helpful to distinguish four different, interrelated components of every political decision: (1) a normative framework; (2) a broad study of society and the world; (3) a political philosophy; and (4) detailed social analysis on specific issues.

#### *Normative Framework*

If our political activity is to be genuinely Christian, then the guiding norms for our politics must come from the core of our faith. Since biblical faith teaches that some sense of the true and good is embedded in the human conscience, common wisdom (call it natural law, if you like) can offer some guidance. Some Christians, especially Roman Catholics, believe that it is still possible to derive major input for one's normative framework from general revelation.[5] My own inclination is to think that since the fall has deeply clouded the understanding of God's law written on all hearts, general revelation by itself cannot be the primary source of the Christian's normative framework for political engagement. For clarity, therefore, I turn to the revealed truth of the Scriptures.

Discovering relevant biblical norms for specific political issues is not, however, a matter of simple proof-texting. The Bible is full of commands, stories, proverbs—in short, a wide variety of materials written over many centuries. To develop a fully biblical perspective on political issues, we need two things: (a) a biblical view of the world and persons (I call this the biblical story); (b) an understanding of biblical teaching related to many concrete issues—for example, the family or economic justice (I call these biblical paradigms). To develop a normative biblical framework, we must in principle examine all relevant biblical passages, understand each text according to proper principles of exegesis, and then formulate a comprehensive summary of all relevant canonical material. The most sweeping comprehensive summary would deal with the biblical story. The other comprehensive summaries (or biblical paradigms) would cover things such as the poor, the family, work, justice, the dignity of persons, etc.[6]

### Broad Study of Society and the World

By itself, however, the biblical framework is insufficient. Nothing in the Bible talks explicitly about the pros and cons of a market economy or multinational corporations or the impact of 6 billion people on the natural environment around them.

In addition to a normative framework, we need a broad, comprehensive study of our world. That study takes many forms. It includes reflection on the historical development of society, the economy, political systems, etc. (As finite historical beings, we come to see some things more clearly as history unfolds.) It also includes, in principle, detailed, comprehensive socioeconomic and political analysis of everything relevant to any particular political question.

This careful study becomes central at two stages of analysis. One's analysis of the history of economics, politics, etc., helps to shape one's political philosophy (see below). For example, as the Marxist experiment worked itself out in the course of the twentieth century, it became more and more clear not only that Marxist philosophy contradicted the biblical view of persons but also that in practice Marxism led to economic inefficiency and political totalitarianism. Similarly, it is becoming increasingly clear that substantial injustice accompanies the functioning of today's market economies. Detailed social analysis of everything relevant to a particular politician or piece of legislation is also crucial (see below).

### Political Philosophy

In addition to a biblical framework and a broad study of society and the world, Christians engaged in politics also need a political philosophy. It is simply impossible, every time one wants to make a political decision, to spend days (actually years) reviewing the mountains of relevant biblical material and complex studies of society. We need a framework, a road map, a handy guide—in short, a political philosophy. But we dare not adopt our political philosophy uncritically from some non-Christian source. It must emerge from our normative biblical framework and painstaking, extensive socioeconomic and political analysis.

### Detailed Social Analysis on Specific Issues

Even after a Christian has a political philosophy shaped by both a normative biblical framework and careful study of society and the world, he or she still needs to do detailed social analysis on everything relevant to a particular legislative proposal or a specific election. Two people could, in principle, have identical normative frameworks, identical historical analyses of modern society, and identical political philosophies and still disagree on whether or not, for example, to raise the minimum wage. Why? Because they rely on different economic analyses of the actual effects of raising the minimum wage. The only way to make progress on settling such a disagreement is to go back together and do further detailed economic analysis. Careful social analysis of all the available information relevant to any specific political judgment is the fourth essential ingredient of responsible Christian political engagement.

## Other Introductory Points

### Complexity and Political Necessity

The method just described is complex—in fact, far more complex than I have been able to suggest here. Every one of the four steps intersects with all the others. Our reading of history shapes the questions we put to the Bible as we seek to develop a normative framework. That framework, in turn, shapes everything else.

In real life we cannot wait to make political decisions until we have completed all the study that is desirable. We must make decisions based on our best current understanding and then keep open to further insight and information.

### Cooperation and Humility

The kind of study required for faithful Christian political engagement is far too complex for any one individual. We need communal activity, teams of scholars and activists, and organizations and networks working together to develop a common vision and agenda. For successful Christian political engagement, then, we need groups of Christians who can integrate a normative biblical framework, study of society and world, a political philosophy (derived from the former two ingredients), and detailed social analysis as they all approach every major issue of contemporary political life. That means working out concrete public policy proposals on everything from welfare reform to family policy to peacemaking.

Knowing the complexity of such political judgments and the possibility of mistakes at every step, we must always hold our specific political conclusions with great humility and tentativeness. But we should dare to advocate boldly for specific policies because we have sought to ground our specific conclusions in a biblical framework and responsible social analysis even as we invite friend and foe alike to help us improve our analysis of both the Scriptures and society at every point.

### Resolving Disagreements

It would help immensely to reduce political disagreements among Christians if we would be more precise about where we disagree. It is unhelpful to confuse a disagreement over the proper interpretation of Matthew 25 with lack of compassion for the poor or disagreement over the relative merits of more or less government intervention in market economies. To the extent that we can be precise about exactly where we disagree, we can make more progress in overcoming our differences.[7]

### Common Language

In a pluralistic society one additional crucial step is essential. Many citizens have no interest at all in political proposals advocated on the basis of a biblical framework. Therefore, we must develop a common language grounded in the common good of all citizens when we take our specific proposals into the public realm. We must try to develop reasons for our policies that are intelligible and convincing to all people, not just Christians.

### The Starting Point—the Christian Community

It is absolutely crucial, however, that Christians first articulate and develop their political agenda and concrete proposals within the Christian community on the basis of biblical norms. If we do not, we will end up adopting secular norms and values and their corresponding political ideologies. The result will be a compromised, often fundamentally unChristian, political engagement.

That is exactly what has happened with many Christians in politics. Too many Christians have uncritically adopted left-wing or right-wing politics. The result has been a sub-Christian religious right that correctly championed the family and the sanctity of human life but neglected economic justice for the poor, uncritically endorsed American nationalism, ignored environmental concern for God's creation, and neglected to struggle against racism. Equally sub-Christian has been a religious left that rightly defended justice, peace and the integrity of creation but largely forgot about the importance of the family and sexual integrity, uncritically endorsed Marxism, the sexual revolution, and almost everything championed under the banner of gay rights, overlooked the fact that freedom is as important as justice, and failed to defend the most vulnerable of all, the unborn and the very old.

This essay is written first of all for the Christian community. Therefore, it first outlines a normative biblical framework and then sketches a political philosophy. Little attention is given to developing the common language for advocating these policies in the larger pluralistic society, although that is also an essential task.

## Normative Biblical Framework

### The Biblical Story

The biblical story provides an essential framework for Christian political thought. The entire created order is good and precious because it comes from the hand of a loving God. Persons created in the image of God are called to a servantlike stewardship of the rest of the Creator's handiwork. Tragically, humanity rebelled against God, and the results include selfish persons, twisted social relationships and institutions, and even a groaning, disordered creation. Unwilling to forsake fallen humanity, however, the Creator began a long historical process of salvation to restore a right relationship among God, persons, and the creation around them. At the center of that redeeming grace is Jesus Christ, Nazarene carpenter and eternal Word, who models perfect humanity, atones for our sins, and rises from the dead to break the power of evil. History is moving toward the risen Lord's return, when all things will be restored to wholeness.[8] This biblical story provides a foundation for thinking about the nature, dignity, and destiny of persons, the status of the nonhuman world, the importance of the historical process, and the ultimate meaning of all things.

From this biblical story as well as all the other relevant biblical material, we can develop comprehensive biblical summaries or paradigms of specific topics that are especially relevant to politics. The following are some of the most important.[9]

### Biblical Paradigms

#### The Special Dignity and Sanctity of Every Human Being

Every human being—and only human beings—is made in the image of God, called to stewardship of the nonhuman creation, made to find fulfillment only when rightly related to God, neighbor, the earth, and self, summoned to respond in freedom to God's invitation of salvation, and invited to live forever in the presence of God.

We must act on the belief that from the moment of conception, we are dealing with human life. No extended biblical passage explicitly teaches that; none denies it. A number of texts use words for the unborn that are normally applied to those who have been born. For nineteen centuries the Christian church has been overwhelmingly opposed to abortion. Modern science now demonstrates with astounding detail that from the moment of conception a genetically distinct human being with a continuous biological development exists. If one is uncertain whether this developing fetus is a human being, one should adopt that view as a working assumption. To do otherwise would be like shooting blindly into a darkened theater with the justification that we cannot know whether we will hit empty seats or murder innocent persons. The directly intended taking of innocent human life—whether in abortion or euthanasia—is wrong.

#### Freedom of Belief

Throughout biblical history God gives persons enormous freedom to respond in obedience or rebellion, unbelief or faith. Jesus' parable of the wheat and tares shows that God chooses to allow this freedom to persons until the final judgment. Therefore, religious freedom is an essential element of a good society.

#### The Family

Strong, stable families (persons related by blood, marriage, or adoption) are essential for a good society. Keeping marriage vows, accepting God's design that sexual intercourse be reserved for a man and a woman united in a lifelong marriage covenant, and valuing singles in the extended family are all important aspects of strengthening the family.

#### Justice

The two key Hebrew words for justice (*mishpat* and *tsedaqah*) are used to call for both just courts and just economic arrangements.

Fair courts require honest witnesses and impartial justice that is not biased toward rich or poor.

Fair economic arrangements[10] require—as the Old Testament treatment of the land (the basic capital in an agricultural society) shows—an arrangement where all families and persons have access to the productive resources needed to earn a decent living and be dignified participating members of society. Sometimes, of course, wrong personal choices rightly result in the loss of these productive resources for a time, but God does not want that to continue forever. Frequently, too, according to the Bible, powerful oppressive people seize these resources from the poorest. Justice requires restoration of equitable arrangements where all have the opportunity to work and thus obtain a generous portion of the necessities of life.

In addition, those who are unable to work and provide for themselves must be cared for by their family and the larger community.

### A Special Concern for the Poor

Hundreds of biblical texts declare God's special concern for the poor and demand that God's people imitate God's concern. One crucial measure of how obedient people judge societies and policies is by what they do to the poorest, weakest, and most marginalized. This special concern to strengthen the poorest is not a bias toward the poor but rather a concern for equal justice for everyone.

### Work

Work is essential to the dignity of human beings, who are called to be coshapers of history with God. Every able person has the responsibility to work, and people have the obligation to structure society so that every person can work in a way that respects human dignity and earns a decent living.

### Peacemaking

Christians look forward to the time when "nation shall not lift up sword against nation, neither shall they learn war anymore." Until the Lord returns, unfortunately, persons persistently resort to wars and rumors of wars. Many Christians believe they should, as the lesser of two evils, engage in just wars for the sake of preserving some order and peace. Other Christians believe that killing is always contrary to the teaching of Christ and that he calls us to overcome our enemies with suffering love rather than the sword. But all agree that Jesus' words "blessed are the peacemakers" are urgent in our time.

### Individuality and Community

Biblical faith holds together the inestimable value of each person, each person's freedom to shape his or her own life, and the fact that persons are made for community and only achieve wholeness in right relationship with others in the family and the larger society.

### Rulers

God ordains rulers both to restrain evil and to promote good. In biblical thought, the justice that God calls the king to do (Ps. 72:1–4, 12–14) includes nurturing both fair courts and economic systems that strengthen the poor.

God stands far above every political ruler. No politician or government has ultimate authority. The story of Naboth's vineyard demonstrates the rights of individual families over against the king. When the king defied God's law, the prophet challenged and condemned him. Everyone and everything, including rulers and government, have only a limited authority that is subordinate to the divine Sovereign.

## Political Philosophy

The Bible does not prescribe any particular political philosophy. Political philosophies emerge as people in community over a period of time integrate a normative framework and careful study and reflection on historical experience. As long as we understand our political philosophy as a useful guide (to be improved by further normative reflection and social analysis) rather than an unchanging dogma, it can be a helpful tool for navigating complex political decisions.

The following components of a political philosophy are, I hope, consistent with biblical revelation and rigorous social analysis.

### Decentralization of Power

There is both a positive and a negative reason for decentralizing all forms of power. Each person is called to exercise his or her creation mandate and become a coworker with God in shaping history. If a small elite makes most decisions, the majority cannot exercise their God-given mandate. Negatively, as Lord Acton pointed out, power tends to corrupt and absolute power tends to corrupt absolutely. Sinful people in a fallen world will almost always use unchecked centralized power to benefit themselves unfairly and oppress others. Therefore, to avoid totalitarianism and injustice, power must be decentralized.

The principle of subsidiarity in Catholic social teaching rightly stresses that, other things being equal, activity should be undertaken by a lower level of government or by a smaller societal institution rather than by a higher or larger unit. At the same time, it must be clearly recognized that some things can only be done (or at least done well) in a more centralized way. Careful analysis is needed in each situation.

### Democracy

A concern for human rights, individual freedom, and the decentralization of power leads to a democratic political order. When freedom of speech, secret voting, and universal suffrage exist, people—at least in theory—have the political power to shape society for the benefit of the majority. Separating legislative, administrative, and judicial functions and balancing national, state, and local governmental realms also decentralizes power.

### Nongovernmental Institutions

A large group of institutions intermediate between the individual and government decentralize power and provide smaller contexts for human communities to flourish. These include the family, the church, the media, the schools, the economy, and a host of smaller voluntary associations. These intermediate centers of power provide a check on governmental power and thus are a significant foundation of freedom.

### Private Ownership and a Market Economy

The history of the twentieth century has shown clearly that when the state owns and controls most of the economy, economic and political power is so centralized that totalitarianism is almost guaranteed. Genuinely decentralized private ownership, on the other hand, nurtures free individuals and serves as a counterbalance to political power. Determining prices and production via supply and demand has also proven to be far more efficient than central planning.

Huge privately owned corporations, of course, can also become centers of enormous economic power. When the same corporations own the media and provide most of the funding for election campaigns, economic and political power is again dangerously centralized.

A concern for justice and freedom demands a continuing vigilance against all forms of centralized economic power and constant effort to strengthen smaller centers of economic life, including family-owned farms and businesses, cooperatives, and widespread home ownership.

### Religious Freedom and Church/State Relations

The First Amendment's prohibition against the government's establishing any official religion or preventing its free exercise is a crucial aspect of a society that truly respects human dignity and individual freedom. Religious freedom is a gift from God, not the state. Government can only acknowledge and defend it.

Avoiding established religion, however, does not mean that religious expression is banished to the private sphere. Everyone, including religious people, should be free to develop and state the implications of their deepest convictions for public policy. Faith-based institutions have a long and venerable history of engagement in education, health care, and social welfare. When government adopts programs to enable the voluntary sector to serve the public good in these areas, there should be no discrimination in eligibility on account of religion, nor should there be exclusionary criteria that force these providers to engage in self-censorship or to otherwise abandon their religious character.

### Human Rights

The right to life and freedom are inalienable because they come from God, not government. Government should recognize and protect the freedom of religion, speech, and political activity.

### Family

Government rightly recognizes and favors the family (those related by blood, marriage, and adoption) and especially the nuclear family (wife, husband, and children) with its larger circle of extended family (grandparents, etc.) as an essential element in a stable society. The family, not government, has the primary responsibility for raising children. Religious institutions can do far more than government to strengthen the family, but government should do what it can. That includes discouraging (although not preventing) divorce and sexual promiscuity and recognizing that children are best served when they live with both of their parents. It also includes not broadening the definition of marriage to include gay partners and not defining family as any two or more people cohabiting. Government rightly offers tax and other benefits that favor marriage rather than cohabitation or divorce.

### Care for Creation and a Sustainable Planet

Responsible care for creation flows from a biblical worldview. We face a long-term environmental crisis. Utilitarian attitudes must be balanced by a recognition of the intrinsic worth of all God's creation and human responsibility to act as God's faithful stewards. Human beings have far more worth than plants or animals. But very seldom, if ever, do we have to choose between taking a human life and destroying an endangered species. Usually it is a choice between growing affluence and obliterating the handiwork of the Creator.

We must aim to develop sustainable economic practices that reduce the stress on natural systems and make it possible for us to pass on a lovely, sustainable planet to our descendants. The needs of the poor and most vulnerable must be central in all environmental decisions; the rich must pay the major cost of reducing environmental damage. We must encourage alternative sources of energy that decrease our reliance on nonrenewable sources. We must balance the needs of workers and the environment.

### The Role of Government

Government should both restrain evil and promote the common good. Nurturing an economic order where everyone, especially the poorest, has the resources to earn a decent living is a central concern of good government. Government is responsible for providing the legal and social framework in which the other institutions in society can flourish. Government should carefully strengthen rather than replace society's intermediate institutions when they experience trouble.

What should be legislated and what not? Why should there be laws against something like racial discrimination in the sale of housing and not against an act of adultery? The following considerations are relevant: (1) individuals should normally be free to harm themselves (e.g., get drunk regularly at home) but not be free to harm others (e.g., drive while drunk); (2) laws must be enforceable in a way that does not undermine other important values (e.g., even if it were good, in spite of the first principle, to have a criminal penalty for adultery, it would be impossible to enforce such a law without the kind of police state that would destroy freedom); (3) laws have a teaching function—to some extent people think (wrongly) that what is legal is moral.

### Work and Workers

Since work is essential to human dignity, every able-bodied person should have the opportunity to work at a job that pays a wage that can support a family. An unemployment rate that denies the dignity of work to people other than those properly in transition from one job to another is immoral and socially destructive. Conversely, people who can work have an obligation to do so in order to earn their living. Welfare policies should assist those who cannot care for themselves but dare not discourage work and responsibility.

Workers have a right to safe working conditions, a living wage, and reasonable job security. The legal right of workers to organize unions counterbalances corporate economic power, encourages justice, and nurtures dignity and self-respect.

### The Priority of the Poor

Poverty has many causes. Those who are poor because they are unable to provide for themselves should be given a decent living by their family and/or other nongovernmental groups where possible and the government where necessary. Those who are poor because of personal irresponsibility should suffer appropriate consequences. Those, however, who are poor—whether through accident of birth or the neglect or oppression of others—because they lack the education and the capital to be productive, self-sufficient members of society should be empowered by both private institutions and government.

Justice demands that every person has equal opportunity to acquire the basic capital (whether land, money, or education) that will enable that person to earn a decent living and be a dignified participating member of society. Strengthening the poor by providing such opportunity should be a central concern of government. Every significant governmental decision should be judged by its impact on the poorest.

### A Consistent Ethic of Life

The first and most basic human right is the inviolable right to life of every human being. The first and most basic responsibility of civil law is to ensure that this right is recognized and protected.

Abortion involves the direct, intentional, and violent taking of human life. No law that legitimizes the direct killing of innocent human beings through abortion can be just. Therefore, we must work for the legal protection of the unborn and oppose all public funding of abortions.

At the same time, we must develop a wide range of alternatives to abortion—both to reduce the evil of abortion and also in recognition that two people are directly involved, not just one. A caring society will surround women who have unwanted pregnancies with love and concrete support, including financial assistance and better adoption alternatives.

Euthanasia—the direct killing of the aged and infirm either with or without their consent—is wrong. That does not mean that it is immoral to refuse or withhold extraordinary medical treatment when death is imminent or inevitable. But we dare not blur the distinction between *allowing* a person to die and *killing* a person.

Concern for a consistent ethic of life does not end with abortion and euthanasia. Life does not begin at conception and end at birth. Tens of millions of people die unnecessarily each year of starvation and malnutrition. Tobacco kills millions of people prematurely each year. Capital punishment kills human beings. We should seek to protect the sanctity of human life wherever it is threatened and violated.

That is not to deny a significant moral difference between abortion and death from lung cancer caused by smoking. The direct, intentional taking of innocent human life in abortion, euthanasia, and genocide is morally more grave than the indirect, unintentional taking of human life in starvation or death from smoking. But all are wrong and all reflect disregard for the inestimable value of human life. Respect for human life is a seamless garment. A consistent ethic of life opposes and seeks to reduce not only abortion and euthanasia but also capital punishment, starvation, and cigarette-induced cancer.

### *Peacemaking*

Those who threaten society, from within or without, must be restrained. Historically, that has usually been done through lethal force as a last resort. Historically, too, it is true both that vast numbers of people have been killed and also that a variety of nonviolent methods of conflict resolution have successfully replaced lethal force. The courts, for example, replaced dueling. In the twentieth century, Gandhi, King, and a host of others successfully used nonviolent techniques to end oppression and seek justice.

Christians today disagree over the extent to which nonviolent models of conflict resolution can successfully replace most or all use of lethal force. But all agree that the search for nonviolent alternatives must be greatly strengthened. Wherever possible, nonviolence must replace lethal force.

### Toward an Evangelical Political Philosophy

I have tried to sketch, very briefly, my own developing understanding of some of the principles for an evangelical political philosophy. But I am not content simply to have individual thinkers work on this in their academic and professional colloquia!

I think evangelical leaders in this country need to come together and try to hammer out a declaration—let's call it "Principles for an Evangelical Political Philosophy"—that could be endorsed across a broad range of evangelical traditions. I think the same needs to happen in every country where substantial numbers of evangelicals exist and are engaged in politics. It also needs to happen at a global level so that people from other countries can help us overcome our one-sidedness and blind spots.

How might we arrive at such a declaration that would help us? It would be foolish to try to sketch a detailed process for developing a document on principles for an evangelical political philosophy widely embraced by a broad cross section of evangelicals in the United States. The venture is enormously difficult. Success can come only at the end of a lengthy journey that will inevitably involve detours and land mines. Pilgrims on the journey will need to improvise at each stage.

However, three things, at least, seem clear to me. The process must include a wide range of evangelical voices; the goal should be limited; and the engagement of major evangelical gatekeepers is indispensable.

If the result is to be of any lasting significance, then we must involve a wide range of evangelical voices. I could sit down today and sketch an evangelical political philosophy that many members of Evangelicals for Social Action would largely endorse. James Dobson could do the same for Focus on the Family. What would help, if it could be developed, is a broad framework that both James and I, plus a wide cross section of people who identify themselves as evangelicals, could embrace as a guide for our concrete political engagement.

Second, our goal must be limited. Not even this raving optimist supposes that we could agree on a detailed, full-blown evangelical political philosophy across the range of views that exist within the evangelical community.

For example, we do disagree, however incoherently, about the proper role of government. Therefore, a comprehensive, common statement on the role of government would be impossible. But would it not help if a broad range of evangelical voices could together reject both libertarianism and socialism and then together define some general criteria for when and how government should and should not intervene in market economies?

The same would be true in a variety of areas. It would be helpful if we could agree together on the basic parameters of a consistent pro-life position, on how to balance the free exercise and nonestablishment clauses of the First Amendment, and so on. If from the beginning we agree that our goal is a limited, incomplete evangelical political philosophy that different groups can develop further in divergent ways, we might at least be able to state a basic framework that would help us overcome some of our naïveté, confusion, and disagreement.

At first glance, our task appears to be nearly impossible. Evangelicals do not have a pope or bishops who can, with some authority, articulate an evangelical political philosophy. Instead, we have a confused babel of more or less influential gatekeepers whose words are respected within their larger or smaller constituencies. Thus, the project will succeed only if leaders representing this broad spectrum within the evangelical community endorse the process and sign the resulting document.

I have no illusions that most evangelical political disagreement would disappear even if multiple miracles produced a widely accepted set of principles for an evangelical political philosophy. Finite sinners that we are, we would still argue about its implications for specific public policy proposals. A common framework, however, would help in several ways.

First, agreement on a basic framework would help us identify more common ground on specific issues, which could help us have a greater impact.

Second, only if we develop a common vision that can sustain evangelical political engagement over the long haul will we produce any lasting political change.

Third, if evangelical Protestants (I include African Americans and theologically orthodox Christians in the older Protestant denominations) developed even the beginnings of a common political philosophy, we would be in a better position to cooperate with Catholics in shaping public life. Few potential political developments are more important. If evangelicals and Catholics learn how to cooperate, this majority could significantly reshape American politics.

That brings me to my last point. I think one of the most urgent political tasks for American Christians is for white evangelicals, Catholics, and African American and Latino Christians to discover how to work together politically around a pro-life *and* pro-poor, pro-family *and* pro-racial justice agenda. A well-organized coalition of those groups could significantly reshape our public life for the better.

I see the beginnings of this kind of new coalition in several quarters. From the liberal side, the Call to Renewal, and from the conservative side, the signers of "We Hold These Truths" have formally embraced this four-part agenda. In practice, of course, conservatives still tend to major on pro-life and pro-family issues and liberals still emphasize economic and racial justice. These one-sided approaches need to end.

I think the approach that I have sketched in this paper could help that happen. If a wide cross section of evangelical leaders prayerfully and thoughtfully sought to listen to what the Bible and historical experience tell us about principles for an evangelical political philosophy, including the kind of balanced political agenda that reflects the full range of God's concerns, then I believe we might be able to overcome some of our differences and work together in a way that could bless this society and the world.

# 7

# POLITICS AFTER THE CULTURE WARS

## HARRY L. POE

On October 19, 1974, I went to Pawley's Island to relax instead of to Anderson, South Carolina, to have supper with the newly sworn-in president, Gerald Ford. At the time, I was the finance director of the South Carolina Republican party. That year—1974—was a dreadful year to be Republican anywhere in the United States. Richard Nixon resigned in July and the Republicans were poised to lose every election in the country. In South Carolina it was worse. We were in a governor's race and our candidate had only a 20 percent recognition factor among the voters, and we had not elected a Republican governor since Reconstruction.

When I first got involved in a political campaign in 1962, South Carolina did not have a single elected Republican official. In those days the Republican party in South Carolina consisted primarily of Yankees who had moved south and disaffected Democrats who had supported Eisen-

Harry L. Poe (Ph.D., Southern Seminary) is Vice President for Academic Resources and Information Services at Union University. Before entering the ministry, he served as Finance Director of the South Carolina Republican party and as a member of the Committee to Re-Elect the President (CREEP).

hower and gained the power of patronage for appointive positions in South Carolina during Ike's administration. In 1964, however, Strom Thurmond switched parties and the germ of a new Republican party began. In 1966 I joined the TeenAge Republicans (TARs) and was elected vice chairman for Greenville County. We elected seven Republicans to the South Carolina House of Representatives that year, but Republicans suffered humiliating defeats in every other election in the state. In 1966 and 1970, Joseph O. Rogers and Albert Watson were trounced in their bids for governor.

Those of us who got involved in politics as teenagers did so from a profound sense of duty. We saw southern politics as the festering remains of a corrupt one-party system that held the South in a stranglehold. Defeat did not discourage us. We discovered that there were others like us all over the state. I was elected state treasurer of the TeenAge Republicans, and my group formed bonds with others across the state that would continue to be strong thirty years later. Then our vision broadened. I went to Washington as Strom Thurmond's page, and there I witnessed in October 1967 the march on the Pentagon. It was an exciting time. For the first time in my awareness, they closed the huge bronze doors to the rotunda of the Capitol—to keep the hippies out! Hundreds of thousands of hippies descended on Washington for the weekend, and I received my first full exposure to the counterculture.

Many Christians today are preparing to fight the culture wars. They do not realize that the culture wars were fought between 1963 and 1973. For the most part, Christians did not even take part. Consider the changes that took place. When the movie *In the Heat of the Night* came out in the mid-1960s, it hit the country like a blockbuster with its treatment of race relations. Thirty years later, however, young people who see it for the first time are left scratching their heads. The climax of the movie comes when a white southern lynch mob decides not to bother Sidney Poitier. What force could possibly be stronger than the emotion of racism? The mob's revulsion comes when they discover that Poitier's accuser is involved in an abortion operation. The movie worked because in the mid-1960s virtually all Americans held a common view of abortion. The success of the counterculture changed all of that, so that by 1973 the Supreme Court could reflect the growing popular opinion that abortion was an expression of freedom. And as Janice Joplin sang in "Me and Bobby McGee":

> Freedom's just another word for nothing left to lose.
> Freedom's just another word to me.
> Feeling good was good enough when Bobby sang the blues.
> Feeling good was good enough for me,
> Good enough for me and Bobby McGee.

By the time I got to college in 1969, the counterculture had already dramatically altered the moral compass. What most people did not realize, however, was that the counterculture involved more than hippies. Movies like *The Graduate* and *Goodbye, Columbus* had shattered the old taboos of sexuality.

In the spring of my freshman year, college campuses all over the country erupted into riots following the Cambodian incursion and the shootings at Kent State. The radicals at the University of South Carolina called for a student strike. A small group of us immediately announced the creation of the Student Strike Back Coalition and claimed to represent 95 percent of the student body. I was chair of the Carolina College Republicans, and my co-conspirator, Richard Hines, was president of the senior class by default because all of the other candidates had been disqualified. He would later be the rationale for abolishing class officers at Carolina. Invitations to go on television came from all over the state, and money poured in to help our cause.

It is intriguing to study the anatomy of a riot. Carolina should not have had one. The radicals could only drum up forty-nine hippies to march to the Horseshoe for their demonstration. My friend, Richard Hines, met them there, and as they gave their speeches, Richard declared, "Don't you dare try to take down this flag" as he flung himself in front of the flagpole and proceeded to make a speech. Unfortunately, while waving his arms in flamboyant and dramatic gestures, he tangled himself in the ropes just as one of the radicals yelled, "Hey, let's take down the flag." In the melee that ensued, Richard yelled out, "Don't you dare try to take over the Student Union Building," which prompted another radical to shout, "Hey, let's go take over the Student Union Building."

A carnival atmosphere prevailed as thousands of Carolina students turned out to watch the hippies take over the Student Union Building. Whatever possessed the highway patrol to fire tear gas into the crowd one will never know, but Carolina joined the schools that had their very own riots that year. After the riots, breaking with tradition and old values became an easy matter.

During the summer of 1970, the Charles Edison Youth Fund and the Young Americans for Freedom began an initiative to bring the best and the brightest of America's young conservative leadership to Washington for the summer to study comparative political and economic systems at Georgetown University and work as interns in congressional offices. We went on full scholarship plus a stipend, or "walking-around money" as we used to call it.

I learned something that startled me about the young conservatives. On Sunday morning I was the only one awake. That summer I was the only one under fifty at the Georgetown Baptist Church. The young conservatives were true clean-cut anticommunists and laissez-faire capitalists, but in terms of lifestyle and values, they were just like the hippies.

In 1971 I succeeded Richard Hines as state chairman of the South Carolina College Republicans. On November 19 we had a fund-raising dinner with Martha Mitchell, the notorious late-night-telephoning wife of the attorney general, as the featured speaker. Two important things happened that night. I was asked to head up the college campaign for the Committee to Re-Elect the President (CREEP) in South Carolina, and Hal Derrick from Newberry College brought a brand-new recruit to the dinner, Lee Atwater. I remembered Lee because he was quite drunk and he tried to pick up the wife of a party chairman from one of the smaller counties.

Becoming a member of CREEP involved quite an initiation, which played to our vanity and need for recognition. Harry Dent came down from Washington to meet with the members of the South Carolina committee. We were the most influential Republicans in the state. He gave us each a felt-tip pen with the presidential seal and Richard Nixon's signature emblazoned across the side. Then he gave us a blue button with white lettering that read, "TOTAL COMMITMENT." Then he gave the sermon. We were totally committed to the reelection of Richard Nixon. Nothing on earth was more important. The future of the nation and the world depended upon it. And until his reelection, everything else in our lives would have to come second: our job, our family, our church. I had heard the sermon many times, but it had always been at a revival meeting, and in the past the preacher had been talking about Jesus instead of Richard Nixon.

By now the political process had given me a profound education. I had seen the role of personality conflict, ego, pettiness, manipulation, humiliation, distortion, innuendo, misrepresentation, suspicion, mistrust, treachery, and compromise. When Watergate occurred, I had a cold, numb feeling about it, because I knew the national CREEP office well enough to know the break-in looked like our work. In July I resigned from CREEP and Lee Atwater took my place. Lee was not very smart, but he knew how to take advice. My Uncle Frank used to say, "He who tooteth not his own horn, getteth not his own horn tooted." Lee sounded like the brass section of the New York Philharmonic. I had distanced myself from politics, but like a junkie, I could not quite let go. The next year the party chairman waved dollar bills in front of my face and offered me the number-two position in the party, which brings us back to October of 1974.

One balmy Thursday afternoon I was driving through the countryside, minding my own business, when God spoke to me. He reminded me that at the age of ten I had heard a call to preach and had agreed to do it. It had been our little secret for fourteen years, throughout my rise in politics. For fourteen years he had been reminding me of my call and my promise, and for fourteen years I had been rationalizing and negotiating as any good politician does. After all, God needed Christians in politics. That was the fundamental flaw in my reasoning, because God does not need anything.

This time, however, God said something different. This time he said that if I was determined to be a professional politician, he would not bother me anymore. It intrigues me how often we do not appreciate something until we lose it. Instead of driving to Anderson to hobnob with the president's advance team, I drove to see my pastor in Greenville to tell him I was leaving politics to enter the ministry.

We often forget the proper role of a Christian in politics simply because the presence of power and fame confuses us. Christians sometimes believe they can use the power and fame for Christ. Actually, the power and fame are nonissues in terms of effectiveness for Christ and his kingdom. The power of a Christian in politics comes not from human instruments of government and law, of election campaigns and public opinion, or of influence and patronage. The power of a Christian in politics is the same as the power of a Christian in business, art, education, farming, sales, or auto mechanics. The power lies in the witness of one in whom Christ richly dwells.

Probably the example of the four Hebrew eunuchs, Daniel, Shadrach, Meshach, and Abednego, gives the best model for involvement in politics. It is important to remember that in politics you have entered enemy territory, and the devil takes no prisoners. An old political adage that was drummed into my head goes, "Destroy your enemies or they will come back to haunt you." This proverb was the faith commitment behind Nixon's hit list and Clinton's FBI investigation of Republican donors. The Hebrew eunuchs were willing to die for their faith, but too often we face the temptation that suggests it is more important for us to remain engaged in the process where we can continue to do good and exert a positive influence than to lose everything over a matter of conscience. Pontius Pilate taught us well that we can take the high road, make the necessary compromises, and wash our hands of any personal taint. He sacrificed just one man for a higher good: he kept the peace and preserved his political career.

Government and other human institutions are established by God to provide for public order. They provide an important function in restraining the violence and covetousness of people. Government can provide the coordination of effort that allows for the free flow of communication and travel. Government can provide for basic human services that lead to an educated and productive citizenry. No government, however, has ever successfully dealt with the corruption and decay that infects its own society. No government, institution, or culture has ever survived permanently. God has raised them up and pulled them down. History tells

102      CHRISTIAN POLITICAL ENGAGEMENT

the story of those that have fallen, and prophecy describes the fate of those that have not.

Whenever Christians believe that politics and government can be allies in the solution to spiritual problems, we have deluded ourselves. Christians have never handled power very well. We handle persecution and suffering exceedingly well. Augustine of Hippo warned us sixteen hundred years ago that there are two cities: the secular city and the city of God. The one will perish while the other is eternal. He was only reflecting the teachings of Paul that our citizenship is in the commonwealth of heaven. Nonetheless, we must live in this world until we die, doing all to the glory of Christ. Our error comes when we think that the secular city can become the city of God by secular means.

Spiritual problems cannot be solved politically. The Puritans of England tried from 1642 until 1660, but they only created a civil and religious mess. Christians involved in politics can address the issues of sewage treatment, road construction, national defense, and the economy, but government cannot address the issues that relate to the complete moral collapse of the nation and Western culture.

When I left politics, it was hard to find a Baptist preacher in the South who was a Republican. Now it is hard to find one who is not. The Grand Old Party I devoted my youth to establishing in the South has had a remarkable success story beginning with that governor's race in South Carolina in 1974. We elected a Republican dentist as governor for a strange reason. The Democratic candidate, a young mortgage banker who had never been involved in politics, ran the first successful media campaign in the South to take the Democratic nomination from the lieutenant governor and a veteran congressman. Just before the election, the state Supreme Court (elected by the Democratic-controlled state legislature) disqualified the young contender on the grounds that he had not lived in the state long enough. A state convention was quickly called at which the old congressman called in his chips and gained the nomination. To punish the old politicians, the people of South Carolina elected a Republican.

That election did not simply mean the arrival of a two-party system in the South. It meant the triumph of the counterculture and the destruction of all the old traditions and values. By rejecting the action of the Democratic party, the people of South Carolina rejected their own tradition and identity. With that break, the Old South began to unravel. In the past, Southerners had behaved because of "what the neighbors might think." Now, the neighbors do not care, so there is no basis for morality anymore.

Nathan Bedford Forrest said he only had one strategy: "Get there first with the most." In the recent Southern Baptist controversy, the moderates never understood that maxim. For the last twenty years, since the birth of the Moral Majority and a variety of successor political groups, conservative Christians have misunderstood the maxim. They have tried to become a national force to be reckoned with by leveraging a shrinking percentage of the population for a place at the table. In exchange for the small extra boost at the ballot boxes, conservative Christians have been invited to prayer breakfasts, briefings, and goodwill tours, and have always had planks in the national Republican platform, none of which has translated into action on the major social and moral issues.

The last time I had lunch with Lee Atwater was in May of 1985. He had twenty-four hours to decide whether to manage the presidential campaign of Howard Baker, Jack Kemp, or George Bush. Howard Baker was out of office and Martin Van Buren was the only vice president in the history of the country to succeed the president of his own party by election. Therefore, Lee had decided to work for Kemp, the young, vibrant candidate. I simply said, "Who?" Only Bush had a significant recognition factor, and besides, there were no prominent governors likely to take the Democratic nomination. Americans have always preferred a governor to serve as president if one was available. Lee got the message.

But he also gave me a clear message. I asked him about the role of a Christian bloc in the Republican party. He said they could never get more than scraps because it would upset too many others. Besides, he saw a new kind of religious mind-set emerging in the United States. He talked about a nebulous mysticism and a declining influence of Christians. The Republican party dare not be too clearly identified with a Christian agenda or it would suffer a tremendous setback when the backlash hit.

In the late 1980s George Barna and George Gallup were describing the United States as an increasingly Christian society. By the mid 1990s, however, they had begun to understand that belief in God and prayer by huge numbers of Americans did not mean people were Christians. Instead, America has become increasingly pagan. The United States will not be rescued from its spiritual malaise by government restoration of Christian values. What is fundamentally wrong with the country will not be solved by the ballot box but through the baptistry.

The only strategy that matters is "Get there first with the most." I have been warning my friends in politics for years that they cannot expect to rally the same dwindling group of people by attacking those with different values and expect to win when those with different values become the majority.

Christian approaches to politics in the past have assumed a common understanding of God and Christ within the country, even when people did not choose to live their lives in submission to the Lord. Christians have now missed two generations of Americans and are quickly losing a third in terms of acquainting them with the gospel. Moving from most favored religion status to that of a barely tolerated minority position will be a tremendous challenge for Christians who have grown accustomed to power and privilege.

Every vocation has its dangers for a Christian. Politics is fraught with the dangers of vanity, pride, power, and conceit. Like other vocations, however, the call is to faithfulness rather than success.

Having lost the culture wars, we now have the opportunity to do what we have always done best. Christianity is a subversive movement. Rather than live remote and isolated lives, we were put here to infiltrate the new culture with the message of Christ. That message is the only power that will transform this culture.

Lee Atwater did not understand what that last statement meant for the longest time. Some commentators have cast doubts about Lee's sudden and dramatic conversion experience shortly before his death from cancer. To the contrary, it was one of the longest, drawn-out, belabored conversions I have ever witnessed. I did not have anything to say to Lee about faith when I was still active in politics and he was eager for any recognition I would give him. I was too busy looking at the big picture and the tremendous issues at stake to notice Atwater, other than to dismiss him. Not until January 1985 did I ever mention Christ to Lee. By then he was a deputy in the Reagan White House and had just established himself in the GOP as the heir to Lyn Nofziger. I was working in my study at the Simpsonville Baptist Church in Kentucky on a sermon about jealousy when the most unmentionable horror struck me. I was jealous of Atwater. As I meditated on it, I noticed something amazing about sin. I was jealous of Atwater for doing all the things I had no interest in doing anymore. Sin always has an irrational dimension in the light of day. I wrote Lee a note to confess my sin, and the most remarkable thing happened. He wrote me back, and we continued an intermittent correspondence until he died. I was not his evangelist, but I was one of his evangelists. Oddly enough, Harry Dent, who had pinned the TOTAL COMMITMENT button on me, prayed with Lee often, as did Chuck Colson, the instigator of so many of CREEP's dirty tricks.

Was it a tragedy that Lee did not become a Christian until just before his death? Think how much good he could have done as a committed Christian serving as chair of the Republican National Committee! I do not think that line of thought leads anywhere. Oddly enough, Lee turned out to be one of the ancient witnesses who was called upon to die. Shortly before his death, he wrote an account of his conversion that appeared in *Life* magazine. According to Harry Dent, the RNC managed to have it edited to remove the overtly Christian dimension so that it sounded like the vague, nebulous mysticism that Lee saw coming. But Lee had the last word. He died on Good Friday. It's hard to control the spin on an exit like that.

# 8

# EVANGELICALS AND POLITICS IN THE THIRD WORLD

## PAUL FRESTON

My interest in the theme of this chapter is twofold. First, in my career as an academic, it has been my major area of research, starting with a doctoral thesis on Protestantism and politics in Brazil, and then broadening out to other Latin American countries, in several of which I have been able to do fieldwork, and finally to Africa and Asia. I am just finishing a book on the subject, the first attempt as far as I know to map out evangelical political engagement in what is still often called the third world, and in some evangelical circles is referred to as the two-thirds world, since far from being an appendage, it contains the great majority of the world's population. Second, as a practicing evangelical and as a citizen of a third-world country, I am myself involved in politics.

Why could some familiarity with evangelical politics in the third world be of use to those who are wrestling with the way forward in the American context? First of all, and obviously, because of America's position in the world, and because the world is shrinking through globalization. But

Paul Freston (Ph.D., University of Campinas) is Lecturer in Sociology at the Methodist University of São Paulo, Brazil.

also because of the reality of the global church today, in which the vast majority of evangelicals live in the third world. It is parochial to imagine that what happens in Anglo-Saxon evangelicalism is still determinative globally. Besides, evangelicalism is a decentralized religion, with no Rome or Mecca. Evangelicalism is polycentric and culturally diverse. And last but not least, because of the Christian ideal of a universal body in which we can arrive at fullness only by learning from each other, in which there is no sacred culture or land, but rather "the priesthood of all cultures," Christianity as a universalism that affirms the particular. Evangelicalism's combination of universalism and particularity may be uniquely powerful in creating global community, a very different global community from the one being created by the dominant trends in the market and the media.

However, my work is not only about the other side of the world; it is also sociological, concerned to map out and analyze the reality of evangelical politics. This means avoiding the conspiracy theories and blanket condemnations found in some literature as well as the romantic and triumphalist image found in many evangelical publications. Like Marco Polo, I run the risk of being called a liar—indeed, I might not have believed some of the things I have read about some countries if I had not seen them with my own eyes in Brazil and elsewhere.

I shall not try to summarize the vast range of sociological material available on this issue. Evangelicalism is being put to an immense variety of political uses across the globe. That is not surprising when one considers the history of Christianity in general. Evangelical religion means different things to different people. It holds different positions in the social and religious field of each country, and varies from church to church. One cannot read off a person's politics from his religious doctrine; between doctrine and political practice many factors come into play. One cannot talk about "evangelicals" in the abstract, globally. The reality of third-world evangelicalism is that the social location of the churches has been very determinative, constraining political possibilities and affecting political behavior.

But there are common denominators. First, we are talking generally about evangelical communities that have grown rapidly in recent years. They are not old, well-established groups with strong institutions and traditions. Second, they are situated in poor countries and are often mostly the poor from those countries; evangelicalism is largely a religion of the third-world poor. So their cultural and educational resources are limited. Third, they are usually divided into many churches, so it is impossible to establish a normative "social doctrine" among them. Fourth, they operate in a religious market situation, so they are in competition for members and resources, and this does not encourage deep thinking or ethical teaching or self-denying politics. Fifth, they often do not have many international contacts and are cut off from the history of Christian reflection on politics. Sixth, they live in social contexts that are the product of increasing differentiation, which opens up space for them but also means they are often religious minorities with little political legitimacy (especially in Asia and to some extent Latin America). Seventh, the global context is the end of the Cold War, the onward march of global capitalism under neoliberal auspices, and the "third wave" of democratization.

One notes in general a lack of theorization about their political engagement. This contrasts with many other Christian currents in worldwide politics: liberation theology, Christian democracy, reconstructionism, the Christian Coalition, etc. While this situation has been effective at producing ecclesiastical leaders with a good presence in political crises, it has not been good at producing lay leaders of caliber. At a moment when many churches reach social visibility, they break out of their sectarian limits and broaden their concept of mission. They have to answer questions they have never tried to answer, and for this they need laypeople with training in a series of areas. The training needed for the third-world church now is not so much the conventional pastoral and evangelistic training but the formation of people who can interface with society in various areas of expertise. In a third world that goes from the tigers in crisis to the would-be tigers, to the extreme inequalities of Brazil and South Africa, to the critical cases of Africa, what does evangelical politics attempt to say that has any specificity and is not just "local subversion" (the subverting of the values of the worldwide church community by local interests, e.g., the Dutch Reformed in South Africa supporting apartheid) or "global subversion" (subordination to the trends of existing globalization)? What does it have to say about economic systems (from the standpoint of those who are on the sharp end), about geopolitical questions, about democracy, about gender? What concepts of the state, the market, and civil society does it work with?

Over all three continents, perhaps the central question is the relationship of evangelical politics to democracy. This includes questions such as religious pluralism and religious equality, but it goes much further. In Africa and parts of Asia, questions of ethnicity and national identity are also key and extremely complex. In Latin America, a key question has been the advisability of evangelical political parties.

I want to illustrate some of these questions by looking at case studies: Brazil, Guatemala, Colombia, Zambia, Kenya, Rwanda. Obviously, I cannot do justice to any of these countries; I shall merely highlight some aspects of each case to illustrate trends. I shall finish with a few ethical and theological considerations; as I am not a theologian, you will take those with a pinch of salt.

## Brazil

Brazil has the world's second-largest community of evangelicals. The social characteristics are illustrated in a recent survey of Rio de Janeiro: the rapid growth (almost one new church per day) is largely among the poor (the needier the district, the more churches per capita) and is popular (independent of social elites). Denominational creation is definitively nationalized; no newly arrived foreign church has established a significant presence in over forty years. Evangelical religion is a national, popular, and rapidly expanding phenomenon.[1]

In Brazil, historical Protestants have been elected to Congress since the 1930s, but their presence was always small (around twelve) and discreet. Some had a basically Protestant electorate, but none had official endorsement from any denomination. They were dispersed among the parties and had no strong ideological concentration. Pentecostals were almost totally absent from Congress.

Redemocratization in 1986 changed all that. Since then there has been a marked increase in the number of Protestant congressmen (up to as many as thirty-four) as well as a change in their composition. Pentecostals are now two-thirds of the total. The great majority of these are official candidates of their denominations, especially of the Assemblies of God, Four-Square and Universal Church of the Kingdom of God. (Other large Pentecostal groups, such as the Christian Congregation and God Is Love, have remained aloof from electoral politics.) The Assemblies of God have been the most important. In 1985, their general convention decided to elect one member from each state to the Constituent Assembly. Eighteen state conventions chose official candidates (occasionally a Pentecostal from another denomination), fourteen of whom were elected. Official Pentecostal candidates are usually one of the following: prominent itinerant evangelists, singers, or media presenters of evangelical programs; sons and sons-in-law of head pastors; and Pentecostal businessmen who make agreements with their ecclesiastical leadership.

The basic causes of Pentecostal politicization have to do with the religious field itself. The main beneficiaries of this corporate politics have been the church leaders themselves. Unlike the historical churches, with their traditions, middle-class clientele and professional and bureaucratic standards, the Pentecostal field is young, fast-growing, popular, and sectarian. In addition, Pentecostal pastors often suffer from a status contradiction: they are leaders in the church but marginalized by society. Going into politics, or sending in a relative or protégé, can reduce tensions and help professionalize the Pentecostal field. The public connection helps internal structuring, strengthening certain positions and organizations. Politics also helps increase access to the media (half of the

Protestant congressmen since 1986 have had links with the media). Politics and the media reinforce each other in structuring the Protestant world in Brazil.

In 1986, Assemblies of God leaders explained their unprecedented political involvement by talk of a "threat to freedom of religion" and a "threat to the family." "Religious freedom" should be understood not as the battle for basic Protestant civil rights (as is still the case in a few Latin American countries) but as the intent to join battle with Catholicism for space in civil religion. Claiming to have almost an equal number of practicing members as the Catholic church, Pentecostalism now demands equal status in public life. The "threat to the family" represented, as elsewhere, an act of cultural defense, a reaction to changes in the social milieu that threatened to undermine the group's capacity to maintain its culture. Thus, the dominant strain of Pentecostal politicization seeks to strengthen internal leaderships, protect sectarian socialization, tap resources for religious expansion, and dispute spaces in civil religion. It is assisted by aspects of the political system (federalist structure, relatively open mass media, weak parties, and a proportional electoral system) and the economic crisis (placing strain on traditional urban clientelism).

Time serving, vote selling, and, at times, straightforward corruption have characterized Protestant politics since 1986 and are closely related to the corporate Pentecostal model of official candidates. Corporate politics gives access to both concrete and symbolic resources that help to structure this vast popular religious field whose rapid expansion is always producing new leaders anxious to strengthen their positions.

Protestant congressional behavior has also been characterized by an emphasis on questions related to the family (abortion, homosexuality, divorce, and censorship) and the media (against democratization of the government-controlled concessionary system, which has so favored Protestant access in recent years). On economic issues Pentecostals could not initially be classified as especially right-wing. The tendency has, however, increased over time. Electoral surveys show that, while the Protestant electorate is far from uniform, there is a tendency (even after taking social and demographic factors into account) to be more unfavorable to left-wing candidates than the population as a whole. The Protestant electorate may have swung the close 1989 presidential election in favor of right-wing populist Fernando Collor. In 1992 the evangelical caucus in Congress was relatively unfavorable to Collor's impeachment for corruption.

However, Brazil is unique in Latin America in also having an active and growing evangelical left wing, largely situated in the historical churches but expanding among Pentecostals. Two figures exemplify this segment. Benedita da Silva, former shanty dweller, member of the Assemblies of

God and of the Workers Party, is the first black woman senator ever. Around 20 percent of her 2 million votes in Rio de Janeiro in 1994 seem to have come from Protestants. Although she entered politics by another route, her evangelical electorate has increased at each election.

Although Benedita is at present the only representative of the evangelical left in Congress, there has been an increase in the number of candidates in left-wing parties, including the former Communist Party. In 1995, Wasny de Roure, a Baptist state deputy, became the finance secretary for the Workers Party administration in the federal district. He is typical of the new evangelical left, which has founded the Evangelical Progressive Movement, distinct from the old Protestant left of the 1960s and 1970s, which was linked to ecumenical organizations and nonconservative theologies.

The existing sociological literature offers few clues for interpreting Brazilian evangelical politics. The American religious right, although it may have a certain demonstration effect, functions in a very different religious and political context. Despite similarities, such as the concern with questions of sexuality and the family and the link with the mass media, the differences (of methods and demands, of background and of prospects) are more decisive. In Brazil the key figures are denominational heads, and not leaders of agencies like the Christian Coalition, which mobilize Protestant opinion. Nor is there in Brazil the nostalgia for a lost past. Brazilian leaders are in a different position in the Protestant field; Protestantism has a different position in the religious world and a different relationship to civil religion and national identity.

The history of Christian sectarianism does not give us many parameters. In Catholic Europe all Protestant groups remain small. In Protestant Europe the established churches inhibited the growth of sects, or else secularization and unfavorable electoral systems politically marginalized religion. In the United States, Protestant sects became denominations (and were sociologically transformed) within a generation or two. Brazilian sects, however, grow rapidly but do not win social and cultural respectability. It is in this context that they have launched themselves into politics.

Even in Latin America the Brazilian case is so far unique. In Peru, the sudden entry of evangelicals into politics in 1990 owed a lot to a secular initiative and affected above all the historical churches. In Guatemala both Protestant presidents were politicians before their conversion to high-class charismatic churches. In Brazil, on the other hand, the political vanguard are leaders of popular sects that have grown so much and so fast that they begin to use the state for their own ends.

In the most recent elections (October 1998), the Universal Church of the Kingdom of God, founded in 1977 in a funeral parlor in a poor suburb of Rio de Janeiro and now present in over fifty countries, elected fifteen congressmen. This is an astonishing achievement, by far the most impressive electoral presence of any Protestant church in Latin America. Their candidates are dispersed among seven parties of the center and right and received a total of 1.17 million votes. Half of all the evangelical congressmen are now connected with the Universal Church, a disturbing trend since this church is highly controversial and clearly intends to dominate the whole Protestant field. It is rigidly hierarchical (no internal democracy) and owns the third-largest television network in the country. As one of its politicians told me: "I am here to defend the interests of the church."

## Guatemala

The Guatemalan case is also characterized by guerrilla warfare, a fragile democracy, and a large indigenous population. But the Protestant field is different. Guatemala is over 20 percent Protestant, overwhelmingly Pentecostal-charismatic. There was a sizable upper- and middle-class inflow to new charismatic churches after Vatican II reforms in Catholicism. The 1976 earthquake stimulated the arrival of charismatic groups from the U.S., among them the Church of the Word (Verbo), which soon recruited future president Ríos Montt. The model was copied by members of the Guatemalan elite, such as the founder of El Shaddai, from which was to spring another future president, Jorge Serrano.

The first of Guatemala's two evangelical presidents to date was General Efrain Ríos Montt. He had been a presidential candidate in 1974. In 1978, having failed to regain the nomination, he joined Verbo. In 1982, after a military coup in which he denies involvement, he was invited to take power. He governed for just over a year before being deposed. He had few evangelical ministers but made weekly presidential sermons on television, exhorting civil servants to honesty. American televangelists launched an aid program, though impact was minimal. At the same time, human-rights abuses worsened in the countryside as part of the antiguerrilla campaign. Even so, Ríos was the favorite in two presidential campaigns (1990 and 1995) in which he was subsequently impeded from running (as a former coup participant). He did manage to become president of Congress, and his party is one of the largest in the country.

Jorge Serrano was a businessman who became a Protestant in 1977. A family tie with a Verbo elder earned him appointment as head of the council of state under Ríos Montt. With the return to democracy, he stood for president in 1985. At the time of his successful presidential campaign in 1990, his church was engaged in a spiritual warfare project of national

112 CHRISTIAN POLITICAL ENGAGEMENT

exorcism known as "Jesus Is Lord of Guatemala." Promoted by Serrano, the project sought to free the country from a three-thousand-year-old curse related to pre-Christian religion. Being an elite church, members rented planes to exorcize the part of the national territory they were flying over. In power, Serrano had to face harsh reality. In 1993, facing opposition in Congress to his stabilization plans, and with his reputation scarred by revelations about his private life and personal probity, Serrano tried to suspend the constitution. He was overthrown within a week. In a last-ditch attempt to retain power, he tried to bribe members of Congress. That was the melancholy end of the first elected evangelical president in Latin America.

Both Ríos Montt and Serrano were politicians before conversion to charismatic churches. "Born-again religion has percolated upward into social strata habitually engaged in politics," says David Stoll.[2] In Guatemala it was evangelicalism's extension upward in the class scale that brought it into politics, whereas in Brazil it was the initiative of leading pastors of the mass popular churches, and in Peru it was the solicitation of secular politicians. Serrano's election does not appear to have been due especially to the Protestant vote; it reflects Protestant penetration of the elite and the degree of social respectability acquired.

Guatemala, the most Protestant country of Latin America, thus gives us a pioneer example of what can happen when Protestantism begins to be practiced by significant numbers of the elite. But the questions Stoll asks in the early 1990s (Is self-reform afoot in the ruling class? Can charismatic-led top-down reform substantially change the political and economic reality of Guatemala?) seem to be given a negative answer in a later work. The social capital generated is wasted in costly experimentation at taking over power rather than altering the basic landscape of politics by encouraging the spread of trust.[3] Grenfell shares this pessimism: "How small is the space that Guatemalan evangelicals have carved out for themselves. In the US a flourishing evangelical subculture helps to broaden the influence of social capital and simultaneously to reinforce its benefits. Guatemala, by contrast, has neither the resources nor the minimal political space necessary to begin the construction of this necessary second stage."[4]

## Colombia

In Colombia, torn apart by the drug traffic and guerrilla warfare, and with a Catholic church that has massive institutional power, the previously small Protestant church is now enjoying significant growth. The elections for a Constituent Assembly in 1990 were the catalyst for political involvement, coordinated by the Evangelical Confederation, for the conquest of evangelical civil rights. Since then, with the effective end of the old two-party system, the many new parties formed around special interest segments have included several evangelical ones, little more than vehicles for the political ambitions of leaders of charismatic megachurches.

Mostly, these evangelical parties have revolved around such leaders, who are well placed to capitalize on the possibilities of party fragmentation in a situation of noncompulsory voting and massive abstentionism. The president of one of these parties talks of "a strategy for taking power with a view to extending the Kingdom of God." Or as another leader said: "We are very special people, and this automatically makes us a political alternative."

In 1998, the outgoing president Ernesto Samper, for years prohibited from entering the U.S. due to his links with the drug cartels, signed an agreement with twelve evangelical churches, known as the "Evangelical Concordat," conceding them the same privileges the Catholic church enjoys in various activities.

Colombia exemplifies the virtual impossibility of unified evangelical politics once evangelical civil rights have been achieved. The tendency for the future seems to be for each large denomination or grouping to present its own candidates, who will be more susceptible to specific denominational interests. The Colombian experience shows that in a context of pulverization of the political world it is easy for "evangelical parties" to become little more than personal vehicles for ambitious ecclesiastics. The process of party formation and the subsequent internal procedures are often not democratic, and the interests defended are often particularistic rather than universalistic. In addition, behind the facade of independence, these parties are often linked into clientelistic practices that enable them to channel concrete benefits. Although reflecting a broadening of democracy, the practices of these parties contribute little or nothing to this process. "What democratic novelty are we talking about if neither the objectives nor the procedures are democratic?" asks Helmsdorff.[5]

## Rwanda

The importance of Rwanda lies in the fact that it was the cradle of one of the great evangelical revivals, the East African Revival of the late 1930s and early 1940s. The Tutsi court and aristocracy had become Catholic, so evangelical Protestantism, transmitted through the Anglican Church Missionary Society (CMS), inherited the mantle of the Nyabingi prophetesses as the Hutu dissident cult. The revival, which became increasingly independent of mission control, was a translation of the CMS teaching on the radical sinfulness of man and of pagan society, plus an emphasis on the Holy Spirit, into the medium of witch calling and Nyabingi shamanism.

Today, Rwanda is about 18 percent Protestant. How could such a country go through a genocide such as that of 1994 (up to 1 million dead, 2 million refugees, and 1 million displaced within the country)? There are different versions of Christian involvement. One seems to be favored by most Christian Hutus: it was a mutual genocide; Christians had to be killed first to be got out of the way; church leaders in exile have to minister to exiles, and it is dangerous to go back. Tutsi Christians usually give a different version: Christians did nothing to prevent the massacres, it was a failure of the church, and Hutu church leaders fled because they were intimately involved with the Hutu government and even with worse things.

I shall cite two articles here. The first is Longman's account of Christianity and politics in Rwanda, written before the genocide. The leaders of the Protestant churches remained silent during earlier periods of ethnic violence. In fact, they are generally even more hesitant to criticize the government than the Catholics. However, in 1991 Catholic and Protestant leaders formed an ecumenical council (with the participation of the Adventists and Pentecostals) to bring the government and opposition together and end the war. Nevertheless, Longman presciently says the churches were ominously silent about human rights, and even about massacres carried out by practicing church members. He describes one Presbyterian parish where pastors and lay leaders were known to be involved in a right-wing Hutu nationalist group implicated in violent attacks on Tutsi. The adepts of the revival, the *abarakore,* the saved, generally preach against involvement in political parties. They see Rwanda's crisis as foreshadowing the second coming of Christ, and thus impossible to oppose.[6]

The second article is by Roger Bowen, who was general secretary of Mid-Africa Ministry (part of CMS), the main Anglican evangelical missionary society in Rwanda. It talks of the "close involvement of Christians and Churches in the horrors of that ethnic violence. . . . For Anglican Rwandans, the evangelical heritage of the East African Revival, for all the blessings associated with it, failed to equip the churches to challenge the conditions which led to mass murder. . . . Revival . . . by and large . . . was unable to deal with the ethnic and power issues within the Christian community itself, let alone in the wider society."[7] The combination of pietism and dispensationalism can lead either to withdrawal or to uncritical support of whomever is in power. Both reactions are discernible in Rwanda. Anglican church leadership was exclusively Hutu. There were glorious exceptions to this triumph of ethnic feeling, and the stories have yet to be told of heroic faith and courage where Christians who were also Hutu helped and protected their Tutsi neighbors from the militias. However, as Bowen stresses, mere growth in numbers without costly discipleship is powerless to confront the pressures of evil. There is little awareness of the solidarities of sin in which we are all embedded as members of society. Sin tends to be simplified to the sin of the individual; the corporate nature of humanity is lost to view, and the full magnitude of evil is most seriously underestimated. The revival doctrine of sin underestimates the power and depth of evil. In addition, Bowen blames teaching methods within the church that discourage reflection and questioning, and also authoritarian styles of church leadership.

Presumably there were innumerable cases of quiet heroism in saving those fleeing for their lives or in defending nonviolent solutions. Even so, Rwanda is a vivid example of the impotence and collusion of antipolitical evangelicalism, of the terrible price that can be paid for the lack of a theology of the public sphere. Whatever the dynamics at work in the original revival, there were several decades of opportunity to teach about the public dimensions of radical sinfulness. The genocide was not at all unforeseeable; there had been dress rehearsals without, it seems, a reading of the signs of the times. But many evangelical communities of other nations could scarcely throw the first stone.

## Zambia

Since 1991 Zambia has had a charismatic evangelical president who has brought great public visibility to his faith. It is thus a laboratory for studying some typical tendencies in a certain kind of evangelical politics in action in highly favorable circumstances.

When Frederick Chiluba defeated incumbent Kenneth Kaunda in a free election in 1991, it was hailed as a new dawn for democracy in Africa. He had risen through the trade union movement, a sort of Zambian Lech Walesa, leading the Zambia Council of Trades Unions more and more into a directly political role as a de facto opposition. In 1981 he was imprisoned for four months. At the end of 1989, Chiluba declared that Africa had to get rid of one-party rule since Eastern Europe had already done so. He became involved heavily in the organization of the opposition Movement for Multi-Party Democracy (MMD).

A member of the United Church of Zambia on the Copperbelt, Chiluba had a born-again experience while in prison in 1981. After he was released, most of his political speeches contained biblical references. Later, he received the gift of tongues at a Reinhard Bonnke crusade.

The MMD was a temporary coalition of unionists, students, businessmen, commercial farmers, and religious leaders. For the elections, a monitoring committee was formed by several groups in civil society, including the Christian Council and the Evangelical Fellowship. In the end

Chiluba beat Kaunda by a comfortable margin, and the latter conceded defeat. It was the first time ever that a former British colony in Africa had changed a president through democratic multiparty elections. It seemed as though a new era had dawned, not only for Zambia but for Africa.

The high hopes were not to be realized. In the opinion of many, a golden opportunity was lost. It was true that Chiluba faced a difficult task in terms of meeting expectations. The coalition of businesses, unions, students, and churchpeople could not last. The size of the MMD parliamentary victory meant there was no credible opposition. Above all, the critical economic situation and the need to carry out radical reforms to please the international donor community meant that, paradoxically, many of the social forces that had organized the transition ran the risk of being weakened by the actions of the new regime. As Nolutshungu says: "Political reform was not always, if ever, identified with the unlimited opening of national economies to foreign penetration, the reduction of public expenditure on social welfare, or the large-scale privatization of national assets."[8] The Chiluba government is increasingly dominated by business interests, divided between more reformist elements and more cronyist ones. Reforms have made a narrow elite close to the MMD hierarchy extremely rich. Only ministers and their business colleagues have gained from privatization. The MMD acronym took on other meanings in popular parlance: Make Money and Depart (but they have not departed) or Mass Movement for Drug Dealers. No ministers linked to high-level corruption and drug trafficking have been sacked.

Election promises have not been kept, such as the commitment to sell off the public media (now a mouthpiece of the MMD) and to abolish the one-industry/one-union policy. The latter betrayal has cost Chiluba much union support. Tribal favoritism, a blight of Kaunda's latter years, has returned under Chiluba, this time favoring his own Bemba. Most serious of all, all the tactics of a virtual one-party state have reappeared. Little more than a year after taking power, Chiluba decreed a state of emergency in order to detain leaders of Kaunda's opposition party. In 1995, after Kaunda had announced he was coming out of retirement and would be a candidate for the 1996 presidential election, Chiluba made a botched attempt to deport him to Malawi. Most of the main opposition leaders survived strange road accidents during the same year. Finally, Chiluba had the constitution changed so that Kaunda would be excluded from running; the law now states that a candidate must have been born in Zambia of Zambian parents, a criterion Kaunda cannot meet. Safely reelected, Chiluba began to talk of introducing a law to regulate all nongovernmental organizations, as well as a controversial press council bill. The home affairs minister said he would not allow "careless talk on the streets any more. . . .[9] People cannot be allowed to talk anyhow against the state." As soon as the 1996 elections were over (Chiluba, 82 percent), police invaded the offices of election monitors, the leaders of the second-place party (a schism from the MMD) went into hiding, and Chiluba placed the security forces on the alert. At the end of 1997, Chiluba finally arrested Kaunda himself.

All of this happened within a unique relationship of evangelicalism to national politics. The MMD 1991 campaign manifesto had said that "the MMD government recognizes and accepts that Zambia is a Christian country which is tolerant of other religions. . . . The MMD acknowledges the particular significance of churches and religious communities [and] shall welcome criticism, ideas and practical cooperation from religious groups."[10] Several ministers in his first cabinet (as well as some provincial governors) were evangelical pastors. One of them, the information minister, soon banned Muslim programs on radio. But he did not last long in his post; as a white Zambian of East European origin and a wealthy businessman, he was dismissed from government for alleged racist treatment of his employees. In 1996 the head of the Evangelical Fellowship claimed "about five born-again [government] ministers."

After Chiluba's 1991 victory, one of his first official acts as president was to proclaim Zambia a "Christian nation." Saying "a nation is blessed whenever it enters into a covenant with God," he repented on behalf of the people of Zambia "of our wicked ways of idolatry, witchcraft, the occult, immorality, injustice and corruption. . . . I submit the Government and the entire nation of Zambia to the Lordship of Jesus Christ. I further declare that Zambia is a Christian nation that will seek to be governed by the righteous principles of the word of God. Righteousness and justice must prevail in all levels of authority, and then we shall see the righteousness of God exalting Zambia."[11]

The announcement took people by surprise, and its implications were unclear. The Catholic hierarchy and the Christian Council of Zambia had not been consulted in advance. Some leaders of the Evangelical Fellowship may have known about it. The idea was either Chiluba's (denied to us by the head of the Evangelical Fellowship of Zambia in 1996) or was Brigadier General Godfrey Miyanda's, who is now the vice president.

It is difficult to assess the reception of the "Christian nation" pronouncement by the churches, though one author says born-again sectors were "euphoric." Old Testament theocratic ideas have wide currency in some evangelical circles, and history would lead us to expect some such reading to be popular among the less sophisticated.

At the same time, Chiluba established diplomatic links with Israel, and in 1993 severed links with Iran and Iraq. This is presumably attributable to dispensationalist Christian Zionism, the view that a nation can prosper only if it is pro-Israel. In 1996 the preamble to the new constitution included the declaration of Zambia as a Christian nation. This was at Chiluba's behest, going against the review committee, which had said it was not desired by most Zambians. A joint letter by the Catholics and Christian Council argued that it would create second-class citizens, would not foster authentic religious practice, could lead to abuse and bring discredit, and that Zambia would become a Christian nation not by declaration but by Christians living their faith.

The declaration of Zambia's status as a Christian nation seems to have been politically empty, since it was not intended to introduce new substantive laws nor to establish any church. It seems to be purely symbolic, in tune with much charismatic political theology, which talks of benefits accruing mystically from such acts, since they attract the blessing of God.

President Chiluba has personally invited certain leading evangelists to visit Zambia for crusades, and he speaks at their rallies. However, evangelical leaders have responded that such invitations should be made through the churches and not by the government. The reaction is highly significant: a partisan "evangelical" government ends up dividing even the evangelicals themselves, besides alienating others. There are two main reasons for this: the divisions and rivalries of the evangelical field, which such a government will find it impossible to mediate; and the undetermined border between what should properly be church initiatives and what should be done by an "evangelical" government. This border problem would be especially acute the more such a government is regarded as having a duty to govern in favor of the evangelicals. Zambia's most famous evangelist, Nevers Mumba, denounced media criticism of Chiluba in his crusades. "Chiluba is part of the household of faith. His victory is our victory." Speaking at a Mumba rally, the president said problems had arisen in Zambia because the Christians had stopped praying and started grumbling.

A clear example of evangelical aspirations from an "evangelical" government came in a meeting chaired by the vice president, Miyanda. Miyanda rejects the idea that Chiluba should have carried out a public consultation before the "Christian nation" declaration, on the grounds that "if you have accepted Jesus, you follow his teaching. Any Christian who condemns the declaration, I question whether they are for Jesus." Whatever has a supposed biblical mandate need not be subjected to democratic procedures—an interesting view of the political function of the Bible. Church leaders then raised many possible interpretations of the "Christian nation" declaration: that pastors should have positions in government; that the religious education syllabus should be replaced with the Bible; that churches should be given land to build on; that the building of mosques should be halted.

The reaction of evangelicals to the Chiluba government seems to be divided. Many leaders are embarrassed at their "Christian" government because scorn for it extends to them as well. This suggests only a self-protective, rather than a principled, distancing. But there may also be another reason for some evangelicals' dissatisfaction: a feeling that "their" government has not brought them the access and influence they expected. Some wanted a ministry of Christian affairs, or some pastors among the ten ministers of parliament appointed by presidential nomination, or at least unlimited access of pastors to State House and a president willing to take pastors' advice. Bishop Mambo of the Church of God said, "The state and church are partners in terms of governance in any democracy. . . . Pagans must not be voted for. . . . The church must . . . run the affairs of this country." Yet Chiluba seemed periodically to change his confidants among the clergy (probably wisely, since he did not owe his presidency to the churches), and the Evangelical Fellowship of Zambia leadership came to be marginalized.

For some evangelical leaders, the disappointed hope of a career boost is compounded by a theology of hierocracy: that God's agents on earth are basically church leaders and that the government of the people of God, promised in the Old Testament, is to be exercised through the direct political power (whether by holding government posts in person or through proxies dependent on them) of evangelical church leaders. Lacking is an idea of diverse ministries of the people of God, including laypeople involved in politics in subordination to the Word of God but not to ecclesiastical hierarchies.

An interesting article by an evangelical minister of parliament pleads for a critical evaluation of recent events. She says that after Zambia was declared a Christian country, people did not expect to see greed, selfishness, and corruption. Some have dismissed Christianity as a result. She concludes by recommending that evangelical leaders maintain distance from government and exercise a prophetic role, educating people in democracy and human rights and being open to working with the Christian Council of Zambia and the Catholics, as it is the latter who have mostly stuck their necks out and defended the people. This evangelical MP's plea does not seem to have been heard. We read nothing about the churches mediating or protesting the bar on Kaunda in 1996, although we do hear of such attempts by other sectors in civil society.

As Gifford says, in some places in Africa, "Christianity is considered an unalloyed good; to describe something as Christian is to forestall all criticism."[12] Is there, then, a possibility that political phenomena such as Chiluba will hasten a future weakening of Christianity due to its poor public performance?

Chiluba was, it seems, a good union leader but "went wrong" in government. Why? Of course, he did not face an easy task, but he could have done much better. His evangelical connections do not seem to have helped him much. Evangelical leaders will, of course, dissociate themselves from him and will say he went wrong because he did not listen to them. But that is unconvincing; what did they have to say to him that would have made him a better president for Zambia, and not just for institutional evangelical interests?

## Kenya

The *Guardian* newspaper of July 8, 1997, has a photograph that takes us immediately into the world of evangelical politics in Kenya. It shows pro-democracy demonstrators fleeing as police open fire. Among them, and in the foreground of the picture, are several Anglican priests clutching Bibles and also starting to scatter. In fact, the police chased demonstrators into the Anglican cathedral. The following day, the evangelical archbishop held a special service to cleanse the cathedral from its profanation by the police.

Kenya is a predominantly Protestant country in which the Anglican Church of the Province of Kenya (CPK) is the most important religious institution and in which evangelical Anglicanism holds a key public position. It is also a country that, while avoiding African socialist experiments and military coups, followed for as long as possible the one-party model. President Daniel arap Moi, a practicing evangelical, has learned how to manipulate the opposition and make sufficient gestures to the international community to earn the approval of foreign donors. Moi is an example of a leader who knows how to play the Christian card to full advantage: the state media portray him as God-fearing and show his presence every Sunday at some church or other. The honor of his presence is usually recognized publicly by the flattered church leader. When he attended the Redeemed Gospel Church in February 1992, at a time of great pressure to lift the ban on opposition parties, the preacher proclaimed: "In heaven it is just like Kenya has been for many years. There is only one party—and God never makes a mistake. . . . We have freedom of worship. What else do we want?" More direct political support was forthcoming at the Africa Church of the Holy Spirit, where over 1,200 people registered as Kenya African National Union (KANU) members during the service. The apotheosis came when the internationally known Korean Pentecostal leader David Yonggi Cho, conducting a crusade in Nairobi, said in the presence of Moi that "Kenya is a blessed country because it has a God-fearing leader."

But in Kenya the Anglican church is largely evangelical. The East African Revival had great effect on the church from the 1930s onward. But another tendency was at play: an increasing Erastian tendency toward subordination to the state. Jomo Kenyatta's brother-in-law had been the first African CPK bishop. No church leader spoke out when the opposition Kenya People's Union was banned. Thus, writing at the end of the Kenyatta period, Lonsdale, Booth-Clibborn, and Hake warned: "The indigenous Kenyan tradition of evangelical Revival, clear-sighted in crisis and prophetic in its defense of Christian autonomy when need arises is, because of its very suspicion of hierarchy and organization, peculiarly ill-fitted to perceive, let alone guard against, such routine envelopment."[13]

Another reason for amicable church-state relations under Kenyatta was that the CPK and the Presbyterian Church of East Africa (PCEA) had become increasingly dominated by Kikuyu churchmen. But Kenyatta's successor, Daniel arap Moi, was not a Kikuyu, and in the early 1980s he began to reduce Kikuyu influence, revitalizing the only legal party, KANU, under his own control and with a new ideology known as Nyayo.

From 1982 to 1991, Kenya was a *de jure* one-party state under the Nyayo ("footsteps") ideology of President Moi. Nyayoism is basically a doctrine of top-down mobilizational leadership, suspicious of debate. Nyayoism "treats the church as 'part and parcel of the government.' Church leaders are . . . just leaders; and all leaders must be part of the leadership corps. . . . The church is not considered as an entity over against the state."[14]

Erastianism (the doctrine of state control over the church) was thus taken to new lengths. What resources could Kenyan evangelicalism bring into play to resist it? The churches historically had a very limited theology of secular power. On the other hand, they had a very well developed tradition of evangelical biblical hermeneutics. Evangelicals in the CPK believed themselves obliged to measure any state's actions by the standards of the Scriptures and to compel the state to attend to the Scriptures by lively preaching. But they only critiqued the practical consequences and not the theory of Nyayoism. Archbishop Gitari, for example, believes the church cannot support one system of government against another; it is the church's duty to engage in critical collaboration with any state that attempts to respect God's purposes. It may not develop a root-and-branch critique of any political system that is not explicitly organized to do evil. As the Nyayo state tottered in the early 1990s, the church had no coherent alternative system to put in its place.

The significant Protestant contribution to the defense of democracy and human rights in Kenya came from four notable church leaders, rather than from the churches as institutions. Unlike the Catholic tradition of collective pastorals, it was courageous individuals who spoke out, perhaps because of the revival heritage of institutional suspicion, plus the CPK's position as an autonomous national church within the Anglican communion rather than as a branch of the worldwide Catholic church with an authoritative social magisterium. Three CPK bishops and a prominent Presbyterian minister have been the main critics. One of them was killed in a mysterious car crash in 1990; the others have all suffered various sorts of harassment and have been criticized in the state press and by members of the government. Even so, the fact is that for many years it was only possible to criticize the government without risking detention or worse if one was a church leader—and even then, only if one's church had international connections that would make the government think twice before acting. The CPK and the PCEA "have preserved close contacts . . . with the wider Christian world and can less easily be intimidated than the Kenya-based independent churches."[15] We thus see the importance of ecclesiastical global links, and the cultural capital that usually accompanies them, in making possible resistance to oppressive governments. While theology is undoubtedly important in Christian political action, it is but one factor among many. Before we make any generalizations about evangelicalism and politics, we must take into account variants such as ecclesiastical position and international connections.

The CPK, PCEA, and Catholics offered a primary political challenge to the Moi regime, generating and sustaining a public discourse on democracy and change. This discourse covered a definition of politics and of the legitimate exercise of power, as well as questions of corruption and local conflicts. Although some authors say that criticism of government must be vociferous and broad-based before senior religious leaders will add their weight to it, this hardly applies to some CPK bishops. It was often they who took the forefront.

As transition to some sort of multiparty politics loomed, the CPK and PCEA clergy were often identified with the incipient opposition parties, and the association with Kikuyu interests had not been totally overcome. As the 1992 elections (the first multiparty elections since 1963) approached, pamphlets were produced on quite a broad range of topics: "Why You Should Vote"; "Toward Multiparty Democracy in Kenya"; "Issues to Consider in the Forthcoming Multiparty Elections"; and "A Guide to Election Monitoring."

The most influential figure has been David Gitari, the most articulate representative of Kenyan evangelical hermeneutics, whose controversial sermons have been published as *In Season and Out of Season: Sermons to a Nation* (1996). This work, published soon before his election as archbishop in 1997, contains sermons dating back to his election as bishop in 1975. He is a product of the third-world evangelicalism that came to prominence at the Lausanne Congress of 1974, a sort of Vatican II of world evangelicalism both in the new vistas it opened up and in the subsequent internal battles over its interpretation. Gitari, like many Latin Americans, represented a more thoroughgoing sociopolitical emphasis than much establishment, first-world evangelicalism was prepared to swallow for very long.

But if Gitari is a product of this international wing in evangelicalism, he also represents an almost uniquely direct and influential application of it to political reality. This is made possible by the degree of the Christianization of Kenyan society, the institutional position of the CPK, and the discrediting of the monolithic political system. But Gitari's own initiative and personal courage were also necessary, since not all CPK bishops have acted in anything like the same manner.

Gitari's sermons are direct, usually starting with the exposition of a biblical passage, which is then applied to recent political events, such as the introduction of a one-party system, the queuing system for voting, rigged elections, or specific cases of corruption or violence. He is always diplomatic, often praising as well as condemning, and calling on Christians to pray for political leaders and "give them a chance" to do good even if, for example, they have been "selected" and not elected. He often uses ad hominem language, adopting the slogans of the government and making them mean what they purport to.

However, Gitari is direct in his denunciations based on biblical hermeneutics. In July 1982 he preached on Esther 4 ("Who knows but that you have come to your position for such a time as this? Only do not keep silent!") to criticize the docility of members of parliament toward the bill making Kenya a one-party state. On another occasion, the story of Naboth's vineyard, appropriated by King Ahab, "urges us to know our fundamental human rights and to defend those rights at whatever cost. The story also serves as a warning to all land grabbers. . . . We cannot be mere spectators watching a few rich people and politicians grab as much land as they want. . . . Was there no Naboth to say 'no' [on the city council]?"[16]

As Gitari and other outspoken clerics were often referred to as troublemakers, he uses King Ahab's reference to the prophet Elijah ("Is that you, you troubler of Israel?") to ask: "Who are the troublers in Kenya? They are the land-grabbers, the election riggers, the councillors who . . . participate in wrong decision-making and lack the courage to say 'No!' . . . [who] wish queueing method of elections . . . [who] plan unwarranted transfers of civil servants who do not support them politically . . . [who] organize thuggery and raiding of people's homes at night . . . who refuse to improve our human rights record."[17] Similarly with Ezekiel 34 ("You are doomed, you shepherds of Israel"): "The leaders in Kenya today are no different from the leaders of Israel . . . in caring for themselves. . . . African leaders keep millions of dollars in foreign banks." And "we have in this country been building a tower of Babel . . . the monolithic KANU party. . . . The idea was that by speaking a 'one party language,' Kenyans would be united in accordance to the wishes of 'Nimrod' [a favorite biblical symbol for Africa's rapacious rulers]."[18] Departing from the biblical analogies, he compares the treatment of a political detainee with that given to Steve Biko by the racist authorities of South Africa.

Gitari bases this sort of preaching on "the Church's heavy responsibility to remind a nation . . . of the standard of righteousness and justice which alone can exalt that nation. . . . Christian leaders throughout Kenya must come out of their ecclesiastical ghettos and ivory towers to lead the citizens . . . in giving active practical moral support to the state when it upholds the standards of righteousness. . . . If, however, those in authority depart [from such standards], the Church should follow the footsteps of the prophets and the apostles in declaring boldly the righteousness and judgement of God."[19] To the traditional revival arguments that politics is a dirty game and that, in any case, our duty is to pray and leave things to God, Gitari responds, "When we expect God to do everything, this inevitably leads to prayer without commitment. . . . We have to cooperate with God in bringing about a just, united, peaceful and liberated nation. . . . Isn't a game made dirty by players who are themselves dirty? Politics is about the welfare of the people and it is ridiculous for the politicians to expect Church leaders to . . . merely spectate. . . . We are sailing in the same boat." In the same vein he says, "Politics is so important in human life that it cannot be left to professional politicians alone."[20]

The Kenyan case thus illustrates many points regarding evangelical politics in the two-thirds world. An ecclesiastical institution may become involved in opposition to a dictatorial state because of its own institutional interests, because of its own ethnic base, or because it is led into such a posture by a universalistic understanding of the gospel. In the latter case, there are several possibilities.

The first possibility is the typical revival posture that, as in the Korean opposition to Shinto shrine worship, sets firm and nonnegotiable limits to the state in its totalitarian aspirations when the latter encroach on religious loyalties. The Kenyan examples are Mau-Mau and the 1969 oathing crisis. This is a reactive, not proactive, politicization, and the revival tradition is perhaps second to none at it. But it is ad hoc and temporary.

The second possibility is the evangelical biblical hermeneutics position exemplified by Gitari. Kenya is considered one of the few cases in Africa in which church leaders have gone beyond mediation to direct contestation—and this was done under evangelical aegis. Kenya thus shows that evangelicalism, given the right institutional location, can undergird a contestatory role. Kenya is thus a key case for showing the possibilities and limitations of such evangelical politics in the most favorable circumstances as far as location in the religious field is concerned. The lessons could illumine much for evangelical political militancy in other parts of the two-thirds world. Are there intrinsic limitations to such politics under the auspices of an evangelical theology, even in the best of circumstances?

If the Kenyan leaders worked with the third possibility, a theology of power, would they be better placed to make a more integral contribution to Kenyan politics? And would institutions similar to the Catholic justice and peace commissions help?

Many other questions suggest themselves. How can (and does) Christianity help consolidate democracy in a multiethnic state without a democratic tradition? The relationship between faith and ethnic identity is a key theme for assessing the political impact of the churches in Africa. What do the church leaders actually do, not just to speak out in times of crisis when other channels may be lacking, but to educate and empower the laity for ongoing political roles? How do the churches' internal structures aid or hinder this?

**Ethical Implications**

The wave of evangelical growth in the third world has several possible outcomes. Like some waves, it may disappoint by breaking before reaching the shore. Or it may invade the shore and cause destruction. Or it may be a beautiful spectacle, bringing joy and life to multitudes. It is interesting that in both Guatemala and Korea, church growth seems to have stagnated, with the percentage of Protestants having leveled off at around 20 percent of the population; one of the possible explanations is that institutional growth without social concern and an adequate political theology can lead to church decline through loss of attractiveness.

In many countries, evangelicalism is going through a peculiar moment of arriving unprepared at new levels of social visibility and becoming a mass religion. The evangelical community has become an attractive market and a political trampoline.

The great challenge today in third-world evangelicalism is thus the ethical challenge. Not that ethical problems did not exist before, but they did not appear so much. Now our deficiencies are projected onto a giant screen. The scandals and absurdities are not basically individual problems. They are deficiencies of teaching and of models of leadership. The evangelical politicians are not an aberration; they are the face of the church we do not want to see. Romans 12 talks of the transformation of the mind as the basis of a nonconformist Christian ethic. But when there is no teaching, we fall prey to conformity. And many churches do not teach ethical principles, but only casuistic rules. But for the legalist who depends on rules, when he enters a sphere for which his church has not elaborated rules, he becomes literally unruly. That is one reason why many evangelical politicians become corrupt: they are legalists and therefore people without principles. Like the Pharisees in Luke 16:14, they are "friends of money."

A community that goes from apoliticism to political involvement without teaching on biblical political ethics will be susceptible to the prevailing political culture. They may not be the greatest villains, but they certainly are not what their rhetoric says they are—the salt of the earth and the answer to their countries' problems.

Another factor is that, like many minority groups with a strong sense of mission, we are fascinated with the idea of converting power. Power is understood as a person, not as a system. We have a weak theology of sin—that is why we are messianic, we dream of converting the person in power, or of putting one of ours there, rather than following the traditional Protestant doctrine of sinners controlling each other in a system of mutual accountability. That is why democracy is so important. But among many third-world evangelicals, the concern for democracy is reduced to religious freedom, which is something that interests us. So we show our collective egotism, because there can be religious freedom without democracy but not democracy without religious freedom. Awareness of the dark side of power will prevent us from imagining we can exercise power in the name of God.

Linked to this is the question of the specificity of politics. One of the evangelical members of the Constituent Assembly in Brazil said: "Everything that is praised in the Bible should be prescribed, everything that is condemned should be proscribed." Really? Not even in Israel were there laws for everything God ordered or condemned. The Bible does not exist to substitute for the creative elaboration of forms of social organization. Political morality is specific: it has to do with the action of governments. It is not enough to know that certain behavior is wrong; we need to know whether it constitutes matter for legislation (political work) or for evangelism and teaching (cultural work).

I believe the heart of the matter is the absence of the Protestant ethic in huge swaths of third-world evangelicalism. In Brazil many nonevangelicals used to think it would be a good thing for Brazilian politics when the evangelicals were sufficiently numerous to make an impact in politics. They do not think that any longer.

By Protestant ethic I am referring to three things. First, the vision that biblical revelation has to do with all areas of life; that Christ is the "transformer of culture"; that structures, and not only people, are corrupt and need reform; that the Word of God, and not the institutional church, has authority in the public sphere. Second, the classical attitude of diligent work and frugal living, of seeing secular life as a sphere for fulfilling God's will. Third, the biblical worldview that impelled modern science, of the world as the home of humankind and open to our creative and responsible action.

But in many evangelical circles in the third world today, instead of the ethic of social transformation, we have the triumphalism that dreams of taking power. Instead of the ethic of diligent work and frugal living, we have the prosperity gospel of enrichment through ritual means. And instead of the biblical worldview, we have the current concept of spiritual warfare, which is a return to a pagan view of the world, preaching ritualistic solutions for problems that should be faced ethically.

A few phrases from Brazil will show how far we are from the Protestant ethic. The leader of one of the largest denominations says: "As spiritual beings, born again, we are the 'cream of society.' The church is on a higher level to normal people . . . because the church has the answers which the politicians are looking for." Once I attended a congress of evangelicals in politics, organized by some evangelical politicians. It was peppered with phrases such as "we have the answer to Brazil's problems." I spent two days waiting eagerly to hear what that answer consisted of, but not even five minutes were spent in discussion of national problems.

"Only the elect of God should occupy the key posts in the nation," says a leader of the Assemblies of God. It is hard for the sect to imagine any other political role for itself. It has always seen itself as morally superior; so, in relation to temporal power, it cannot really accept that it is one player among many others. It must either be indifferent or be in charge.

Another example is the declaration of a young televangelist, now a member of Brazil's Congress, which I heard at a rally in 1994: "If we evangelicals are one day going to literally dominate on earth, why can't we start taking power now, as a foretaste?" This divine right to govern is linked to theological concepts of spiritual warfare, a strongly dualistic worldview. "The social, political and economic chaos is due to spiritual curses lying on our country [idolatry, spiritism]. . . . The transformation of Brazil will begin with spiritual restoration. . . . God is raising up men full of the Spirit to take over the positions of power."

We need to be suspicious of all vanguards, Marxist or evangelical! Theologically, we confuse the imperative with the indicative, which leads to triumphalism. We *should be* the salt of the earth, but are we? We can't presume we are just because we carry the evangelical label. We need to apply the parables about the surprises in the kingdom of God to ourselves. Read Jesus' denunciations of the religious leaders of his time against ourselves. Learn to think about society biblically, in terms of values and not in terms of groups that have this or that label. The doctrine of common grace teaches us that, just because we are Christians, it doesn't mean we have privileged knowledge of social reality.

Another phrase is from an evangelical congressman, who received a concession for a radio station from the government in exchange for having voted an extra year onto then-president Sarney's mandate. "If Sarney wanted a mandate of one hundred years in exchange for one hundred radio stations, as long as it was to preach the gospel I would vote for it." This is the classic recipe of politics placed at the service of ecclesiastical expansion, as the Catholic church did for centuries. This suggests evangelical growth is not going to change things very much. The label on the bottle will be changed, but the liquid inside will be the same. In Brazil the rise of a large evangelical community has brought many benefits to the country, but the entry into politics of some denominational leaders has not. We need a vision of what the evangelical presence in society could be: altruistic, without an inferiority complex or a superiority complex; neither a marginalized minority nor an enlightened vanguard, but a transformative minority; not trying just to place "one of our people" at the top, but investing over the long haul in changing evangelical political culture.

# PART 2

# CURRENT ISSUES
# DEMANDING
# CHRISTIAN RESPONSE

# CHRISTIAN FAITH
# AND EDUCATIONAL POLICY

## *Key Questions*

## CHARLES L. GLENN

There is no single biblical teaching that can be applied to every dimension of educational policy, nor are many of the issues that arise easily resolved by appeal to Christian tradition. In fact, education raises complex issues for Christian and non-Christian alike, and the application of biblical principles to each of these issues requires careful discernment of specific situations.

I am not going to attempt to provide a systematic treatment of this subject—really, of the two subjects of social ethics and educational policy in their intersection—because it seems to me more useful to raise and attempt to answer some of the questions that are likely to be on the Christian reader's mind. I am assuming that these are not necessarily the same questions that I might attempt to answer in the secular context where I have worked for the last thirty years, and that in answering them the reader will allow me to draw upon both "secular" and "religious" considerations.

Charles L. Glenn (Ed.D., Harvard Graduate School of Education; Ph.D., Boston University) is Professor of Educational Policy and Chairman of the Department of Administration, Training and Policy Studies at Boston University School of Education.

## Public Schools

### *Should Christians Entrust Their Children to Public Schools?*

It depends. Some will do so because they believe that God is calling them and their children to a ministry of presence and of witness, to be the salt of the earth and the yeast in the dough. They will stay closely involved with the school and with their child's teacher, will discuss homework assignments with their child, and will help their child to understand that to be a Christian means sometimes disagreeing with the messages the world is presenting. Parents who make this choice will be gentle and patient but firm in their convictions.

My wife and I have made that choice, and it has given us many opportunities to teach our children about how being a believer makes a difference—opportunities we might not otherwise have had. The other evening I was helping my fifth grader with a homework assignment that asked about human differences and whether any of them were undesirable. The expected answer, I assume, was that of course all differences were just fine (the future teachers that I teach at Boston University tend to be convinced that we must never "impose our values" by judging what others do). I helped my daughter to understand that one of the human differences is how we behave and, underlying that, what we believe about how we *should* behave. Christians are called to be loving and forgiving but not relativistic.

Here, parenthetically, we touch upon a central theme of the history of education over the past two centuries: the bitter disagreement between those who believe that schools should focus upon truth and those who believe they should focus upon process. Beneath this lies a fundamental philosophical disagreement about whether there is such a thing as truth that we can at least seek to approximate, truth upon which we can build a firm foundation, or whether there is only the mist of constantly shifting perspectives. We must not imagine that this disagreement is a feature of our own time only; the fashionable theorists of education have long insisted that schools should not seek to convey the accumulated wisdom of humankind but rather encourage children to discover for themselves the "truth" that works for them, to construct their own reality.

We don't agree. Some differences, Christians believe, are undesirable, and we should not hesitate to say so, whatever messages our children receive in school. That's a small example of the sort of daily attention we need to pay to the teaching opportunities that arise when our children attend a public school, and that might not arise so explicitly if our children were in a Christian school.

Other parents make a different decision, to home-school their children or send them to a Christian school. They are concerned that all of the instruction their children receive be within the context of a Christian worldview, and that their classmates and friends be from families that share the same beliefs. The controversial new book by Judith Harris lends support to the idea that we should take great care about the influence of peers; she argues that this influence is much more important than that of parents themselves in the way a child turns out.[1] Of course, we would want to add that the wise arrangements and the example of parents help to determine which peers children will associate with and be influenced by. Decisions about schooling are part of that process of parental guidance.

Home schooling and Christian schools are good choices, though neither of them is the choice that my family has made (we are grateful that our teenagers are active in a Christian youth group and in mission trips). Those choosing a Christian school can't simply relax and leave everything up to the teachers, however. Nor should they assume that the school has not been penetrated by some of the ideas in the surrounding culture that are contrary to the gospel.

I believe that this is one of those questions to which there are several right answers, and that we should respect parents who make one choice or another in a serious and committed way.

### What Should Christians Expect and Demand of the Public Schools?

Whether we have children in the public schools or not, we have a right to expect that they uphold high standards of academics and of teaching about character, and we have a duty to be active citizens and "critical friends" of the public schools.

We also should expect the public schools to make a special effort to overcome the learning gap in our society that is based upon social class and race and that is larger than the gap in comparable societies. That is, the achievement gap between high-scoring and low-scoring schools in the United States is substantially larger than that in other industrialized societies with many immigrant children in their schools, like Australia or the Netherlands or France. E. D. Hirsch Jr. has argued convincingly in *The Schools We Need . . . and Why We Don't Have Them* that this is in large part the result of the incoherence of our educational standards. Poor children are especially at the mercy of schooling that fails to provide them with knowledge and skills that middle-class children acquire in part at home. The schools that serve poor children need to be *more* effective than those that serve middle-class children, rather than less so, and Christians should be insisting that public-school officials face up to this responsibility.

### Should Christians Seek to Influence the Curriculum of Public Schools?

Yes, and we should not be dissuaded by the cry of "censorship." Censorship is what school officials do when they do not include religious titles in school libraries, for example, not what parents do when they object to material they find offensive. But we need to be careful not to attempt to remake the curriculum to advance our own particular religious beliefs. Our concern must be with fairness. Just as African American groups have argued successfully that the curriculum and the materials used should reflect the participation of black Americans in all aspects of our society, so Christians (many of whom, of course, are African American!) should insist that the role of religious convictions should find as prominent a place in the curriculum as it has played in shaping our history and present society. Children could easily come away with the impression that this role ended with the first Thanksgiving, if not before.

It is better to be in the position of seeking to add perspectives to the curriculum and to the school library than of seeking to remove others. The angry reaction of many parents in New York City several years ago to a new curriculum promoting a positive perspective on homosexuality, single parenting, and other "lifestyle choices" was fueled in part by a sense that the public schools had for decades been failing to say anything positive about the choice of heterosexual marriage. One study, a few years ago, found that the words "marriage," "wife," and "husband" did not appear at all in a number of the commonly used textbooks discussing the family, nor were there any images offered of mothers who were full-time homemakers. Such curriculum materials give a deeply distorted view of the lives that millions of Americans live, often with heroic determination, and should be challenged in the name of truth, not of special interests.

### Should Christians Use the Political Process to Promote "School Prayer" or the Teaching of Religious Beliefs in Public Schools?

No. There are two reasons why this is a bad idea; one is based on principle, the other on prudence. The first is that Christians are not in the business of seeking to use government to promote their religious beliefs, least of all in a setting where young children are present involuntarily. The prudential reason is that two can play at that game, and most of us would not want our own children exposed to the sort of New Age spirituality that would be likely to make its way into public schools from a culture that seems, like the Athenians to whom Paul preached, always eager to hear something new.

### Are There Any Circumstances under Which It Would Be Appropriate for Public Schools to Have a Religious Character?

Most legal and educational policy specialists would say no, but I believe it is possible to imagine a scenario under which it would be appropriate, both legally and ethically, for a public school to be distinctively religious, at least in some respects. A charter school, as I'm sure you know, is a public school that is not under the direct control of local elected officials but rather of its own board of trustees, who have received a charter from the state (or, in some cases, from a local school system or a public university) to operate as an autonomous institution with a distinctive character and with full funding from tax revenues. All of the pupils who attend a charter school do so as the result of a free choice by their parents, who have the alternative of sending them to one or more public schools operated by the local school system.

What would happen if the board of a charter school decided, with the full support of parents with children in the school, to include regular study of the Bible or to conduct religious exercises at the start of the school day or at other times? It is very likely that the state would threaten to revoke their charter. Would the board have a legal defense? I believe that it would, leaning upon recent decisions by the federal courts that call for state action to be neutral between religious and secular messages.

The board's position would be strongest with respect to curriculum decisions that had a religious character. After all, charter schools are free to choose many different approaches to teaching. For the state to allow, say, an ecological or a Native American theme, but not to allow a biblical theme, would arguably be a form of "viewpoint discrimination," which would go beyond its authority. Even to inquire closely as to whether the teaching was too religious would require the state to overstep appropriate limits on its role. The board's position would be weaker with respect to "school prayer" or other religious exercises not directly related to its curriculum. It may be that the board would need to show that these religious aspects were funded separately from the regular instruction, perhaps by voluntary contributions, or took place outside of the instructional time supported with public funds.

### Is "Outcome-Based Education" a Sinister Plot against Traditional Values?

"Outcome-based education" (OBE) is a good idea that was spoiled—let us hope not permanently—by the attempt to use it to grind various axes. The original idea was to lift the burden of regulation that falls so heavily upon public schools, thwarting the efforts of conscientious teachers and principals. It would be replaced by accountability for results. In a 1986 report by the National Governors' Association, Lamar Alexander of Tennessee spoke for his colleagues in offering "some old-fashioned horse-trading. We'll regulate less, if schools and school districts will produce better results."[2] It was a good idea then and is a good idea still.

Despite our prevalent self-image, the staff of American schools typically have far less real autonomy than do those of schools in other democracies. The real power in American education is exercised at the level of the school system or local educational agency, where the fact that administrative and supervisory staff are relatively close to the school encourages a much higher degree of interference than is possible in an educational system that is centralized on the regional or national level. This is evident from the comparative data collected a few years ago by the Organization for Economic Cooperation and Development, which showed that staff of American public schools have very little scope to make decisions compared with those in other countries.

Different nations have struck different balances between centralized direction and the independence of each school; American education has managed to have the worst of both approaches to the organization of schooling. The low level of autonomy and thus of professional discretion in schools has been combined with an equally low level of clarity about what every school should teach and every pupil learn.

The difficulty with switching over to accountability for results is that we have so little agreement about what those results should be or how they should be measured. And here's where the mischief came in. The effort of a number of states—Pennsylvania and Virginia among others—to set up outcome standards against which school performance could be measured became an opportunity to advance various agendas. Charles Sykes has shown in *Dumbing-down Our Kids* how the process was perverted to propose outcomes that had more to do with attitudes than with skills and knowledge. Suspicion was aroused among parents who saw this as opening the door to imposition on their children of a "secular humanist" agenda or requiring approval of "alternative lifestyles," such as single parenting and homosexual cohabitation.

In March 1992 the Pennsylvania State Board of Education issued a list of more than five hundred proposed outcomes in fifty-one categories, intended to replace course credits as the basis for high-school graduation. Many of the outcomes were unexceptional, but critics zeroed in on those that seemed to go beyond what could be measured accurately or that government should seek to prescribe, such as that "all students understand and appreciate their worth as unique and capable individuals and exhibit self-esteem" and that students "should act through a desire to succeed rather than a fear of failure while recognizing that failure is part of everyone's experience."[3] Desirable as it might be for every student to have such attitudes, it is difficult to see how they could be made the basis for educational standards or measured in an objective and reliable way.

Pennsylvania had a tradition of examining such aspects of learning, going back at least to 1967, when the Educational Quality Assessment program was established, "charged with developing assessments based on 10 very broadly stated goals." The assessments included hypothetical situations in response to which students were asked to select responses based either upon peer pressure or upon fear of punishment; convictions about what is right and what wrong were not among the multiple-choice options. A critic of this program wrote that "personal opinions are being assessed for 'correct' responses in a pluralistic society that supposedly treasures the concept of individual differences."[4]

The danger is that appropriate resistance to promotion of an ideological agenda through standards and testing will result in resistance to the very idea of external standards for schools. This would be a serious mistake, especially for the interests of poor children. Middle-class children will do pretty well even in the absence of a societal consensus about what they should know and what they should be able to do, but poor children will suffer. They will be cheated of an effective education because most attend the schools with low expectations and little capacity to close the gap, which will have lifelong consequences. As Hirsch has written, "In the United States, the all-too-consistent correlation between low academic performance and low economic status shows that something more than innate talent is determining the results."[5] Part of the gap is caused by the lack of standards that insist poor children be taught what more fortunate children are already learning at home and in their high-expectations schools.

The frustration over the attempted abuses of OBE and over the "political correctness" that is rampant in many textbooks should not discourage us from working for high common standards for all children and from holding all schools accountable for seeking to meet those standards.

## Nonpublic ("Private") Schools

### Should Government Have a Role in Relation to Nonpublic Schools?

Certainly. Christians prize liberty, but we are not ideological libertarians; we recognize that government is appointed by God to ensure justice (Rom. 13), including the right of every child to receive an effective education and to be protected against unethical forms of discrimination.

That does not mean that government has to be in the education business, as it is now on a massive scale, but it does mean that government should provide the resources to make good schools available to all children, and should be vigilant to ensure that race or sex or handicap or poverty or family dysfunction does not result in any child failing to attend and to profit from such a school.

But the role of government should be carefully limited to ensure that schools can express a distinctive character without interference or influence. My latest book, called *The Ambiguous Embrace,* explores both the dangers and the possibilities in the relationship of government and faith-based schools and social agencies. I show that schools that insist upon the religious dimension of their mission are generally successful in preserving it despite government regulation and (in other countries) public funding, but that too many engage in what Luis Lugo calls "pre-emptive capitulation," surrendering their distinctiveness unnecessarily and at a high cost to that mission. I show also that funding mechanisms like vouchers place a protective layer of parent decision making between government and schools.

### Should Christians Support Vouchers and Other Public Funds for Nonpublic Schools?

Yes, and we should do so even if our own children and those of our church would not benefit directly. We should do so in the name of justice, since vouchers would enable poor parents to make the same sorts of decisions about the education of their children that we take for granted. We should do so in the name of educational effectiveness, since schools that must be responsive to parents and that have the organizational autonomy to do so are likely to be more focused upon getting the job done.

### But Won't Vouchers Lead to Segregation and Social Division?

Has the public school monopoly led to integration and social harmony? Of course not. Public schools are in fact more racially segregated than nonpublic schools, because they tend to draw their pupils from geographically defined residential areas. This counterintuitive phenomenon, pointed out by the late James Coleman years ago, has recently been confirmed by Jay Greene of the University of Texas at Austin. In 1992 he found that 36.6 percent of private school pupils, but only 18.3 percent of public school pupils, were in classrooms whose racial makeup was within 10 percent of the national average. The greater integration of private schools held up in urban, suburban, and rural areas in all parts of the country, except in the rural South. Even there the reality is exactly the opposite of what we would expect from remembering "segregation academies" and "white flight": rural southern private schools are less integrated than comparable public schools because they have *too many* minority pupils, not too few!

Greene has also asked whether this physical mixing is accompanied by positive changes in racial attitudes, and he suggests that it is. He looked at the behavior of students at lunchtime and found those in private schools were more likely to sit in racially integrated groups than were students in public schools.[6]

To take another example, studies of the new phenomenon of charter schools have found that they serve significantly higher proportions of minority students and low-income students than does the regular public education system.

Avoiding negative consequences from increased parental choice of schools is largely a matter of intelligent design and sound policies.

### In the Design of Voucher Programs, What Considerations Should Be Primary?

First, rules for participation by families that ensure fairness in having the opportunity to participate and to be admitted to a particular school, but that also allow school staff to make clear to prospective parents that the school's curriculum and common life have a distinctive pedagogical or religious profile. In Massachusetts we established information centers through which parents apply to public schools in a dozen cities that have made choice the basis for school assignments; this model could work well for a voucher program as well.

Second, parents who choose to participate should be given vouchers redeemable by any approved school that accepts their children, amounting to the average expenditure for a pupil of that category (for example, more is spent on secondary than on elementary pupils, and on pupils with special needs) in the public schools.

Third, rules for participation by schools should be based upon their demonstrated effectiveness over time or—in the case of new schools— upon approval of a plan comparable to that required of charter schools. Schools participating should have a right to maintain and to express their religious or other identity in employment and in program decisions, consistent with the charitable choice provision of the 1996 federal welfare reform act. Upon application from parents, school leadership should be required to arrange for excusal of pupils from religious exercises, though not from any aspect of instruction that, in the judgment of the school leadership, is essential to its academic program.

Finally, schools participating should be required to provide accurate and appropriate information to prospective applicants, to parents, and to the general public about school policies, practices, and outcomes. If the state requires low-performing public schools to close, it should apply the same standard to denying eligibility to receive vouchers.

### Should Christian Schools Accept Public Funds If They Become Available?

Yes, if the terms under which the funds are available do not require that the school change its goals, its curriculum, or its hiring policies. If it is essential to the mission of a school that it accept only children whose parents are members of the sponsoring church, the school should not seek public funds, since legal conflict over admissions is sure to ensue. A Christian school that is open to any family that will abide by its goals and ways of doing things should not hesitate to accept public funds through a well-designed voucher program, but it should insist upon control over hiring decisions (an issue on which no compromise should be entertained) and the freedom to maintain and to publicize a distinctive educational approach. These measures, consistently applied, should be enough to ensure that a school is able to maintain its distinctive character. Few of us feel comfortable applying religious criteria to employment decisions, but to do so is a fundamental requirement of "truth in advertising" for schools that claim a religious identity. Otherwise, it is very unlikely that their character will continue to have any real meaning, and parents will be misled in choosing those schools for their children. This does not have to mean, of course, that evangelical schools should hire only evangelicals—better a Catholic teacher or a Jewish teacher who takes religious conviction seriously and is willing to teach within the context of the school's mission than a wishy-washy Protestant! Indifference is the poison that seeps into a school's life if shared convictions are not front and center.

This distinctiveness is always under threat, whether or not there is any entanglement with government as a result of public funding. Teachers and principals in Christian schools, and those who train them, are often insufficiently clear about how to incarnate their beliefs in the specifics of curriculum and school culture. Expressing and living a religious character is by no means a simple matter for a school community, given the fears of "imposing our values" that are so prevalent today. But some values are worth standing up for, and the availability of a choice of schools based upon a range of understandings of the moral and philosophical foundations of education should remove all hesitations on that score.

## *Is Supporting Distinctively Religious Schools Good Public Policy?*

Yes, and there are welcome signs that this is increasingly recognized. Curiously, while the American Constitution's First Amendment privileges the free exercise of religion as especially worthy of protection, the effect of Supreme Court decisions over the past forty years has been to treat religion as the only forbidden motivation for school choice. Parents may choose among publicly funded schools because of ambition for their children or pedagogical theory or fear of minority children, but they have not been able to choose because of religious conviction. This reverses the legal situation in other Western democracies, which generally privilege and support school choice based upon religious convictions over other motivations. Such policies recognize that religion has a way of encapsulating, for many parents, a whole range of hopes, moral convictions, and loyalties that they want above all to transmit to their children.

It would not do to leave the impression that religion is the only basis upon which a school can develop and express a distinctive ethos, a moral coherence that makes it as effective at educating children as it is successful at attracting like-minded parents. There are many fine schools that have achieved such coherence on the basis of a shared understanding of education that is thoroughly secular, although even a secular ethos may be understood as functionally religious. Perhaps such schools have to work a little harder at keeping the ethos fresh and effective.

What does the future hold for Christian schools? They have the potential of making an even more significant contribution to American education in the future than they have in the past. Whether this will happen is to a large extent in their own hands, dependent upon how faithfully they express a distinctive—and worthy—character in the myriad details of their life and work. If they fail to rise to that challenge, no changes in the political and legal climate will make them capable—or deserving—of survival.

# 10

# THE DIVORCE EPIDEMIC

*Evaluating Policy Options That Can Reduce Divorce*

## DAVID P. GUSHEE

Other contracts may be modified, restricted, or enlarged, or entirely released upon the consent of the parties. Not so with marriage. The relation once formed, the law steps in and holds the parties to various obligations and liabilities. It is an institution, the purity of which the public is deeply interested in, for it is the foundation of the family and society without which there would be neither civilization nor progress.

—U.S. Supreme Court, *Maynard v. Hill,* 1888

## Prolegomena

Serious theologians usually begin with what they call "prolegomena"—a fancy prologue, as it were, in which instead of talking about theological convictions, they talk about talking about theological convictions.[1] They offer an often elaborate discussion of why one talks about theology, how

David P. Gushee (Ph.D., Union Theological Seminary, New York) is Graves Professor of Moral Philosophy and Senior Fellow of the Center for Christian Leadership at Union University.

one talks about theology, who has the privilege of talking about theology, and so on.

My task in this relatively brief discussion will be to examine, assess, and propose legal changes that might strengthen marriage and prevent divorce.

There is much prolegomena to such a discussion that, in a lengthier essay, I could and would offer. In particular, I would need to show several things, in approximately this order:

1. that the goal of strong and permanent marriages is an important dimension of any fully biblical Christian social vision;
2. that current realities in American family life fall significantly short of this Christian moral vision;
3. that Christians—even in a structurally, confessionally, and morally pluralistic society like our own—are permitted and even obligated to work for social change where gaps exist between the biblical social vision and current realities;
4. that in terms of our own faith and in terms of the rules that govern American public life Christians may legitimately employ a nuanced and limited legal reform strategy as at least one among many means for effecting the social change we seek;
5. in addition, assuming the successful demonstration of the foregoing, I would need to discuss which aspects of marriage and divorce law ought to be reformed and which public policy mechanisms should be employed with regard to each aspect of the laws in question.

In the interest of getting to the heart of my subject rapidly in this brief chapter, I simply am going to offer items 1–4 here as presuppositions. I will focus my attention on item 5. The substance of my work will consist precisely of an exploration of marriage and divorce law reform, which I do believe is one appropriate form of Christian response to the rise in marital dysfunction and divorce in American society over the past thirty years or so.

## Entry Points for Marriage and Divorce Law Reform

Christians and others who are interested in the reform of divorce laws tend to concentrate their fire on the legal regime known as no-fault divorce. I believe that this focus is much too narrow. No-fault divorce, as we will discuss in more detail later, has to do specifically with the issue of how and on what grounds an individual or couple may enter into divorce. Yet if we want to think coherently about addressing the divorce problem through legal means, we must look at the entire marriage and divorce law system.

Marriage is a relationship governed by state law in our federal system of government. Each of the fifty states offers a comprehensive regime of laws governing the full range of activities related to marriage:

- The *entry into marriage* is regulated primarily through qualification and licensing procedures as well as provisions for regulating officiants at marriage ceremonies.
- The *conduct of marriage* is regulated through a welter of laws related to finances, children, domestic violence, and so on.
- The *entry into divorce* is regulated through provisions related to residency, grounds for divorce, waiting periods, and counseling or mediation.
- The *postdivorce relationship* of the now divided family is regulated through provisions related to property, spousal support, child custody and visitation, and child support. (I will allude to these issues only briefly here.)
- Finally, in its shaping of laws related to each particular pressure point in the marriage and divorce process, as well as in its broader approach to marriage and divorce as social practices, government communicates either a coherent or an incoherent public ethic that cannot help but have an impact on public attitudes and practices. This "constitutive" or "bully pulpit" dimension of public policy response must also be considered when thinking about divorce law reform.[2]

## Available Public Policy Levers for Legal Reform

Below I will consider potential reform measures that apply to each of these pressure points in the marriage and divorce law system. But before doing so, it is important for us to be reminded of the particular levers that policymakers have available to them when constructing public policy.

Essentially, with regard to any particular social practice, policymakers can do one of the following:

### *Remain Neutral*

Policymakers can decide that there is no governmental interest in either encouraging or discouraging a particular action. Or alternatively, they can conclude that any attempt to interfere with this action would exceed the boundaries of their jurisdiction and authority.

### Create (or Permit) Options

Policymakers can choose to open up a range of options or choices to citizens for the accomplishment of a particular social goal or practice, while remaining essentially neutral concerning which options citizens avail themselves of. For example, government has a legitimate interest in seeing that its citizens receive an adequate education, and almost every family wants to see their child educated. But government permits and sometimes creates a diversity of options for individuals and families in accomplishing that goal (though in our current system public education is clearly favored). On a different issue, federal environmental and energy policy includes among its stipulations the mandate of progressively higher fuel efficiency targets for automakers. But it leaves to the automakers' discretion how they will meet this target. They can choose to make an entire fleet of cars, all of which meet the target; or they can make cars with a range of fuel efficiencies and then simply manipulate the sales mix to accomplish the target.

### Offer Incentives or Disincentives

Government can move out of neutrality toward the expression of a particular set of values through the creation of incentives and/or disincentives by which it can encourage or discourage behavior. The "incentive set" that government has available to it is impressive. Most compelling, most of the time, is the power of the purse. Government can create incentives by offering money to those who perform the behavior government seeks. These dollars can be delivered, for example, via the tax system, in the form of direct cash grants, or through the reduction or waiver of licensing fees. Likewise, government can also create disincentives using the same financial levers.

Government also has the ability to create and offer nonfinancial incentives or disincentives. It can offer public honor or dishonor, praise or blame. It can, for example, publish a list of the fifty companies in the state who are doing the best job of putting former welfare recipients to work and then hold a press conference in which their CEOs are featured.

### Regulate Access

Another policy lever available to government is its ability to regulate access to some product or benefit. Thus, while cigarette smoking is permitted in our country, access to cigarettes (at least officially) is limited to those over a certain age. The same holds true of access to alcohol or to R-rated movies. These examples immediately bring to mind the limits of law in accomplishing its objectives, for each of these particular regulations of access is routinely violated. Yet access regulation is an important policy mechanism that must be considered here.

### *Mandate or Prohibit*

Finally, policymakers can decide that an action or practice is of sufficient importance that it must be either prohibited or mandated. Because mandating or prohibiting certain behaviors limits personal freedom, in our system a higher burden of proof must be met to justify this particular policy lever. The social benefit gained (or harm prevented) must exceed the cost to personal freedoms that it entails. Most often, the move to this level involves a prohibition rather than a mandate. We are required not to kill, not to rape, not to steal, and so on. However, it is easy to think of a range of things we are required to do, such as wear our seatbelts whenever we drive.

Public policy signals its level of seriousness on such matters in part through the harshness of the consequences of violations. The same principle holds true with regard to all of the policy mechanisms just discussed—they can be employed with various degrees of intensity depending on their public significance as determined by lawmakers.

In the ongoing debate about divorce law reform, variations of each of these public policy levers have been proposed, as we shall see. Christians, especially those who are passionate about particular issues, tend to move immediately to the "mandate or prohibit" level. Quite frequently, however, such demands are morally or practically inappropriate to the issue under consideration or are politically infeasible. We must remain open to less dramatic measures.

## The Entry into Marriage: Reform Options

Let us turn now to a consideration of particular legal reform proposals and possibilities, as well as two proposals that might be viewed as systemic reforms. We begin with entry into marriage.

Most states currently regulate the entry into marriage very lightly. States neither mandate nor prohibit marriage. Those seeking marriage must obtain a license by filling out a brief form and paying a small fee. There is generally a one- to five-day waiting period that the American Bar Association legal guide says is intended "to give a brief cooling-off time during which the parties can change their minds if they wish."[3] This might be viewed as a modest access regulation strategy, as are provisions restricting the marriage of close blood relatives. Those marrying must have the legal capacity to do so, in terms of mental and psychological competence. Most states also regulate access to marriage by age, generally requiring both parties to be at least eighteen years old (sixteen with consent of parents; some states lower the age if the woman is pregnant and the parents consent). Currently all states prohibit same-sex marriages, though that is under intense debate nationally.

One reform option is to attack the problem of marital quality and divorce through more vigorous regulation of the entry into marriage. A number of different strategies have been proposed.

First, some scholars and policymakers are proposing either the requirement or the encouragement of a program of premarital preparation, including testing, counseling, and education. Such an initiative could be undertaken in tandem with another measure, the strategic use of extended waiting periods prior to the granting of a marriage license. The counseling could be provided by the state itself or by others and certified by the state. In the summer of 1998, Florida became the first state in the nation to pass a law—the Marriage Preparation and Preservation Act—with precisely this approach. Couples who take a marriage preparation class can receive a $32.50 reduction in the cost of the marriage license.[4] Legislators in several states have introduced bills, with variations, along these lines.[5] For example, Rep. Jessie Dalman (Michigan) proposed a $20 fee and a three-day waiting period for counseled couples, and a $100 fee and a thirty-day wait for those without counseling.[6] No state thus far has mandated premarital counseling—only voluntary or incentive-based approaches are currently under serious consideration.

Another strategy related to the entry into marriage is to address the age issue. States could choose to use one or another lever of public policy to increase the age at which couples marry, reasoning from all relevant data that teen marriages are likely to be less stable and enduring than those begun later. In March 1998 a Missouri legislator proposed an incentive-based law along these lines. Rep. Pat Kelley's bill would have the state offer a $1,000 bonus to any couple who delay marriage until both are at least twenty-one.[7]

Close kin to this kind of approach would be a strategy aimed at encouraging or mandating longer courtships.[8] States could require couples to show that they have known each other for at least, say, six months or one year, or could offer incentives to those who have had that kind of time together. Again, such an approach would reflect the recognition that marriages are more likely to succeed if preceded by a significant courtship period.

How are we to evaluate all of these entry-type proposals? Critiques can be offered at both practical and philosophical levels. At a practical level, such policies would routinely require the state to create a new or expanded administrative apparatus for this area of the law. If the state actually provides premarital counseling, there is the question of the expansion of state payrolls to accommodate hordes of official marriage preparers. There is the issue of how or whether state funding would be provided for those couples unable to pay for counseling (at least for counseling offered by someone other than the state) or perhaps for all couples. There is the question of possible abuse through the filing of false affidavits on the belief that no one at the county clerk's office will find the time to verify all the information submitted. Finally, some argue that premarital counseling is ineffective even in the best of circumstances in that such couples rarely view their relationships realistically. It is certainly the case that coerced premarital counseling would be less likely than voluntary counseling to have a positive impact on the couple involved.

Philosophically, some see this kind of regulation as an intrusion of the state into what is legitimately the private sphere—the "nanny state" run amok. Indeed, this libertarian-type objection will likely doom purely mandatory measures in most states. As Illinois Republican James Durkin said, "It's not our place to dictate how people will enter into the sanctity of marriage. For the state to mandate premarital counseling is just going too far."[9]

Further, even those who support the basic concept here must be aware of the "iron law of unintended consequences." Given the rising rate of cohabitation in our society and some of the problems that it produces, it can be argued that nothing should be done to increase its frequency. Putting "speed bumps" in the path of marriage could lead some couples simply to live together instead, thus making the cure worse than the malady.

Despite these objections and concerns, I personally support an incentive-based approach focused on significant premarital preparation, though the concept of also rewarding longer courtships and later marriages is intriguing as well. I do not believe that an incentive-based approach violates the boundaries of the state's jurisdiction. I believe that the administrative time and costs are worth the trouble and can be limited through the use of streamlined procedures. Generally, I do not think the state should be in the counseling business itself, except perhaps as the provider of last resort. Instead, the state should accept the counseling offered by any certified counselor as long as his or her work meets certain minimal standards. This includes religious-based counselors— church/state issues on this front should not be seen as a problem, as this ground has already been plowed in the charitable choice debate. Counselors (of whatever type) would affirm via affidavit their participation in the counseling, reducing the possibility of abuse of this part of the process. States should offer tax breaks for couples who undergo premarital counseling in any given year, unless the counseling was the free, state-sponsored type.

I would broaden the difference in the way counseled and noncoun-seled couples are treated: a sixty-day waiting period and a $200 fee for those not receiving counseling, for example, would raise the level of incen-tive to undertake the premarital program. It would require experimenta-tion to see exactly how high a fee and how long a wait could be employed without negative side effects vis-à-vis cohabitation. A state could defend higher fees and longer waiting periods by spelling out the social and gov-ernmental costs of divorce and the state's legitimate interest in discour-aging it and encouraging marital permanence. All fees could be officially designated for divorce-related government expenses (court costs, wel-fare, child support enforcement administration, counseling and social services, divorce-related abuse and violence, etc.).

One final note about church involvement is needed. Religious leaders, congregations, or larger bodies could contribute mightily to the rate of participation in a state-encouraged premarital preparation process sim-ply by offering high-quality programs themselves and refusing to marry anyone who refuses to participate in them. This decision would be pub-licly announced as church policy. I believe this should be the stance of ministers and congregations with regard to premarital preparation in any case, regardless of state law.[10] But where states move in this direction, the churches can partner with government by this means.

## The Conduct of Marriage: Reform Options

Current state laws regulate the conduct of marriage in three basic are-nas: finances, children, and domestic violence.

In terms of finances, a maze of regulations cover all aspects of the finan-cial partnership that is marriage. Property, debt, and taxes are among the issues that garner most attention. (These issues become central dur-ing the divorce process as well.) The decision concerning whether or not to have or to adopt children is left to the couple, as are most decisions concerning how to raise children. The rights of children themselves are also a subject of law. Domestic violence statutes prohibit murder, assault, rape, or robbery between spouses or against children.

Other than these aspects, the states at this time tend to demonstrate no particular interest in the quality or well-being of the marriages within their jurisdiction. Again, the state remains neutral, or as Milton C. Regan puts it, "agnostic," about behavior within families.[11] While it is certainly true that states must not micromanage relationships between husbands and wives, it is no less true that states have a compelling interest in mar-ital harmony and permanence—and we are a long way from that goal as a nation.

Given this, states should move from neutrality to a clear public stance of encouraging high-quality and lasting marriages, and their public policies should reflect this value. As Sylvia Ann Hewlett and Cornel West have put it, "Government should get back into the business of fostering the value of marriage as a long-term commitment."[12]

In particular, I suggest the following modest initiative: states should use financial and nonfinancial incentives to encourage couples to undertake legitimate and effective marriage enrichment and marriage counseling activities during the course of their marriages. There would be no need for states to develop such activities or programs themselves, though they certainly would be free to do so. All they would really need to do would be to offer a modest tax incentive to couples who in any given year can certify their participation in such a program. Church/state and funding issues raised by this kind of approach were discussed above. The only real policy debate here is not whether such programs would benefit marriage but instead whether or not public will exists for investing tax dollars for this purpose.

At a much broader level, one could argue that we need to consider a wide range of measures that taken together would offer public policy support for stable and permanent marriage and family relationships. Hewlett and West, in their provocative recent work entitled *The War against Parents,* have proposed a "parents' bill of rights"—a set of measures that would, in their view, demonstrate societal support for the honorable, sacrificial, and absolutely critical work of parents. They group their proposals under the following categories of what parents are entitled to: time for their children, economic security, a pro-family electoral system, a pro-family legal structure, a supportive external environment, and honor and dignity.[13] Other analysts and advocacy groups have for some time been constructing entire public policy programs around the vision of strengthening families, though particular proposals vary widely—usually along ideological lines.[14]

To pursue this issue further here would take us outside the focus of this paper, but I concur with the basic claim that public policy has a legitimate role to play in offering broad support for strong and healthy marriage and family life.

## The Entry into Divorce: Reform Options

Now let us consider the critical issue of how states regulate the entry into divorce.

Today, most states approach this issue with the same agnostic neutrality that marks state laws related to the entry into marriage. Most,

though not all, states require residency or domicile of one or both parties to the divorce in the state in which the divorce is being sought. Residency requirements range from none to one year. A residency requirement could be seen as a very modest access regulation strategy.

All state statutes specify the permissible legal grounds for divorce.
Here one finds, in contemporary state law, two basic but very different
patterns: no-fault and fault-based grounds. Since 1985, all states have had
no-fault statutes; some have fault-based grounds to go with no-fault
approaches. There is an important history behind the rather strange current structure of our divorce laws.

Through most of our nation's history, divorce was available only to a
husband or wife who could demonstrate that his or her spouse had committed an offense against marriage that was serious enough to merit the
dissolution of the marriage. It is hard at this point perhaps to even imagine a divorce law system built on this premise. But the presupposition of
the law was that the marriage relationship was a matter of significant public interest that extended well beyond the interests or feelings of either
husband or wife. Marriage was viewed as a status that imposes—through
the momentous voluntarism of choosing to marry—a permanent set of
obligations on all who are embedded in the relationships that marriage
creates.[15] The law legitimately held people to those obligations, releas-
ing them from these only when one partner's behavior constituted a fundamental offense against the marriage. Clearly, this legal theory was
closely tied to the religious/moral legacy of the Western Christian tradition, with its understanding of the permanence of marriage.

Early in American history the list of offending behaviors, or grounds
for divorce, tended to be relatively short and closely tied to a reading of
biblical teaching. Thus, for example, the first and premier ground for
divorce has always tended to be adultery. Over time those grounds
expanded incrementally, with great variations across the fifty states.[16]
But what these codes held in common was the view that the dissolution
of a marriage was a grave act that should be limited to particular offenses
against marriage.

Quietly and with relatively little fanfare, a revolution in divorce law
was successfully undertaken in the 1970s. The first to take the plunge was
the state of California in 1969. Marking a clean break with the entire history we have been outlining, non-fault-based divorce (popularized under
the label "no-fault divorce") became the new benchmark for divorce law.
It swept not only the U.S. but most of Western Europe as well.

It is important to understand what the framers of no-fault divorce
intended. They were not trying to argue that no one is ever at fault when
a marriage collapses, nor that the end of a marriage is not morally significant. However, they did believe that no one's interests were being

served by a system in which divorcing couples had to go to court to prove to a judge that each other was to blame for a marriage's problems. They believed that the adversarial nature of this structure only aggravated conflicts and was particularly hard on children.

As well, they were aware that as the demand for divorce began to increase in the 1960s (*before* the laws were changed), the strictures of then-current divorce laws were creating an environment of duplicity in the legal process. Couples genuinely and mutually wanting to divorce were having to pretend that one or the other was guilty of some particular marital offense. These "disguised mutual consent" divorces generally involved the offering of perjured testimony under oath. As well, the demand for divorce was leading some judges to stretch the permitted grounds beyond recognition; for example, "cruelty" as a ground for divorce now became "mental cruelty," which could be recognized whenever one or the other partner appeared miserable.[17]

The reformers' idea was to eliminate all of this duplicity by waiving the requirement of showing fault. Much like no-fault auto insurance, which was introduced at the same time and clearly influenced the public perception of this divorce law reform, no-fault divorce would simply remove the legal system from the role of sorting out blame and guilt for a marital "crash."[18] One might say that the legal fiction of a marital offense as cause of every divorce was replaced by the legal fiction of *no* offense as a cause for *any* divorce. The public interest consisted not in keeping troubled marriages together but in enabling their dissolution to be as painless and fair as possible.[19]

Of course, these legal changes were driven not only by legal logic but also by profound cultural shifts occurring at the time. As Barbara DaFoe Whitehead has argued most persuasively, the nation during the period we are considering rather rapidly transitioned from an ethic of obligation to others to an ethic of obligation to self. Marriage likewise shifted from a lifetime relationship to which we are duty bound to a temporary relationship to which we are tethered as long as we both are enjoying it.[20] Marriage was becoming precisely that consensual, always-up-for-review relationship that the Supreme Court rejected in its 1888 decision cited above. Because my "unhappiness" or "failure to thrive" or "lack of sexual self-actualization" does not necessarily involve fault on my spouse's part, there should be no need to prove that she did anything wrong. I should be free to leave as I continue the search for personal fulfillment that is every American's birthright. Thus the entry into divorce was almost entirely deregulated.

The no-fault vision, if implemented in pure form, would have eliminated all fault grounds from legal codes. However, not all states were willing to go this far: a majority have retained both fault and no-fault grounds.

Yet the fault grounds are at this point largely vestigial; their primary use appears to be in the postdivorce settlement process. Our actual divorce law regime essentially permits divorce to be initiated by either spouse for any reason at any time in the marriage. Simply by claiming "irreconcilable differences" or "marriage breakdown" and waiting a relatively brief period of time, a person can find a way of escape from his or her marital commitments.

Today there is much discussion, especially though not exclusively among Christians, as to whether this thirty-year-old experiment in legal reform should be reconsidered. I believe that it should be. The argument for the abolition of no-fault divorce can be made in at least the following ways:

### Legal Considerations

Milton Regan and others have argued that marriage was once understood as a status relationship but now has become contractual in nature. Yet under no-fault what we have is a very flimsy contract. Contract law regulates the entry of two or more parties into a binding legal agreement, specifies the means by which such contracts may be amicably renegotiated or ended, and metes out punishments to those who violate or abandon contractual agreements. But no-fault divorce allows a person to abandon the marriage relationship (with its many clearly contractual elements, including state licensure) unilaterally, without penalty, and without recourse by the offended contract partner. In legal terms, this is a "terminable at will" relationship. The state's continued participation in the supposed regulation and licensing of marriage is revealed as a sham, little more than "notarized dating." It is more difficult and costly to break a contract to buy a car than a marriage contract.[21] As Bryce J. Christensen has written, "No fault divorce put[s] the state . . . in the absurd position of requiring a license for the pronouncing of public vows which the state subsequently regards with indifference."[22]

### Moral Considerations

The law is a teacher, even if at times we might prefer not to notice this constitutive dimension of its impact. If it is a teacher, no-fault divorce teaches all the wrong things. It teaches men and women that marriage can be casually entered and exited. Yet it is both morally and empirically wrong to believe that this is so. It teaches that contracts—at least this one—can be violated with impunity. By its very name it teaches that no one is to be "faulted" for offenses against marriage, such as adultery and abandonment, where these are present. It permits gross injustices against spouses and children without penalty—indeed, by its structure no-fault divorce allies the state with the irresponsible party.[23] It teaches that marriage itself, as an institution, is not of particular social significance. It thus contributes to the weakening of personal character, relational stability, public justice, and social virtue. It further contributes to weakened links between American law and our common moral heritage.

### Economic Considerations

The ease with which anyone can obtain a divorce places the economically dependent spouse (usually the wife) in a precarious situation. If she is abandoned, the fact that no fault is claimed tends to reduce the value of the property settlement she obtains during the legal process of divorce. Given that 90 percent of divorces leave child custody with the mother, she and her children are at risk of impoverishment, as many are noting today.[24] It is a bitter irony to note that no-fault divorce was, in part, intended to improve the financial situation for divorced women.

### "Speed Bumps"

Despite considerable stirring and unease related to no-fault divorce laws, no state has done away with what by now is a well-established dimension of family law, nor does it appear that any state is likely to do so in the near future. As well, not every antidivorce analyst is convinced that the return to a fault-based system would be constructive.[25] As we shall see later, the "covenant marriage" idea is one new approach for bringing at least the option of limited, fault-based divorce back into family law.

But is there something short of a rollback of no-fault divorce that we can propose related to the entry into divorce?

I suggest four "speed bumps" for consideration: enhanced waiting periods, a more vital role for mutual consent, stronger counseling and education requirements, and modest judicial discretion in granting divorces.

#### Waiting Periods

When states require substantial waiting periods from the time in which a plaintiff files for divorce until a divorce can be legally granted, they communicate a public interest in preventing unnecessary or rash divorces. In Virginia, for example, marriages in which children are present cannot be legally dissolved without a one-year period of "living separate and apart without cohabitation."[26]

I suggest the possibility that each state should include waiting period requirements at least this rigorous as a feature of their divorce laws. Amy Black suggests that these waiting periods should be extended to the two-to five-year range, as is the case in some Western European nations.[27] In thinking about this issue we need to be realistic about what waiting periods can accomplish, as well as the chaos that emerges when the next relationship begins during a spouse's court-enforced waiting period (as already happens frequently now). As well, we must be especially concerned, as most state divorce statutes are, to protect the interests of abused spouses and children. Exceptions can and should be made in these cases. Yet clearly a substantial waiting period is called for under most circumstances. Such legislation was passed in Georgia and is being considered in several other states.[28]

### Mutual Consent

There is much ferment concerning the issue of consent. The legal fiction that a marriage has "broken down" or suffers from "irreconcilable differences" even when both parties do not share that view is under withering assault. Some argue for the reinstatement of mutual consent at every stage of the divorce process in every case. This proposal would probably be unworkable and is politically infeasible. However, proposals are surfacing, such as one in Virginia, that would eliminate (as an oxymoron) unilateral no-fault divorce.[29] Other proposals would eliminate no-fault divorce without mutual consent where there are children involved. Various proposals have surfaced that would permit unilateral no-fault but would treat the process differently than where there is mutual consent. William Galston has proposed eliminating unilateral no-fault where there are children, with the alternative of a five-year waiting period.[30] The principle at stake is important: the decision to divorce is of a fundamentally different nature where there is mutual consent and where there is not, and the law should almost always side with the nonconsenting partner where it can.

### Counseling and Education

A focus of considerable attention in recent divorce law reform efforts has been the strengthening of counseling and education requirements. This is to be heartily endorsed.

Some states require a thirty-, sixty-, or ninety-day period of counseling prior to the granting of a divorce. Others have no such requirements, or limit them to the requests of one party or the discretion of a judge. I advocate a sixty- to ninety-day period of counseling for every divorcing couple, regardless of their interest in it.

Education efforts should be an integral part of any counseling or instruction obtained during the divorce consideration process. Several states have launched recent initiatives requiring divorcing parents to receive some sobering education concerning the effects of divorce on children. Some require the couple to write and have approved a child custody, visitation, and parenting plan. I believe that this education process should also include a prior emphasis on marriage-building practices such as communication and conflict resolution. The bias should first be toward the resolution or management of marital conflict, with the goal of preventing unnecessary divorces, especially where children are concerned.

### Judicial Discretion

While nearly every state involves family court judges in the divorce process, generally they have very little discretion in their decision making. They do not normally have or take the time to undertake a real judicial inquiry into the circumstances facing the couple, but instead the process is generally little more than a summary administrative procedure.[31] Some states permit judges to require counseling, and they are heavily involved in postdivorce financial and custody issues. My suggestion here is simply that judges should be given the leeway at least to delay the granting of a divorce where it is fundamentally frivolous or unnecessary. As Carl E. Schneider has written,

> Many laws now make divorce available where there has been an "irretrievable breakdown" of the marriage. In practice, however, this standard is essentially ignored in favor of divorce on demand. Revitalizing that standard might . . . allow courts to, in effect, send some divorce petitions back for reconsideration.[32]

Mary Ann Glendon has pointed out that several European countries have included "hardship clauses" in their no-fault divorce laws. For example, a 1976 West German law permitted judges to deny divorces "if dissolution of the marriage would impose severe hardship on the unwilling spouse" or if maintaining the marriage was "exceptionally necessary" for the well-being of the children.[33] This sensible provision would be one way of limiting divorce on demand and holding people accountable to the obligations they have taken upon themselves in marriage. Judges should also have the freedom to assess the circumstances of marriage breakdown, especially egregious fault, in determining divorce settlements.

In summary, then, I support the following steps in relation to the entry into divorce:

- Retain the possibility of mutual consent, no-fault divorce for couples without children.

- Retain and use fault grounds where appropriate both for the entry into divorce and for the just determination of divorce settlements.
- Require substantial waiting periods prior to divorce—longer where there are children.
- Eliminate unilateral no-fault divorce, at least where there are children present.
- Require counseling and education prior to granting of divorce, in specialized and more extensive form where children are present.
- Enhance judicial discretion to deny or delay divorce, especially in hardship cases.

## Systemic Reform Option 1: Covenant Marriage

Let us finally consider two systemic reform options. These attack the divorce problem not through one or another pressure point but through an overhaul of the entire marriage and divorce system. We will look first at what has come to be known as covenant marriage.

The 1997 passage in Louisiana of the Covenant Marriage Law (and passage of a similar law in Arizona in 1998) has created considerable public attention to and interest in this particular systemic reform option. Covenant marriage is best understood as an effort to create an optional fault-based marriage covenant as a supplement to the current no-fault regime. It uses the public policy lever of option creation as an expression of public values related to the importance of marriage. The covenant marriage idea can be traced back at least as far as a 1990 article by Elizabeth Scott, a law professor at the University of Virginia, who employed the language of "precommitments" to discuss the possibility of a couple making an advance commitment to marital permanence, or of the state requiring couples to do so.[34] The first legislative proposal related to covenant marriage surfaced in Florida, also in 1990.[35] The communitarian Amitai Etzioni wrote an influential *Time* magazine article in 1993 in which he proposed the use of "supervows," premarital contracts committing couples to do more than the law requires to keep their marriages together.[36] Since that time the idea has picked up momentum, so that by now it is the leading divorce reform concept in the nation. Bills have not only been passed in Louisiana and Arizona but are being considered in at least seventeen other states. Let us look closely here at the pioneering Louisiana law.

As of August 15, 1997, married couples in Louisiana can choose voluntarily to enter into a covenant marriage. The language of the law implicitly recognizes that a covenant marriage contract is a different kind of arrangement than the typical current marriage, and it is to be treated as such by the legal system *at every stage*—this is what I mean by a systemic reform of the marriage law regime. Everything about a covenant marriage is intended to signal the heightened seriousness of this particular version of the marital relationship. Note how each aspect of the marriage law system is addressed in the following provisions.

### The Entry into Marriage

The couple must execute a formal declaration of intent to enter into a covenant marriage. The formal declaration of intent reads as follows:

> We do solemnly declare that marriage is a covenant between a man and a woman who agree to live together as husband and wife for so long as they both may live. We have chosen each other carefully and disclosed to one another everything which could adversely affect the decision to enter into this marriage. We have read the Covenant Marriage Act, and we understand that a Covenant Marriage is for life. If we experience marital difficulties, we commit ourselves to take all reasonable efforts to preserve our marriage, including marriage counseling (LA 3(VII)273(1)).

This declaration must accompany an application for a marriage license. The marriage certificate also indicates whether this is a covenant marriage; witnesses to the marriage must duly certify that this is the case. Those seeking covenant marriage must be able to certify by a notarized affidavit that they have received premarital counseling from a clergyperson or counselor; the law specifies in detail the key elements of the content of this counseling, which includes discussion of a pamphlet from the state attorney general's office concerning the nature of a covenant marriage. The counselor must also offer a notarized attestation of the counseling.

### The Conduct of Marriage

The declaration of intent to enter a covenant marriage requires the couple to seek marital counseling if they experience difficulties.

### The Entry into Divorce

Divorce or separation in a Louisiana covenant marriage is fault-based; adultery, imprisonment for a felony, desertion, or physical/sexual abuse of child or spouse are the only causes listed.

Two years of continuous separation without reconciliation are required before a covenant marriage can be dissolved, though divorce can be granted somewhat sooner for the traditional fault grounds.

How shall we evaluate this innovative legislation? Covenant marriage (at least as we find it in Louisiana) is an attempt to encourage rather than mandate a return to the pre-1969 *status quo ante* in divorce law. The mechanism it uses to offer this encouragement is solely the creation of an optional "marriage deluxe" legal structure. No incentives or disincentives, mandates or prohibitions, are employed. That is one reason why the law was passed: it could be presented in the language of choice rather than mandate.

Even so, a close reading of the law (and the very existence of the law) reveals its clear intent to encourage a return to the moral *status quo ante* in terms of how men and women view the permanence of marriage. The state of Louisiana wants to encourage couples to believe that marriage is a lifetime commitment and to act on that belief. It is prepared to help them do so by structuring its marriage laws in a way that makes it more difficult to exit a marriage if couples contract to play by those rules from the outset. The net result, at least in the short term, is the creation of a two-tier marriage system: intentionally permanent marriages, governed by the covenant marriage laws, and other (implicitly impermanent) marriages, governed by no-fault laws. Clearly, Louisiana hopes that the number of the former will grow and the latter decline.

Criticism of this approach could come from two directions: that Louisiana is going too far, or not far enough. Already there are critics who argue that Louisiana lawmakers have no business enshrining their moral convictions about marital permanence into law. Even the vocabulary ("covenant marriage"), with its clearly biblical overtones, signals the religiomoral convictions that underlie this legislation. The fact that the legislation emerges from the South heightens the suspicions of some here. Predictable choruses of despair concerning the growing influence of the religious right can be heard.

On the other hand, this law can be seen by serious advocates of divorce reform as not going far enough. Louisiana's law does not abolish or even modify no-fault divorce itself but more subtly, and less coercively, seeks to supplement it with an optional fault-based alternative. It can be questioned whether a purely optional system is good public policy—whether it communicates public values in a sufficiently strong and vigorous manner. One could at least ponder the potential of adding a set of incentives and disincentives into the mix.

More broadly, it is a reasonable question to ask whether a two-tier legal system related to marriage is fundamentally coherent. It is hard to think of any other area of the law in which citizens can choose from two sets of rules, unless they are different means of accomplishing a public value, as discussed above. Here lawmakers are attempting to articulate a public valuation of marital permanence but without requiring or even using incentives to encourage anyone to act in a way that accomplishes that goal. It is as if they are saying: "We want you to stay married, but only if *you* want to. If you do, here's a legal option that can help. That's all we'll do for you, but we hope you're interested." That approach may simply be too weak to be very effective. Yet it appeals to our libertarian preference for choice making. Indeed, some are now arguing for a totally deregulated free market in marriage contracts—not just two options but the freedom to make whatever marriage contract we want to make.[37]

Early returns from Louisiana indicate that requests for covenant marriage have trickled rather than flowed in—roughly 2 percent in the law's first year (though hundreds of couples have grandfathered their marriages in, which is also permitted). It is hard to know whether these numbers will increase in the years ahead. The law has encountered a distressing lack of cooperation from many key religious leaders and groups in the state, including the influential Roman Catholic Church in Louisiana, which in a devastating decision chose to remain neutral on the law because it requires counselors to discuss divorce as a legal option.[38] (A clear example of the best being the enemy of the good, in my view.) Some thought that what one Internet wag called "the diplomacy of love" would lead courting couples to agree to covenant marriages rather than admit in advance that they wanted the low-octane variety. So far this hasn't happened.

It may turn out to be the case that citizens will prove to be unwilling to voluntarily bind themselves to laws that are stricter than those that apply to their neighbors. One cannot imagine people doing so in any other area of the law. It may well not work here either, despite the legislature's good intentions. My suggestion is that covenant marriage approaches be strengthened through the intentional use of incentives and disincentives, and that, despite discouraging responses thus far, this experiment should continue to be attempted wherever feasible. And yet I do not consider this voluntary, optional regime the most promising current divorce reform strategy.

## Systemic Reform Option 2: A Child-Focused Two-Tier Marriage/Divorce Law System

The concept of a two-tiered divorce law system could take another potential form: a nonoptional system hinging on the presence of children. With William Galston, I believe that this is the main direction that divorce law reform should take.[39] The presence of children should automatically transform the legal status of marriage and raise the "guardrails" against divorce.

This is not the place to rehearse the complex but compelling evidence concerning the impact of divorce on children. Suffice it to say that the research evidence is strong that divorce has a profoundly negative impact on children, consisting of an abundance of loss, disadvantage, and inequality.[40] This is so even where there has been profound marital and family difficulty prior to the divorce—but especially where there has not, which is the case roughly 70 percent of the time, according to one authoritative recent study.[41] Society has a strong interest in supporting marriages that both endure and are worth enduring, and among the most persuasive supports for this claim is what we now know about divorce's lasting impact in the lives of children. And it is children whose interests are most frequently the last to be considered in our modern culture of divorce.

What would our divorce law system look like if those interests were taken seriously? First, a strong case could be made that because roughly two-thirds of all divorces do involve children, the kinds of "entry into marriage" reforms we have already considered should not only be encouraged but ultimately mandated for all couples. When we consider the engaged couple, we should see not only who they are now but the children they will very likely bring into the world—and the predictable impact of divorce on those children. Those impacts are becoming more and more clear to the generation of children who have suffered the serial monogamy of their Boomer parents.[42]

But let us bracket that proposal and now consider the couple who already have children, either through out-of-wedlock birth or through a prior marriage. A two-tier marriage law system that takes the needs and interests of those children seriously would mandate, rather than merely encourage or make optional, a course of premarital testing and counseling and a lengthy waiting period prior to marriage. The liberty interest of the couple in this case should give way to the well-being of the children involved and to society's stake in that well-being. One added empirical support for this argument is the fact that remarriages, and other marriages initiated when there are already children present, fail more frequently than childless first marriages.[43]

The same basic principle applies when it comes to the decision to enter into divorce. Certainly, where children are involved, states should require lengthy waiting periods of perhaps as much as two years or more (as in Virginia and elsewhere, these waiting periods should be longer where children are present than where they are not present—and of course, abuse situations should always be treated differently). Couples who have children and are considering divorce should be required to attend classes related to the impact of divorce on children as well as all child-related postdivorce issues. The educational process at this pivotal point should operate with a bias toward preserving the marriage and should require reconciliation counseling as well as instruction in communication and conflict resolution. Judges should have the discretion to delay or discourage unnecessary or frivolous divorces where children are involved.

Amy Black has argued that mutual consent should be required in divorces involving children, even if it is not required for other divorces.[44] Galston agrees but would leave a five-year waiting period as an escape clause.[45] While I can see needed exceptions to this approach, I do believe that it is appropriate to return to a modified fault-based system for divorce where children are present. In such a system the presence of children in the home would raise the state's threshold for permitting divorce to something approaching the older fault-based standards that prevailed in American law until 1969. Child or spousal abuse should always be one of the permitted grounds. But a unilaterally initiated divorce for purpose of personal self-fulfillment or career advancement (or whatever) should not be permitted where children will be affected. Or, if an escape clause ultimately is required, the person seeking it should be required to pay dearly for the privilege, both in terms of a waiting period and financial settlement.

With this final proposal I may have stepped over that line of personal liberty that must be carefully guarded in our political system. However, I do believe that a mandatory two-tier divorce law system that takes into account the well-being of children is morally justified and could be politically feasible. Such a proposal would constitute a systemic reform that includes most of the specific incremental proposals outlined above. It is stronger than covenant marriage in that it would be mandatory rather than voluntary and would apply to at least two-thirds of all marriages. Indeed, one might say that it would constitute legal recognition that once children enter the picture, every marriage is, and must be, a "covenant marriage"—because bringing children into the world imposes covenantal obligations on parents that they must not be permitted to evade in the quest for personal fulfillment.

## Conclusion: The Limits of Law

Policymakers can do much to encourage marital permanence and discourage divorce. Beyond the incremental and systemic proposals offered here, government can also use its "bully pulpit" and public education powers to weigh in on behalf of the public good of family stability. In 1998, Florida's state legislators passed not only measures intended to address marital entry and exit but also now require courses on marriage and its skills in the public high schools.[46] One can easily imagine many creative public education measures that could be taken along these lines if the machinery of government at every level was turned to the explicit promotion of this social value.

However, it is important to close with a note of realism and of admonition. The note of realism is this: law cannot produce people of good character, of sound relational skills, of the stuff required to make a lifetime marriage work. Neither can the law force a couple to live out the meaning of the marriage covenant or, ultimately, to live as married persons. Law always has its limits, and those limits are most obvious here. James Fitzjames Stephen was perhaps a bit more pessimistic than I am when he wrote, "To try to regulate the internal affairs of a family, the relations of love or friendship . . . by law or by the coercion of public opinion, is like trying to pull an eyelash out of a man's eye with a pair of tongs. They may put out the eye, but they will never get hold of the eyelash."[47]

Thus a word of admonition must go to individuals, couples, and churches. Ultimately the future of marriage and the well-being of children rests in our own hands. Government can encourage "the better angels of our nature," but we must be willing to live accordingly. Churches, in particular, must do much more to exercise their own leadership in this area. What government cannot mandate or prohibit for citizens, churches can—for their members. And what we mandate we can supply—marriage preparation, marriage enrichment and counseling, divorce prevention tools, and so on.

Real progress in this area of the law is most likely to result from a partnership of individuals, families, churches, government, and other spheres of society.[48] Change must begin with renewal in our hearts and lives of what once were shared values among us. These values must then find creative expression and incarnation in the preaching and programming of churches and other religious organizations. Then and only then can Christians legitimately seek to employ the limited power of government in this sphere of life to enhance public justice and serve the common good.

# 11

# WELFARE REFORM'S CHALLENGE TO THE EVANGELICAL CHURCH

## STANLEY W. CARLSON-THIES

Here you are, a member of your church's mercy committee. One day, an official from the county welfare department comes to your committee and says, "I'm working with a family on welfare, a young mother with two kids. The mother really wants to get off welfare and become a self-sufficient, contributing member of society. But she has not managed to make it with the welfare checks and the training programs we have given her. Her life just isn't pulled together; she can't see her way forward and she has trouble dealing with her kids and with her own depression.

"This mother is crying for a kind of help I can't give. She needs the welfare checks we write and the food stamps and Medicaid we offer. But she needs more help than this. I think you can give the additional help she needs, you and others at your church. I've heard that you already help people in your own congregation with financial seminars, parenting

Stanley Carlson-Thies (Ph.D., University of Toronto) is Director of Social Policy Studies at the Center for Public Justice and currently directs the Center's project to track the implementation and impact of the Charitable Choice provision of the 1996 federal welfare reform law.

classes, automobile clinics, a group for separated and divorced people, and a lot more.

"So here's my proposal: I will match up this woman and her family with a support team from your church. The team will help the family become independent of welfare within six months. To make that possible, our welfare office will transfer to your church a whole year's worth of welfare. The team will control the money, working out a budget with the family and helping them stick to it. The extra funds we are giving can be used to pay off the mom's towing bill so that she can get her car back. And she'll need to use some of it for a few months of specialized training that will equip her for a job that pays enough to support her family. Decide together how the rest of the money can be best used to prepare the family for independence.

"And please help the family with some of your church's rich human and moral resources. Help connect her with jobs. Help her learn what it takes to keep a job. Help her develop better parenting skills. And please welcome her into your supportive network so she has somewhere to turn for advice and help when she runs into trouble.

"The welfare department will work with the team to make sure the family sticks to the agreements it makes with you. We'll help you, too, with our experience in working across cultural and racial divisions. And we'll help your team and the family connect with other important resources, such as subsidized child care.

"We in public welfare have a lot to offer this family, but we can't do everything it needs. We can't offer social connections. We aren't very good at providing encouragement and 'tough love' warnings. We don't do well in giving moral guidance. We can offer a lot to the family, but your church can offer much that is just as important. You could provide the key that helps this family gain independence. Please, will you do it? This family really needs what you can provide. Will you join with us to help this family?"

What would your church say to a county welfare official who came to you with this plea for help and this offer of a partnership?

When I sketched this scenario for an adult Sunday school class on social issues in an evangelical church in my county in Maryland, the class members were shocked that I would even suggest such a thing in their church. They had two main reactions: (1) we don't believe any official would ever ask the church for its support, and (2) we wouldn't cooperate with public welfare anyway, because helping the poor is the task of the church and not government's responsibility.

This negative response, I fear, is not due to some peculiarity or hardheartedness of this particular Sunday school class. Rather, I think it is an all-too-common instinct for American evangelicals, for theologically conservative Protestants. Our sense of how God works is intensely centered on a person's heart and on the church. This is right, as far as it goes. Human hearts, which are sunk in sin, must be restored to a right relationship with God. And the church, the gathering of those who seek to be faithful to God, is a central part of God's work in the world. However, by concentrating so much on the heart and the gathered church, we may lose sight of the larger picture of God as Lord of all creation and Christ as the Reconciler of all things. We may forget that God is concerned with more than hearts and that he is active in many ways beyond the walls of the church.

Our tendency to look inward instead of outward is no doubt encouraged by the circumstances in which we live. Our society, it appears, has turned its back on biblical standards and is rapidly sinking into a moral cesspool. So while we may agitate for government to make laws that will stop the cultural decay and uphold righteousness, and while we may celebrate America's Christian heritage and pray for national repentance so that our society will again become, as we suppose it once was, a city on a hill, we really have little expectation that God is at work in the wider world. When it comes to expecting anything really dependable and good, anything that will really please God, we are sure it will come only to the remnant, that it can happen only in our own midst, only inside the church.

So why in the world would we expect public welfare officials to come ask for our help, and why would we want to connect the church with government, that engine of so much evil?

Yet the truth of the matter is that public welfare officials are in fact knocking on the doors of churches around the nation asking for assistance. In my own county in Maryland, public officials have been making speeches like the one with which I started, inviting churches to form support teams and paying into church bank accounts the welfare checks of families desperate for a different kind of help than government can provide.[1] Throughout the nation, public welfare departments are acknowledging that they cannot solve the welfare problem by themselves and they are seeking partnerships with churches and other faith-based organizations. So if we don't believe that government would ever turn to the church for assistance in serving the needy, then we show only that our eyes and ears have been closed and that we have missed a striking historical trend that conflicts with our pessimism about the culture wars of our day.

Yet if we turn down the government's plea for partnership by saying that serving the poor is the task of the church, we will be committing an even graver error. And that is because such a response is wrong. That is the case I want to make here. My argument will be threefold. The claim that serving the poor is the church's responsibility sounds biblical, but it is first of all an inadequate idea; it is, second, too small a concept; and it will, third, lead us astray at this opportune moment. If we evangelicals are unable to get past our negative reaction to government's invitation to cooperation, we will miss a historic opportunity to serve our neighbors and to shine God's light in our culture.

## Recovering Social Concern

By criticizing the concept that welfare is the task of the church, I do not mean that the church should ignore the poor. Quite the opposite: caring for the needy and powerless is a defining characteristic of God's people. The Bible, from one end to the other, is full of the command that we must care for the poor. Indeed, the call to love our neighbor is second only to the commandment to love God entirely (Matt. 22:37–40). More than four hundred verses in the Bible emphasize God's concern for the needy.[2]

So I believe we are hearing a word from the Lord when Marvin Olasky and others urge Christians individually and corporately to become directly involved with the poor. As Olasky emphasizes, true compassion means "suffering with" the needy. In his memorable words, the problem with government welfare is "not that it is extravagant, but that it is too stingy." The poor receive only material benefits, when they need a personal investment in their lives by a Good Samaritan. And people who are commanded to be Good Samaritans let themselves off the hook by shoving their love obligation onto government. Instead, those who love the Lord must turn to embrace their neighbors.[3] As John Perkins preaches, "A conversion needs to occur in the Church to address the many problems of our communities." What is needed is "a powerful army of God's people working together to solve the problems of our cities, problems the government can never solve alone."[4]

Therefore, I believe also that we are seeing a work of the Lord in the growing ranks of churches and Christian nonprofits gathered in the organization John Perkins inspired, the Christian Community Development Association. CCDA organizations and many others around the country have heard the *word* of the Lord and are putting it to *work* by reaching out to families and neighborhoods sunk in poverty and social distress, and sometimes moral confusion and spiritual darkness. Rather than ignoring their hurting neighbors, they follow a three-R strategy of *relocation* to places of greatest need, *reconciliation* across economic and racial divisions, and *redistribution* of talents, money, and social influence.[5]

Might we be witnessing in such examples the beginning of a recovery of the evangelical church's engagement with society that was so prominent in the nineteenth century? We have all heard the stirring story of

William Wilberforce and his fight in the name of the Lord against the British slave trade. And yet, although we don't hear as much as about it, American evangelicals in the last century also fought in the name of the Lord against slavery and vice and on behalf of the poor and powerless.[6] But alas, evangelicals underwent a "Great Reversal," coming to believe that the Good News applies only to the heart and that concern with poverty and social distress is at best optional.[7]

But the Bible is at war with such a truncated gospel. When the Lord assures us through Isaiah (1:18, NIV) that our sins can be washed "white as snow" even though they be "like scarlet," his specific accusation is that his people have blood on their hands because of their neglect of the weak and poor. "Stop doing wrong," the Lord commands us, "learn to do right! Seek justice, encourage the oppressed. Defend the cause of the fatherless, plead the case of the widow" (vv. 16b–17, NIV). And if we do not do this, the Lord says through Isaiah, then our worship is mere "meaningless offerings," "detestable" incense, and "evil assemblies" (v. 13, NIV).

So we must pray and work for a recovery of social compassion in the evangelical church and in our own hearts. The church must be actively involved in service to distressed neighbors and neighborhoods. And yet the idea that care for the poor is the task of the church alone does not do justice to the biblical requirement that we listen and respond to the cry of the poor. This idea is inadequate, too small, and misleading.

## An Inadequate Idea

It is, first, an inadequate idea. It presumes that churches need only to be more diligent, more faithful, in their outreach to the needy. Scandalously, some churches are so turned inward and have so spiritualized the Good News that they have no outreach to the needy nor even a ministry to the hurts of their own members. And when churches do seek to serve the poor and downtrodden, they often do not know what they are doing. All too often churches, out of misguided compassion, see the poor as empty vessels who need only to be filled with the resources churches can supply. So they give a few dollars to keep the electricity from being cut off, and next month a few dollars again, and the next month . . . without asking if something could be done to prevent the recurring crisis. They operate soup kitchens during the week and distribute food baskets at special times, neglecting to wonder if those who come for these handouts might deserve a different kind of assistance that would enable them to earn their own food for their families.

What a family may desperately need is not more dollars but insightful counsel about life; not another food basket but an invitation into a network that leads to employment and offers advice and encouragement when times are tough; or perhaps not material assistance at all but a healing of the spirit and a turn toward the Lord. In the insightful language of Amy Sherman, many churches need to make the shift from "commodity-based" charity that only hands out things, neglecting the causes of persistent poverty, to a transformational approach, "a relational, holistic ministry" that will enable the family to address its deeper problems and move to self-sufficiency and the ability to contribute to others.[8]

A church that is unwilling to look critically at how it has been assisting the needy may, tragically, only be enabling the poor to "manage their poverty rather than escape from it."[9] Of course, that has been one of the chief criticisms of government welfare: that it gives out money but does not really help families achieve self-sufficiency. Public welfare programs are now being reoriented away from income maintenance to empowerment for independence. What a great irony, and a great tragedy, if we were now to substitute bad church welfare programs for a public system that has begun to do the right thing! It is not enough to say that the care of the poor should be put in the hands of the church, because the church's welfare effort itself may need to be reformed.[10]

## Too Small a Vision

To claim that caring for the poor is the church's task is mistaken, in the second place, because the concept is too small. And it is too small in two different ways.

One problem is that it can lead us to whittle down love of neighbor from a matter of calling to only a matter of volunteerism. Volunteering to help people in need is wonderful, of course, and greatly to be encouraged. Who was the Good Samaritan but a person who, seeing another in an emergency, volunteered to help? Ministries that work with people in need, whatever their need might be, whether physical, mental, or spiritual, always need volunteers, people who freely give of themselves, over and above their work and family commitments, to provide a wide range of services to the ministry itself and to those it assists.

Yet love for the poor is a commandment that touches not only what we do with our volunteer energy; it must also shape how we carry out our primary callings in life. It is not an adequate response to the divine requirement if we are zealous to volunteer each Saturday at a homeless shelter but in our five days per week as a zoning official, lawyer, mayor, banker, or day-care operator we neglect to consider the cause of the poor and powerless. How tragic and hypocritical it would be for a business-person to volunteer an evening a week to help welfare recipients become prepared for the world of work, and yet never once consider whether her own company should be willing to hire a mother who never before had a real chance at a job. How sad and wrong when a public official serves energetically as a church deacon but refuses to ensure that the poor receive justice and mercy when the government makes decisions about schooling, the police, or welfare services. Others can serve on a mercy committee or assist with an evening job-skills course, but who else except the businessperson can actually offer a job and who else but the public official has the authority and power to do public justice? Volunteering is good and indispensable, but it must not come at the expense of listening to the call to serve the needy in our occupations, in our primary callings in life.

The idea that the poor are the church's responsibility is also too limited in another way: it ignores the biblical teaching that the requirement to help the needy is addressed not only to the church but also to other institutions. We all do acknowledge that, at least to some degree. We know that families have a responsibility to their poor members. We see that businesses have to be part of the solution to welfare dependency. We say that churches must play a role. Yet our institutional view may not be expansive enough. I would like to emphasize that not only the church and employers and the families of the poor are called to act on behalf of the poor; government, too, has a divine calling to serve the needy.

We evangelicals tend to be very suspicious of government. Perhaps it is because the sins of public officials are all too obvious. Perhaps it is because we know that government too often harasses rather than protects people and organizations seeking to follow the Lord. Perhaps it is because we have seen too many public policies hurt those they are intended to help, or waste money or be ineffectual. Perhaps it is mainly because we are Americans and share the American suspicion of government.

Whatever the reason, I believe our disdain for government cannot withstand biblical scrutiny. That government can do wrong and be worse than useless is the abundant testimony of Scripture. Nevertheless, the Bible also affirms that government is ordained of God, and its ministers are charged to punish evildoers and to uphold those who do right. When government, its officials, and its policies instead do injustice and harass those who would do good, then what is required is that we call government back to its rightful task. The Bible does not give us permission to turn our backs in disgust as if government is now, or ever could be, merely an evil irrelevancy, of no concern to God and of no significance for his work with the world.[11]

What, then, must government do if it is to do good and not evil? One of its prime responsibilities is to act on behalf of the poor. The godly king portrayed in Psalm 72, for instance, defends the poor, delivers the needy, and crushes the oppressor. When Job thinks back to the time before calamity struck, he recalls that he sat "in the public square" and was commended by all because he "rescued the poor who cried for help, and the fatherless who had none to assist him." He was a "father to the needy" and "broke the fangs of the wicked and snatched the victims from their teeth" (Job 29:7, 11–12, 16–17, NIV). Nor is this a charge only to God-fearing leaders: Nebuchadnezzar, for instance, is warned by Daniel that if he is to be restored to humanity, he must, among other changes, renounce wickedness "by being kind to the oppressed" (Dan. 4:24–27).[12]

But why should government be involved at all in helping the poor, when God's people are plainly commanded to love their neighbors? Let me suggest two reasons.

In the first place, some of what the poor need can come only from that institution in society charged to make and enforce laws, that is, the government. A tenant unjustly evicted requires the arm of the law. A person turned away from jobs or housing due to the color of her skin needs civil rights protection. When the only schools that a poor family can afford are incompetent to prepare the family's children for adulthood, then a revolution in the society's educational system is necessary, and that requires government action. Some families are dependent on welfare only because the father of the children has left them and now refuses to pay child support. What such families need is not so much a handout as strong action by government that will compel Dad to play his part by supporting his children, while encouraging him to resume his role as father and, maybe, as husband.

Nor does it take much imagination to think of many other ways in which government's action, or inaction, is crucial for the well-being of the needy. An unfavorable business climate chokes economic opportunity, harming particularly the poor. Excessive regulation can make it impossible for the poor to start small businesses that will give them a way out of poverty. On the other hand, sometimes what the poor require for advance is government action in the marketplace: individual development accounts— special savings accounts that give the poor a chance to accumulate the capital they need for a more secure life; a supplement to low wages, such as the earned income tax credit; government health insurance to make up for what private companies cannot supply; enterprise zones that encourage companies to take a second look at areas that have been written off as unprofitable. Furthermore, because poverty and family structure are so directly related, one of the most important actions government can take on behalf of the poor is to bolster the institution of the family by requiring greater care in entering marriage and by making divorce a less casual process.

Second, government action may be required beyond positive general policies and specific laws that protect the rights of the poor. Government may be the institution that must step in when families in economic crisis require emergency money and services—when welfare is needed. Thanks to disillusionment with government errors and enthusiasm about the revival of private charity, it has become popular with many (not least evangelicals) to talk about closing down the public welfare system, dismantling what is disdainfully called the "nanny state," and turning over all care of the poor to private charity and to the churches. To the extent that this sentiment regenerates church mercy ministries and personal, hands-on service, its practical consequences are good. But as an attack on government, it is pernicious.

In 1995, a year before the federal welfare reform law was adopted, Mississippi governor Kirk Fordice announced his own state's welfare reform. He called it the Faith and Families program. Faith and Families matches welfare families with churches that provide mentoring and other help so that recipients can make the transition to independence. Government welfare, Fordice proclaimed, "does nothing to inspire self-esteem, independence, or healthy family relationships." What was needed was "a completely new approach." "The rationale behind the Faith and Families initiative is simple," the governor said. "If government is causing the problem, let us remove government from the picture; and, we have."[13]

Except that Mississippi had not. Faith and Families is a structure initiated, designed, and funded by government, and far from the churches taking over welfare from government, they supplement what government does. All of the families involved continue to receive their government benefits—their welfare checks, food stamps, Medicaid services, subsidized child care, and more. Now, in addition, they receive from the churches moral guidance, prayer, life-skills training and advice, a network of people dedicated to their success, a witness to the love and truth of God, and informal help, such as an emergency baby-sitter or a ride to work if the car breaks down. The churches are not substituting for government welfare; instead, they are supplementing it, adding other services and benefits, a personal and moral approach, that helps change government benefits from a handout to a hand up. Faith and Families, in other words, despite the libertarian pronouncements of Governor Fordice, is not about abolishing government welfare but rather about making it fruitful by adding the churches.[14]

But why should government continue to play a role? Let me give two reasons: reliability and distribution. I'll start with distribution. What I have in mind is the problem of matching resources and needs. When some suburban church gets energized to serve the needy, we can expect that it will not restrict its attention only to its middle-class neighborhood, but will it even know that its help is most needed not five miles away downtown but rather in the central core of the next big city over, or in a desperate rural region half a continent away? And in deciding on our own where to allocate our resources, aren't we all too prone to be moved by photogenic poverty—the mom and kids abandoned by a faithless husband rather than the drug-addicted teen whose babies had to be removed for their own safety? Yet neither proximity to need nor the strength of the tugs on our heartstrings are reliable guides to where help should be provided. Effective help for the poor is not a matter only of desire and dedication but also of identifying and prioritizing needs and marshaling dispersed resources. And as it happens, we elect, appoint, and hire people to make just such decisions for the whole political community; this mechanism is called government.[15]

I've labeled the other reason for government involvement "reliability." I mean this: whether or not our hearts are moved to compassion at a particular moment, whether or not our church has run all the way through its six-month bureaucratic process of deciding to start a new program, whether or not at this moment we think we can spare a few dollars to help someone else, right now there are children and adults who must be able to count on assistance from others. Essential needs must be met or disaster will result. It may even be a life-or-death matter. So assistance must be reliable, even though the human heart is fickle. That is why there needs to be an institution charged to ensure that the cries of the poor are not ignored. The institution charged with promoting public justice is the government.

It was in just this way that Jonathan Edwards defended the legal requirement in his day that towns must come to the aid of the needy. Desperately poor families, he said, ought not to be left to so precarious a source of supply as voluntary charity. It is fit that there should be something sure for them to depend upon. But a voluntary charity in this corrupt world is an uncertain thing. Therefore, the wisdom of the legislature did not think fit to leave those who are so reduced upon such a precarious foundation for subsistence.[16]

Surely we are all called to voluntary charity. But even when we are not moved, the poor require assistance. So while the call to serve our neighbor comes to each of us personally and also to the church, it also comes to the government, which is charged with upholding public justice.

However, to say that government must protect the poor is not at all to say that government itself must always be the supplier of needs. Indeed, the first, second, and third lines of defense should not be government at all. People should prepare for crises themselves. When their own resources have run out, they should be able to look to their families for assistance. When their need for help is even greater, they should be able to turn to the church and to other institutions in civil society. Yet even when help from such sources is insufficient or unavailable, poor persons and families still require help. And they should be able to count on government, the institution of public justice, for that help.

Yet even when the poor must rely on government for their emergency or welfare help, it may be best that much of the help actually be delivered by others. Government's own means of assistance—its checks and programs—are impersonal, abstract, and morally thin, when what is needed to nurture a renewal of responsible action is personal, direct, and morally authoritative assistance. "The kind of help that is most successful comes from people with deep moral and religious commitments, and very often from those who work for explicitly religious organizations."[17]

Thus a major way that government can best fulfill its own specific responsibility to come to the aid of the needy is by supporting the diverse assistance efforts of the institutions that surround those in need. It is these bodies "that can and should bear [direct] responsibility for people in special need. Government policies should not sidestep or displace families, churches, schools, and independent service agencies. To the contrary, the law and public funds should go, first of all, to support the institutions and organizations that can . . . minister directly and personally to people, helping them recover their own accountability."[18] Government should work with and uphold, rather than neglect or displace, nongovernmental assistance agencies, particularly churches and faith-based nonprofit organizations.[19]

Government must play a role, then, in assisting the poor. Laws and public policies are required that no other institution is authorized to make. And government must ensure that welfare help is available. But most of the time that emergency help can best be provided by, or in partnership with, other institutions in society, including religious institutions. Governor Fordice saw this. Officials in my county in Maryland have seen this. So have many other public officials. The question is, will the evangelical church also see this? If our wisdom on poverty relief is limited to repeating the idea that assisting the needy is the job of the church, we will not be prepared when officials are looking for faith-based organizations with which they can partner for the sake of poor families.

## Faulty Guidance

So we come to my third objection to the notion that serving the poor is the task of the church: this idea steers us in the wrong direction just at the moment when our society is searching for more effective ways to assist the needy.

It is striking that in our current time of dramatic welfare reform, the old conflict about just doing either more or less government welfare has been mostly superseded. What most officials, and also citizens and recipients themselves, are looking for is a different way of doing welfare. The new consensus is that welfare should not be just a handout but should enable and require needy families to take care of themselves. The federal welfare law that Congress and the president adopted in August 1996 made a decisive break from the income-support idea of welfare, putting in its place policies and incentives intended to help welfare recipients move from welfare to employment.[20]

The new consensus has another key feature: the idea that welfare can be provided most effectively when government cooperates with the institutions of civil society. Many now see that the fight against poverty cannot be successful if families keep falling apart, and that the cooperation of the business sector is essential if the needy are to be helped over the long run. Likewise, many now agree that the involvement of the faith community is important if families are to be helped to become self-sufficient and contributing members of society.

This conviction about the importance of partnerships between government and faith-based institutions is not merely a bright idea being bandied about by talking heads on television public-affairs programs. I have already suggested two specific instances where officials are seeking to connect public welfare with the help that can be provided by congregations. And there are many more.[21] In fact, the idea that when government seeks to help poor families, it should work with community organizations, including religious organizations, is a key feature of the 1996 federal welfare reform law that is the basis for the extensive changes being made in all of the states.

That federal law contained a short section, which has come to be called the charitable choice provision, that instituted new rules for how government interacts with faith-based organizations. We evangelicals are very conscious that government has had a pernicious, secularizing impact on society, and that government rules, particularly when government money is involved, have posed a danger to Christian ministries. In fact, government policy is not as negative as we might guess based on some well-publicized horror stories.[22] Nevertheless, there has been at best much uncertainty about whether government can require Christian ministries to downplay or eliminate the Christian aspects of their programs.[23] Given this history, many evangelical churches and parachurch ministries have understandably sought to keep their distance from government money and government influence.

The charitable choice provision is a legislative initiative that addresses these problems. It has put on the books a range of specific protections for the religious character of faith-based organizations, protecting their right to hire only staff committed to their mission, allowing them to use religious concepts in their programs, and ending the foolish requirement that walls be stripped of all religious symbols. And charitable choice explicitly outlaws government discrimination against faith-based organizations that want to compete to provide welfare services using government funds. It is now the law that when any state decides to use its federal welfare funds to serve welfare families by paying independent organizations to provide the services, then evangelical churches and nonprofits, along with other faith-based organizations, have every right to put forth their programs as effective tools to help welfare families become independent.[24]

What is the significance of this legislative action? It means that the government has recognized that in the past it has not been very hospitable to religious organizations, thus forcing many of them to stay as far away as they could lest they become secularized and lose their ability to carry out their mission in obedience to the Lord. And the government has now acted to make itself hospitable, constructing specific legal protections for faith-based organizations that accept government money to provide welfare services—specific legal protections that apply even in states with constitutions that are hostile to partnerships between government and religious organizations. Because these protections are now in place, government officials are hoping that evangelical churches and nonprofits and other faith-based organizations will be encouraged to partner with welfare departments.

And as I have noted several times, in addition to these charitable choice protections and the invitation to consider accepting government money to provide welfare services, many welfare departments are creating networks that bring together welfare families and churches in voluntary relationships focused on mentoring.

So, whether or not we evangelicals would have expected it, government officials have decided that welfare must be provided in new ways, and that those new ways require the involvement of new organizations, in particular churches and faith-based nonprofits. Government is seeking to build cooperative relationships with the faith community. If our idea about serving the needy is just that it is the church's job, then we will not be in a position even to see the significance of this change in the government's attitude toward welfare and toward religious organizations.

## Answering the Call?

So I return to my question from the beginning: What would your evangelical church say to a welfare official who came to you with a plea for help and with an offer of a partnership? The point shouldn't be money or influence. Charitable choice and these mentoring networks shouldn't be seen as ways to build the church's budget or to gain new members. What is important, rather, is that the church is being asked to help create and operate more effective ways of assisting needy people and families.

We say that serving the needy is the task of the church because we acknowledge that God calls us to love our needy neighbors and because we believe that biblical wisdom gives the best guidance about how to rescue people. At this very moment there is before the church a historic opportunity to use its best insights to fulfill the divine commandment by showing love to thousands of families that need more than welfare provides. Surely we must pray that evangelicals will not let this opportunity go by without a vigorous response simply because all we can think to do is to repeat the slogan that helping the poor is the job of the church.

# 12

# REFUGEES

## *Uncertain Welcome*

## CHRISTINE D. POHL AND BEN DONLEY

"Our century is marked by displacements on the scale of continents. ... Never before have so many human beings fled from so many homes."[1] Elie Wiesel, a former refugee himself, now a well-known author and Nobel Peace Prize winner, captures in his comment some of the enormity of the problem. The numbers of refugees around the world are staggering, and the magnitude of their numbers is matched only by their desperation and by the international uncertainty about how to respond to their need.

Today there are over 14 million refugees—people who have left their home countries because of a "well-founded fear of persecution." There are at least an additional 17 million people who live in refugeelike situations—people who have fled their home areas because their lives were in danger but who have remained within the borders of their home country.[2]

Refugee numbers are large for several reasons, but particularly because of the increased violence toward civilians in internal conflicts.[3] Gil Loescher, a specialist in refugee affairs, describes the current situation.

Christine D. Pohl (Ph.D., Emory University) is Professor of Social Ethics at Asbury Seminary. Ben Donley is a graduate of Asbury Seminary in the Missions and Evangelism program.

179

At present, refugee movements are most likely to be the result of ethnic, communal, and religious conflicts. The most common form of warfare in the developing world and in Eastern Europe in the 1990s is internal conflict, fueled by the increasing availability of modern weaponry, sharp socioeconomic inequalities, and human rights abuses.[4]

Those forced to flee are frequently the most marginalized in their own society: members of minority groups, indigenous populations, and others without political voice or influence.[5] Evictions and expulsions of entire populations are increasingly common strategies for establishing "culturally or ethnically homogeneous societies."[6] In many of these civil wars, disregard for international humanitarian law is shocking. Practices include calculated atrocities, methodical rape, forced starvation, intentional destruction of civilian places, and widespread use of land mines.[7] Of the refugees and displaced persons under the care of the United Nations High Commissioner on Refugees in 1997, 80 percent were women and children.[8]

We know the human consequences of these patterns; we stare with bewilderment as news reports describe the latest atrocities or desperate situations. We watch the evening news and listen to another story of personal tragedy or wonder at the shadowy half-starved figures squatting silently in the midst of vast dusty camps. We wince as mothers weep for children lost to disease, starvation, or the latest outbreak of ethnic violence.

The problem is complicated and it requires comprehensive responses. Refugee needs are profoundly important humanitarian concerns, but they are also tied to complex political issues. Concern for refugees cannot be entirely separated from foreign policy and security questions, human rights abuse and protection, and local and international development issues.[9] In addition, historical religious, political, and ethnic tensions and violence sometimes make it difficult to sort out claims of aggression, wrongdoing, and self-defense.

Because of the number of interrelated factors, frequently our political and personal response is to do nothing at all. The involvement of the United States and NATO in Kosovo was unusual in its substantial focus on the needs of refugees. In discussions of public policy among Christians, refugee concerns may be unique in how little attention is usually paid to them.

But complex public policy issues have very human dimensions. Particular persons and families are caught in the middle of political, economic, and social crises they cannot avert. Our attention to their needs might be more focused if we could imagine ourselves as refugees.

For a moment, picture yourself as the father of a Kosovar family, reunited after not knowing for several months whether or not your wife and children were even alive. All of you have been granted refugee status and are beginning a new life in the United States. Although you were a teacher in Kosovo, you will now try to support your children by working in a local factory. Your entire family is struggling with the depth of betrayal experienced as neighbors and friends turned against you and participated in the murder of your relatives and the destruction of your home. But you have begun to make a home in your new land and are grateful for the Christian families that helped you to resettle here.

Or imagine yourself as a woman from Liberia who fled after your parents and three children were murdered by soldiers when your husband would not join their side. Your husband barely survived the attack, which occurred while you were away visiting a sister. You and your husband fled your home and country and through a wildly tortuous path made your way to the United States to request asylum. Without documents and proof of persecution, and because you were not part of an orderly refugee departure program, you were both detained in local Texas prisons. You were held with regular criminals. Neither of you had committed crimes, but you were imprisoned for months awaiting asylum hearings. You are a devout Christian. Your tragic losses in Liberia were compounded by a traumatic trip to the United States and intensified by the prison experience. Once released, you were required to stay in the area while awaiting your asylum hearing, but you were not permitted to work. If not for the kindness of a small Christian organization, you would have had no place to stay.

Or try to picture yourself as a Palestinian boy living in a refugee camp in Lebanon. Your family has been there since 1949 and you have never known anything except the life of a refugee. You were born a refugee, and so were your parents. You are intelligent and your academic potential is obvious, but educational opportunities are scarce and the hope for any kind of professional vocation is bleak.

Finally, imagine yourself as a teenage Rwandan girl whose family was wiped out in the brutal civil war. During the devastation, you were raped repeatedly by soldiers who used rape as a weapon of war. You have found distant relatives who also managed to survive the war, the flight to a neighboring country, and the dangers of the refugee camp. You are part of a large repatriation project; you are going home—but what is home, what is left, where will it ever be safe for you?

The experience of being a refugee—forced to flee all that is familiar, betrayed by one's government and often one's neighbors—is distant from our experience. But refugees ache with the same grief we feel when a child dies or a daughter is raped, when friends betray us, or when all that is familiar is demolished around us.

Given the gravity of the situations, the level of human need, and the vulnerability of persons, it is striking that Christians know so little about this topic. While we might gather a few details during an international refugee crisis that receives wide media attention, have strong opinions on immigration, or occasionally be involved in helping to resettle a refugee family, very few Christians (or non-Christians) know much about the larger public policy questions. Few people are able to distinguish clearly between immigration issues and refugee concerns.

How is it that such a significant human issue touches Christians in the United States so little? Are any people in the world more vulnerable than those who have been forced out of their homes and into alien settings where they are completely dependent on the kindness of strangers? If part of our identity as Christians involves caring for the weakest, welcoming strangers, and being advocates for those with no voice, then we have a responsibility to learn something about the issues. We are obligated to understand them well enough to recognize good and bad policy responses, and to care about the people sufficiently to invest some of our time and resources in helping them. Bad policy decisions and delayed reactions to crises have awful human consequences. Desperate situations in foreign lands must be addressed even as we recognize the gravity of some of our own domestic problems and needs.

The greatest numbers of refugees today are in Africa, the Middle East, and parts of Asia. Increasingly, however, as a result of conflicts in parts of the former Soviet Union and especially in the former Yugoslavia, refugee crises have also become significant in Europe. Most refugees seek asylum or safety in neighboring countries. The largest refugee flows are from poor countries to poor countries. Although desperate people occasionally make their way to wealthier nations to request refugee status or asylum, they often find those countries unwilling to process their requests.

People leave their homes for many reasons. Some leave because of persecution by their government or by groups with power; others are driven out by civil war, "ethnic cleansing," or religious persecution. Still others leave because of environmental degradation, human rights violations, poverty, or hope for a better life. Recently, some persons have fled because of forced abortion and sterilization policies, and because of the practice of female genital mutilation in certain countries. In several nations ruled by Islamic fundamentalists, Christians and other non-Muslims have been persecuted severely, and some have sought refuge in other lands.

In a certain sense, all of these people are refugees, but the term *refugee* in international law also has a technical or legal definition. It refers to a person who,

> owing to a well-founded fear of being persecuted for reasons of race, religion, nationality, membership in a particular social group, or holding a certain political opinion, is outside the country of his nationality and is unable or, owing to such fear, is unwilling to avail himself of the protection of that country.[10]

Two criteria in the legal refugee designation are crucial: (1) the individual has *suffered persecution,* usually interpreted as a deliberate act by a government against individuals; and (2) the individual has *fled his or her country.* The strict definition does not usually include people fleeing war and violence, economic deprivation, or environmental catastrophe.[11]

In the past, the official refugee designation emphasized *individuals* fleeing persecution, but increasingly today there are whole communities or groups displaced by ethnic conflicts. In fact, as Gil Loescher notes, "present refugee crises are complex emergencies, combining political instability, ethnic tensions, armed conflict, economic collapse, and the disintegration of civil society."[12] It has become difficult to reconcile the narrow legal designation of refugee with the very complex social, political, and economic experience of those forced to flee their homes.

For several reasons, not all people forced to flee cross the border into another country. Increasing numbers of people running from armed conflict or persecution move to a different part of their own country. Sometimes they remain in their home country because it is safe there, but often it is because the borders are closed to them. These are *internally displaced persons,* sharing most of the characteristics of refugees but in many ways even more vulnerable because they have not crossed borders. No international agency protects or assists them because they remain within their own state. The crisis is internal to the country, and international agencies as well as other nations have been uncertain about intervention.[13]

Endangered persons who cross a national border seek asylum in a neighboring country. If the border is fairly open and they are culturally and linguistically similar to the local population, they may be able to blend in permanently or until it is safe to return to their home country. However, this practice was more common in the past than it is today because nations have grown more rigid about protecting their borders and controlling immigration.

If a country does not close its borders to those fleeing danger or persecution, it might grant asylum seekers temporary or permanent protection. But the pressures on host countries can be severe. Often these countries are very poor and the influx of refugees can strain limited resources even further. Sometimes refugee influxes can destabilize the host country politically; many countries that receive refugees are themselves in fragile political, economic, and environmental situations. For this reason, the United Nations, international humanitarian agencies, and sometimes other nations become involved. Refugee needs are immediate, substantial, and critical. Local populations and national governments cannot necessarily meet the need.

Protection and care for refugees at the international level are accomplished through the international refugee regime—the combination of "laws, agreements and institutions which have been established to regulate and resolve the refugee problem." The key international commitments were established in the United Nations 1951 Convention on Refugees and the 1967 Protocol that defined refugee status and established certain protections. These documents have now been ratified by about 134 nations.[14]

Central to the regime is the United Nations High Commissioner for Refugees (UNHCR), which assists refugees through protection and coordination of shelter, food, and medical care, often in refugee camps. It helps with repatriation, resettlement, and integration into countries of first asylum. "With representation in some 120 countries, UNHCR is concerned with the well-being of more than 22 million people."[15] Loescher reports that "more than two-thirds of all international assistance is channeled through the UNHCR," most of whose funding comes from the voluntary contributions of national governments.[16]

Many humanitarian and religious agencies work with the UNHCR. Their workers serve in the camps, provide food and assistance, and help in the resettlement of refugees. These nongovernmental organizations (NGOs) include such agencies as World Relief, Church World Service, and United States Catholic Conference/Migration and Refugee Services. Some are large international agencies, others work at a smaller, more local level. "As implementing partners for the UNHCR, NGOs bear the brunt of delivering food and providing shelter, water, sanitation, and health care to refugees."[17]

Under the United Nations agreements, asylum seekers are protected by a principle of international law known as *non-refoulement* (no forced return). Those nations that have signed on to the UN commitments agree that "no state 'shall expel or return [*refouler*] a refugee . . . to the frontiers of territories where his life or freedom would be threatened.'"[18] Under international law, persons have a right to seek asylum and a right not to be forced back into a dangerous situation. However, because of commitments to national sovereignty, there is no corresponding requirement that nations must grant asylum. States are not required to give entry to anyone at their borders; most have simply agreed not to deport those who have made their way in and requested refuge from danger.

For people who have fled to another country, there are basically three options: voluntary repatriation (returning home), local settlement and integration into the country of first asylum, and third-country resettlement for those with special problems associated with repatriation and local integration. Although some refugees are absorbed into neighboring countries for extended periods, most refugees eventually return to their home countries. Many spend time in refugee camps; some people remain in these camps for years.

For a small number of the world's refugees, third-country resettlement is a crucial option. The UNHCR describes these circumstances.[19] Sometimes the safety and security of particular refugees cannot be guaranteed in the initial host country. Refugees faced with forced repatriation, women threatened by sexual violence in the camps, unaccompanied minors, and refugees who continue to be in danger because of ethnic or religious background often need to be resettled elsewhere. Resettlement is also crucial to those who have special needs: life-threatening medical problems, injuries or disabilities, and victims of torture, rape, and severe trauma. Resettlement also allows refugees to be reunited with family members who are already living in another country.

Third-country resettlement is a necessary option for those refugees who have lived in a country of first asylum for some time but are unable to integrate there and yet are also unable to go home. This is particularly true for those refugees from minority groups who, after the conflict is over, have no home to which to return.[20] Nongovernmental organizations are central in third-country resettlement—they are the instruments through which refugees are provided with aid, sponsors, travel arrangements, and preliminary introductions into a new society.

Despite severe needs for assistance, protection, asylum, and resettlement, certain trends are endangering refugees further. The UNHCR reports that "refugee protection standards are currently being undermined: by the denial of asylum by potential countries of refuge; by threats to the physical safety and human security of exiled populations; and by a weakening commitment to the principle of voluntary repatriation."[21] A closer look at each of these trends is important for understanding their impact on the lives of refugees.

## Denials of Asylum

All countries struggle with granting asylum, but denials of asylum are a particularly disturbing trend among wealthier nations. Highly developed countries fear that refugee crises and asylum seekers will come in a never-ending stream. Building higher walls and establishing tighter restrictions, however, do not make the crises disappear—they only move them to other countries, many of which have fewer resources for helping refugees.[22]

While there is no right to receive asylum under international law, "a willingness to provide asylum is the litmus test for the commitment by affluent states to human rights." A. Shacknove, addressing the needs of asylum seekers, explains, "Affluent states cannot expect other, more vulnerable nations to execute demanding reforms or improve human rights conditions and at the same time claim that it is beyond their own substantial means to sustain a commitment to asylum."[23]

Poorer countries, who often host waves of refugees, find the increased resistance to asylum among wealthier nations a double burden. Poor countries have few resources and most of the refugees.[24] Wealthier nations have far more resources but are also more able to distance and insulate themselves from the problem.

The United States has been moderately positive about orderly refugee resettlement, welcoming significant numbers of refugees whose processing had occurred outside its borders. On the other hand, the United States, and increasingly Europe, has been hostile to asylum seekers who, without processing, arrive within the nation's borders. Official policy now includes imposition of carrier sanctions—punishments on shipping and airline companies that transport asylum seekers who do not have the required documents. Governments are sometimes involved in interdictions at sea to turn people back to their home country. For those who manage to get in, there can be harsh detainment prior to asylum hearings.

Another expression of the resistance to granting asylum is the increased emphasis on in-country processing—insisting that those seeking refugee status do so from within their own country. Individuals are expected to file for visas and other documents in the local embassy and to prepare for an orderly departure. Although this may be sensible in a few cases, it is hard to imagine that such an approach actually rescues anyone who is genuinely and immediately endangered. People in the midst of persecution are not usually in a situation that would make it wise to contact embassies and wait for documents.

Partly because of the numbers of countries that now resist offering asylum, many of those forced from their homes are caught within their own country. Current responses often emphasize "confinement and containment" of endangered populations within their home countries. In the past any intervention on behalf of these people was seen as beyond the mandate of the UNHCR. There is now more willingness to consider a multilateral intervention because of the enormous costs to host and donor countries in providing help, and because of the recognition that refugee crises can have an impact on regional and international security concerns. Nevertheless, intervening in the internal affairs of a country remains highly contested, and actual intervention comes slowly at best. When nations do respond to growing difficulties within a country, it is often because they are becoming increasingly worried about the impact of a refugee flow on a neighboring country.[25]

## Increased Threats to Safety and Security

The increasing threats to the safety and security of exiled populations and refugee workers is a second trend that endangers refugees. Refugee camps must be secure if there is to be any kind of orderly resettlement or repatriation, or if even basic needs of refugees are to be met. In a number of the conflicts that have recently produced refugees, however, warring factions have deliberately attacked refugees and exploited the work of humanitarian organizations for military and political ends. A serious problem results when the UNHCR and other humanitarian agencies must deal with refugee crises without simultaneous international effort to end the armed conflicts, demilitarize the camps, or address massive human rights abuses.[26]

It is becoming quite clear that concerned nations and organizations must pay more attention to the quality of asylum in "safe havens," refugee camps, and countries of first asylum. Sometimes "asylum" is both dangerous and inadequate.[27] Assistance without protection is a serious and increasing problem. Refugees obviously need food and medicines, but when these are provided in camps or situations that are not secure from military threat or criminal violence, such assistance can actually increase the danger. Recipients become targets of warring factions. Attempts to provide humanitarian aid without adequate protection also push humanitarian organizations and the UNHCR into compromising positions of cooperation with "local perpetrators of human rights abuses."[28]

## Weakening Commitment to Voluntary Repatriation

In many places the principle of *non-refoulement* is being flouted. Refugees are being returned to their home countries under duress. Sometimes this is because the condition in the host country is deteriorating; sometimes it is because camp situations are very bad. Those who return prematurely face serious dangers because tensions may not have been resolved. Ongoing fighting, continuing socioethnic conflicts, the uncertain legal status of returnees, and questions about property and land access significantly intensify the vulnerability of refugees forced to return.[29]

Within international circles there is presently a strong emphasis on repatriation as the best approach to refugee crises. But repatriation is not a solution for every crisis or every refugee, and when done apart from attention to reintegration issues, it can be very dangerous.

The above-noted trends help demonstrate the complex and interrelated factors in addressing refugee concerns. They help illustrate that refugee crises cannot be neatly extracted from larger political and economic issues. Solutions require attention to questions about migration, human rights, and development assistance, as well as to concerns about the meaning of national sovereignty and the appropriateness of international intervention. Charitable responses are crucial to the well-being of refugees, but refugee crises cannot be solved by humanitarian aid alone.[30]

The end of the Cold War has provided the United States with a significant occasion to rethink its refugee policy. For decades, U.S. policy on refugees was closely tied to concerns about communism and its spread. During that period, almost all of the refugees admitted by the United States were fleeing countries dominated by communism.

In general, governments are more likely to aid refugees "fleeing from their enemies than from their friends."[31] Welcoming refugees from countries who are adversaries reinforces the claim that their regime is bad for their own people. This approach prompted a generous response to persons fleeing communist-controlled lands. U.S. public policy often assumed that persons were persecuted because they lived under communism, and refugees from communism were paroled into the United States in bloc fashion. In all, the United States admitted several million people from Cuba, Indochina, and Central and Eastern Europe.[32]

Concerns about communism's spread made many U.S. politicians, leaders, and citizens unwilling to acknowledge human rights abuses and persecutions in allied, noncommunist countries. For example, despite some protests, the U.S. government concluded that persons fleeing Haiti, Guatemala, and El Salvador were leaving for economic reasons and were thus not refugees. To have designated them refugees would have been to acknowledge that the leaders with whom the United States worked were abusive toward some of their own people. This tension was compounded by fears that, because these people had ready access to U.S. borders, there would be an unending stream of asylum claims.

Today, with the end of the Cold War, the potential is greater for refugee policy to be shaped more directly by humanitarian need and less by foreign policy objectives. While this is a helpful shift for those persons most endangered, it is presently accompanied by reductions in the overall numbers of refugees being admitted into the United States. So now, while policies are more open to persons truly fleeing persecution, the actual slots available to them are diminishing. There is also a second problem. Although refugee policy is now tied less to foreign policy objectives, it is increasingly shaped by economic concerns. Corporations and many citizens resist attempts to condemn human rights violations in countries in which U.S. business interests are significant.

Given the complex trends and history, and the severe human needs, it is important to ask ourselves how Christians in the United States might respond in ways that reflect God's love and wisdom, ways that are helpful and humane. What resources of our Christian faith do we bring to this issue that will help us sort out responses that are faithful to God and responsible to our neighbors?

With no one to protect them, those forced from their homes and communities have little support and few resources. No population is more vulnerable or in greater danger. Refugees and those in refugeelike situations have a special moral claim on us simply because of their great need.

Does the Great Commandment to love our neighbors as ourselves apply to refugees? How can we possibly consider people with whom we have little connection "neighbors" in any meaningful sense of the term? What makes someone a neighbor? In Luke 10:29–37, Jesus answers the question "Who is my neighbor?" with a parable; he tells the story of the wounded man and the Samaritan who rescues him. Jesus makes it clear that it was the Samaritan who acted as "neighbor" to the man in need. The parable reminds us that the question posed for Christians who are able to help is not shaped by careful definitions of "neighbor." The key question for us is whether or not *we* are acting as neighbors to persons in need. In several places, Jesus requires that his followers include even enemies in their circle of care (e.g., Luke 6:27–31). No one is left outside of the scope of Christian concern; the neighbor is anyone who needs help.

Christians recognize that every person is created in the image of God and that we share a common humanity with every other human being. We share similar needs and similar dependence on others for help. Over four hundred years ago, John Calvin wrote that God "has impressed his image in us and has given us a common nature, which should incite us to providing one for the other." Persons who try to exempt themselves from caring for their neighbors should, Calvin said, simply announce that they do not want to be human beings anymore. To care is part of what it means to be human. "To make any person our neighbor," Calvin said, "it is enough that he be a man." In fact, based on the story of the Good Samaritan, "the greatest stranger is our neighbour," and the neighborhood to which we are responsible, Calvin explained, "extends to the whole human race."[33]

While compassion can be costly, kindness to strangers is not optional for Christians. Love and hospitality are fundamental to Christian identity. To give up kindness, to close our hearts, to carelessly assert that we have no room is to risk giving up part of our humanity and much of our Christian identity.

Historically, hospitality has included providing sanctuary or protection from persecution and danger. It has also involved provision—food, shelter, and clothing. But equally important, hospitality has expressed recognition that the stranger is a fellow human being who deserves both care and respect.

In the Christian tradition, the normative focus of hospitality has been on those most in need and on those who appear to have the least to offer. The distinctive Christian contribution to the tradition of hospitality is its separation from concerns about how caring for strangers can benefit the host. In Matthew 25:31–46, Jesus explains that "inasmuch as you have done it to the least of these you have done it to me," and in Luke 14:12–14, he challenges us to invite to our tables those who cannot repay us. These texts shape Christian understandings of hospitality and divorce them from seeking or expecting advantage in return. In hospitality, we respond to strangers with the kindness that we would give to our own relatives and friends.[34] Welcoming needy strangers, without concern about gaining benefit from our hospitality, can be our particular contribution to the refugee debate.

The people of God have always been expected to care for the most vulnerable—widows, orphans, strangers, and the poor. Protection of strangers and sojourners in ancient Israel involved more than freedom from harm. In Leviticus 19:18, and 33–34, when the Great Commandment was first given, the people of God were instructed to love their neighbors as themselves and then, several verses later, to love the alien or stranger as themselves. Calvin interpreted texts from the Levitical law to mean that when strangers were permitted to live in the land, they should be "kindly treated according to the rights of hospitality, for to allow them to *live* is to make their condition just and tolerable. And thus God indirectly implies, that such unhappy persons are expelled and driven away, so as not to *live,* if they are oppressed by unjust burdens." Therefore, he concluded, persons with ability ought to uplift and relieve those who are weak or in poverty.[35]

Whether such persons live among us or at a distance, they should elicit from us special concern because of God's special care for them. In a world that has grown much smaller because of technology, displaced people in Sudan or Kosovo are not so far removed from us. They are our neighbors as they appear on television screens in our living rooms, and although we cannot help everyone, we have far more resources for helping than we are using.

Understanding refugee issues takes work because the problem is complex. Our response is partly a matter of stewardship. Christians have a special responsibility because we have been given much, and from those who have been given much, much will be required. Christians in democratic societies, especially in the United States, have the freedom to speak out and the resources with which to work. We can be advocates for those with no voice. We can be advocates in government, advocates in local communities that feel burdened by immigrants and refugees, and advocates in churches when decisions about ministry focus and budget allocations come along. We can challenge one another to think more carefully about how we use our personal and collective resources.

Christians can also model concern and respect for refugees. We should challenge careless language and heartless utilitarian calculations that weigh our comfort and convenience against other people's basic survival. Because most of us focus on domestic concerns and well-being, simple attention to refugees, knowing their condition and talking about their needs, will matter in public policy. Being a friend to refugees—whether they are on the other side of the world or resettled down the street—is an important public affirmation of their importance and value.

It is often the case that those who are most desperate are pushed aside and hidden from view. Sometimes we choose to ignore such persons and close our eyes to their need. We cultivate an ignorance that keeps us safe; we perceive ourselves to be not responsible if we never even knew about their situation. In a sermon from the eighteenth century, John Wesley observed that one part of the world does not know what the other part suffers. He continued, "Many of them do not know, because they do not care to know: they keep out of the way of knowing it—and then plead their voluntary ignorance as an excuse for their hardness of heart."[36]

Christian believers bring particular commitments to public policy discussions, and we must allow those commitments to frame our interpretations and responses to international, national, and local refugee concerns. Our care for the most vulnerable should translate into strong, active response on their behalf. But in order to have a substantial impact on public policy, we must find points of contact with others in the larger society. On an issue such as refugee policy, this can be done by appealing to certain shared understandings and commitments that are for us undergirded by Christian faith. Other citizens in our society draw on different religious and moral traditions but share some of the same fundamental human commitments.

How, then, might a deep Christian concern for the most vulnerable persons translate into actual public policy orientations regarding refugees?

## Recognize Basic Rights

We must begin with a recognition that every person has basic rights. God's love for each human being establishes every person's equal worth and value no matter what his or her condition or location. Our recognition of persons' equality and value before God can be articulated as an acknowledgment of their basic human rights.[37] Our love for human beings includes recognizing and responding to their needs for food, shelter, and safety. Refugee policy properly attends to the basic human needs of persons endangered by religious or political persecution, ethnic cleansing, civil war, etc. As our commitment is clear on basic needs and rights, we will be better able to resist temptations to assign refugee status or grant asylum only to those who are ideologically or economically useful to us.

## Provide Sanctuary

The practice of offering hospitality to strangers is an international tradition acknowledged and valued by most cultures. Providing sanctuary is the appropriate moral response when people are endangered.

Some of the poorest nations are literal neighbors to the countries producing the most desperate refugee flows. They have traditions of hospitality and generally provide refugees with a place to flee, if only briefly. Because of their own circumstances, however, they are not necessarily able to handle the numbers or the needs. Responses of wealthier nations should be in solidarity with poorer countries that often receive the refugees. Such solidarity can be expressed in two key areas.

First, a continued willingness to be a country of resettlement. Even though industrialized nations resettle small numbers of refugees compared with the total refugee population, it is an important gesture of solidarity and a practical expression of help for some refugees.[38] As we resettle some refugees into the United States, we should expect to provide adequate assistance when they first arrive and support that will help them move toward self-sufficiency.

Second, the United States and other wealthy nations must supply substantial humanitarian assistance and development aid to those nations and organizations coping with large numbers of refugees.[39] The United States should continue our more positive connections with the UNHCR and our support of NGOs. Adequate funding of the UNHCR and other programs that assist refugees in camps and resettlement is essential.

In refugee camps, however, more than humanitarian aid is needed. We should support stricter human rights protection within the camps and strengthen the security of refugees and workers from violence external and internal to the camps. Assistance in many areas will have to be accompanied by an international or well-trained local peacekeeping force.

### Serve as Moral Leaders

The United States possesses great power; it also assumes a position of significant moral leadership in the world. Our example is extremely important. In particular, when asylum seekers come to our own borders, we must not respond with methods we criticize other nations for using— methods such as interdiction at sea or automatic exclusion. Principles of respect and care should undergird our responses to asylum seekers.

The processing of asylum seekers—those who arrive on our shores without prior processing—needs careful attention. While these people must be monitored, and real claims must be sifted from spurious ones, confining them to prison and harsh detention until their claims are heard is deeply unjust. It treats asylum seekers as criminals and sets a terrible example. It is imperative that we develop an adequate framework for offering temporary protected status.[40]

If we expect impoverished countries to continue to provide asylum, and if we expect to have moral authority when we criticize heartless responses in other nations, we must make sure our own actions are framed by justice and compassion. We must also take our share of refugees and asylum seekers.

## Share the Burden

In considerations of public policy, we recognize that no nation can receive or support infinite numbers of refugees. Nations must, however, work together to share the burden. Effective responses require cooperation at the local, national, and international level, and between governments, voluntary organizations such as NGOs, churches, and individuals. To do more than give humanitarian assistance, to actually strike at the causes of refugee flows, requires an even more complex interaction between relief and development work, human rights monitoring, peacekeeping, and conflict resolution mechanisms. Any adequate response to the needs of internally displaced persons will require much careful discussion about the limits of national sovereignty and the appropriateness of international intervention. When entire populations are being attacked within and by their own country, some international response is morally and strategically necessary.

Refugees need a country to which they can belong. Most refugees want to go home, and repatriation is the best solution when it is safe and when human rights can be protected. Repatriation, however, is often difficult and assistance with reintegration is essential. If refugees cannot be repatriated, they must find another home. Long-term residence in camps is not a humane option. To institutionalize a marginal existence by allowing people to remain refugees indefinitely is to break their spirits and waste their lives.

It is easy for individuals to avoid responsibility to refugees by simply allowing those with strongly restrictionist orientations to prevail in community and government. Because this is an international issue, tied to foreign policy, integrity of national borders, multinational alliances, domestic attitudes, identity, and resources, it is impossible to do much without engaging public policy. If we allow policies to close our national borders to refugees and asylum seekers, we are effectively cut off from encountering refugees in our lives and from significant personal action on their behalf.

Obviously the issues are complex and responsibilities and duties can conflict. When we acknowledge an obligation to refugees, we still must take seriously the needs of our own citizens, especially the poor of our own society. Furthermore, caring about refugees does not mean we dismiss concerns about maintaining a valued way of life or particular cultural identities and traditions. No nation is infinitely expandable, but every community can and should accept some responsibility to those in deep distress. While not advocating open borders, we do need to make room for some people.

This is, in fact, a public policy issue that requires a fundamental generosity. Responding to refugee needs requires the sharing of material resources. An adequate response to refugee crises also depends on strong advocacy by those who care and who have taken time to understand the issues. The religious community in the United States has had a key role in resettlement efforts and in keeping the humanitarian concerns in focus. It is crucial that Christians take this issue seriously; without our voice the discussions will be more easily dominated by a limited focus, utilitarian calculations, domestic concerns, and restrictionist arguments.

Americans do not want refugees to suffer or to die, but few Americans take time to learn enough to make a difference. This issue demonstrates the importance of education, awareness, and consensus building in shaping a foundation for a humane public policy. Education and advocacy are essential at the local church level even as we attend to national policy. Parachurch agencies and denominational offices are crucial in raising awareness, providing education, and in connecting concerned Christians with specific ways to be involved.

An important contribution that individual Christians can make is to pray specifically and faithfully about refugees. In small groups in church or with a few friends, concerned persons can target a particular area or refugee population, learn more about the situation, and pray specifically. We can bring the needs to the attention of others. We can learn about possible responses from churches and government. We can pray for and support people and agencies who are responding. We can encourage local newspeople to pay attention to the situation and challenge local politicians to take initiative on the issue in Congress.

Assisting in the resettlement of a refugee family gives the issue a human face and offers healing in the midst of brokenness. Welcoming refugees who have been resettled into our communities and churches and becoming friends with them requires intentionality and commitment, but it also brings significant blessing.

So, what do Christians have to say on public policy relating to refugees? Often not very much. But the potential is there for just, compassionate, and practical involvement tied to the deepest commitments of our faith. Such responses will locate us squarely with the world's most vulnerable people.

# 13

# WHERE CHURCH AND STATE INTERSECT

## Stephen V. Monsma

We are all accustomed to the metaphor of a "wall of separation" between church and state. The United States Supreme Court has on more than one occasion referred to that wall of separation and declared that it "must be kept high and impregnable."[1] But in fact it is not high and it surely is not impregnable. Time and time again religion and government intersect—appropriately and necessarily so. When a church or synagogue building catches fire, taxpayer-funded firefighters rush to put it out. A host of health, safety, zoning, and labor regulations promulgated and enforced by government apply to religious congregations and their buildings and activities. If you doubt this, just try to start a child-care center in your church's basement without obtaining the necessary health and safety permits! Billions of taxpayer dollars go each year to religiously based hospitals, nursing homes, child and family service agencies, international aid and relief agencies, homeless shelters, spouse abuse homes, and many more.

The key issue, then, is not whether or not there should be an impenetrable wall of separation between church and state—we as a society

Stephen V. Monsma (Ph.D., Michigan State University) is Professor of Political Science and Chair of the Social Science Division at Pepperdine University.

decided a long time ago against such a wall. Church and state inhabit the same society; they cannot be kept in isolation from each other; they do intersect. Instead, the crucial question is: By what concepts or theories should the intersections of church and state be governed? What principles should be used to determine what is an appropriate—and an inappropriate—relationship between church and state? There are in the United States two basic theories or principles that are struggling for dominance in answering that question today. The outcome of that struggle for dominance has enormous consequences for religious freedom in the United States and for the ability of Christians to be the salt and light our society needs. In this chapter I seek to describe the two contending principles, why I favor the one I do, and why the outcome of their struggle for dominance is of great consequence.

## No Aid to Religion

One basic principle is the strict separationist, no-aid-to-religion principle. It holds that the religious freedom language of the First Amendment should be interpreted to mean that church and state must be kept in as separate spheres as possible and that government may not subsidize or support religion.

In a series of post–World War II cases the Supreme Court largely embraced this approach to church-state issues. Justice Hugo Black wrote in the 1947 landmark *Everson* decision: "No tax in any amount, large or small, can be levied to support any religious activities or institutions, whatever they may be called. . . . In the words of Jefferson, the clause against establishment of religion by law was intended to erect 'a wall of separation between church and state.'"[2] On this basis the Supreme Court has held that almost all forms of state aid to religiously based elementary and secondary schools, and that almost all forms of religion in public elementary and secondary schools, are unconstitutional. It has frequently reiterated its support for this position, as when, in 1963, it favorably quoted from one of its earlier opinions that stated the First Amendment forbids "*every* form of public aid or support for religion."[3]

The Supreme Court and those who support this strict separationist, no-aid-to-religion approach to church-state issues see it as leading to governmental neutrality on matters of religion. In 1963 the Supreme Court wrote: "We have come to recognize through bitter experience that it is not within the power of government to invade that citadel [of religion], whether its purpose or effect be to aid or oppose, to advance or retard. In the relationship between man and religion, the State is firmly committed to a position of neutrality."[4] In the 1947 decision from which I quoted earlier, it is clear that Justice Black saw his ringing words of no aid to religion as leading to governmental neutrality on matters of religion. Two pages after the quoted words he went on to write that the First Amendment "requires the state to be neutral in its relations with groups of religious believers and non-believers."[5] Justice Thurgood Marshall, in a 1983 opinion, directly linked the no-aid-to-religion and neutrality concepts: "The Establishment Clause of the First Amendment prohibits a State from subsidizing religious education, whether it does so directly or indirectly. In my view, this principle of neutrality forbids . . . any tax benefit . . . which subsidizes tuition payments to sectarian schools."[6]

I believe, however, that there is a basic flaw in the no-aid-to-religion principle, resulting in its being anything but neutral. Instead, it has the pervasive effect of putting religion in a disadvantaged position as compared with secular systems of belief. This is true for two reasons. Political scientist James Reichley expressed one of these reasons well when he wrote that "banishment of religion does not represent neutrality between religion and secularism; conduct of public institutions without any acknowledgment of religion *is* secularism."[7] Common sense confirms this. If, for example, a school teaches such issues as race relations, human sexuality, and civic responsibility without any reference to religion, the message being sent is clearly that religion is irrelevant to such topics, or at the least that such topics can be fully understood and discussed without reference to religion. Most of the world's great religions would dispute this conclusion, while secular systems of belief would firmly hold to it. Thus, it is anything but neutral.

Let me give an actual, concrete example of what I have in mind. In 1987 Phillip Bishop was an assistant professor in physiology and physical education at the University of Alabama. In one of his classes he explained to his students that he was a Christian believer and that "bias"—as he termed it—affected his approach to his academic duties. He also invited his students to an after-class, purely voluntary session where he lectured and led a discussion on evidences for God in human physiology. Professor Bishop's departmental chair sent him a memo in which he stated that Bishop had to refrain from such references. He was aiding religion. The university administration supported the department chair, and a legal battle ensued. The United States District Court ruled in favor of Professor Bishop being able to make such minimal references to the Christian faith, but the United States Court of Appeals overturned the District Court and upheld the university's action. The United States Supreme Court refused to hear the case. Professor Bishop was effectively muzzled.

On state university campuses almost all points of view can be heard—in and out of the classroom. Perspectives reflecting Marxist, libertarian, secular feminist, gay rights, and other views are welcomed, as well they should be. But at least at the University of Alabama the line was drawn against Christian perspectives. But to do so is to favor secular interpretations and perspectives over religious ones. This is not being neutral. Yet this is where the strict separationist, no-aid-to-religion approach to church-state issues has led us.

A second reason why the no-aid-to-religion principle is not neutral between religion and secularism grows out of the changing role of government in society today. Today government is involved in providing a host of services that at the start of the twentieth century it never dreamed it would be called upon to provide. And this is crucial: both secularly based and religiously based groups are also involved in providing many of the same services government is now providing. Examples abound: child-care centers, elementary and secondary schools, colleges and universities, drug treatment programs, homeless shelters, international aid and relief, adoption programs, nursing homes, and many, many more. Government, private secular agencies, and private religious agencies—all three—are today active in providing services such as these. If government provides its own secular services, and if it subsidizes or in other ways assists the private secular agencies but refuses to subsidize or assist the private religious agencies, it is putting the religious agencies at a comparative disadvantage. It is making it harder for them and their supporters to follow their consciences, which have led them to provide those services.

Another concrete example may help. This example is an actual case that came before the Supreme Court in 1995. It deals with the policy of the University of Virginia—a state university—of subsidizing a wide range of student publications. The policy—in keeping with the norms of strict separation and no aid to religion as the means to neutrality—did not permit the funding of religious publications. Thus the university refused to fund *Wide Awake,* a publication put out by a group of evangelical students. *Wide Awake* sought to bring Christian perspectives to bear on issues such as eating disorders, war and peace, and homosexuality. Both the federal District Court and the Court of Appeals upheld the constitutionality of the university's policy of not funding religious publications, even though it was funding a wide variety of nonreligious publications of a similar or competing nature.

The decision of the Court of Appeals is especially instructive on whether the university's no-funding policy was religiously neutral. At one point the court stated that the University of Virginia's proscribing the funding of religious organizations "thus creates an uneven playing field on which the advantage is tilted towards CIOs [that is, the student organizations] engaged in wholly secular modes of expression."[8] The court went on to hold that *Wide Awake*'s "receipt of government benefits [had been made dependent] upon their foregoing constitutionally protected religious expression."[9] Yet that same court went on to hold that this uneven playing field that was tilted against religion was required by the strict separationist, no-aid-to-religion interpretations of the First Amendment currently held by the Supreme Court. It therefore upheld the constitutionality of the university's ban on funding religiously based publications. In other words, in this case the court felt it had to choose between maintaining the no-aid-to-religion standard or insisting on a level playing field where religion is not disadvantaged by government policies. It sadly chose against a level playing field and for the no-aid-to-religion standard.

Happily, the Supreme Court, in a close 5–4 vote, decided that the University of Virginia—if it was to fund the publication of a wide variety of student opinions—could not exclude religiously based ones. It chose for a level playing field. More on this in a moment.

## Equal Treatment or Substantive Neutrality

Competing with the no-aid-to-religion, strict separationist position is the equal treatment or substantive neutrality position.[10] It says that the First Amendment—properly interpreted—seeks to assure the neutrality of government toward persons and groups of all faiths and those of none. This means government ought not to advantage or disadvantage any particular religion, nor ought its actions to advantage or disadvantage religion in general or secularism in general. Only then will full freedom of belief for both the religious and the nonreligious among us prevail. To achieve this goal, substantive neutrality says that a rigid no-aid-to-religion principle should be replaced with the principle that public money or other forms of governmental recognition or support may go to services and programs of religiously based groups that are of temporal, this-worldly benefit to society as long as the same or similar governmental recognition or support is going to similar or parallel services or programs of all religious traditions without favoritism and of similar or parallel services and programs of a secular nature. The underlying principle is that of equal treatment of equal groups or belief systems in equal circumstances.

Thus, in the example mentioned earlier, the Christian student publication *Wide Awake* should receive university funding on the same basis as the secular student publications. It should receive no more than other publications because it is religious in nature, but neither should it receive less. A thin Supreme Court 5-to-4 majority saw things in exactly this light. Justice Anthony Kennedy wrote in the majority opinion:

> A central lesson of our decisions is that a significant factor in upholding governmental programs in the face of Establishment Clause attack is their neutrality towards religion. . . . We have held that the guarantee of neu-

trality is respected, not offended, when the government, following neutral criteria and evenhanded policies, extends benefits to recipients whose ide- ologies and viewpoints, including religious ones, are broad and diverse.[11]

Justice Sandra Day O'Connor described the issue raised by this case in exactly the right terms when she wrote in her concurring opinion: "This case lies at the intersection of the principle of government neutrality and the prohibition on state funding of religious activities."[12] Justice O'Con- nor and four of her colleagues favored in this instance governmental neu- trality over no funding of religion. The four dissenting justices made the opposite choice. They argued that the court ought to adhere "to the pre- eminence of the no-direct-funding [of religion] principle over the princi- ple of evenhandedness."[13] In this case, more than in any other, the two competing principles of First Amendment interpretation clashed and the neutrality or evenhandedness principle won out.

The neutrality or equal treatment principle says the University of Vir- ginia could decide to fund no student publications, but once it had de- cided to fund them, it could no more decide to fund all secular publica- tions and exclude religious publications than it could fund all religious publications and exclude secular ones.

In the case dealing with the University of Alabama and Professor Bishop, the neutrality or equal treatment principle would say that a pro- fessor could make appropriate references to his religious faith as long as other professors were allowed to make references to their underlying belief systems. Normal academic standards would, of course, have to pre- vail, such as a spirit of civility and respect, belief system references being relevant to the subject matter of the course, and no grading bias toward students who disagree with the professor. But as long as those standards are adhered to, the substantive neutrality principle says religion ought not to be singled out for special limitations that do not apply to parallel, competing systems of belief.

### The Neutrality vs. No-Aid-to-Religion Clash

These two principles—the no-aid-to-religion principle and the neu- trality principle—are competing in the courts, in Congress, and in the news media for dominance in the United States today. There is a line of cases—going back to the 1947 *Everson* case referred to earlier—in which the Supreme Court has insisted on the no-aid-to-religion principle. As recently as 1992 the Court ruled invocations at public school graduation ceremonies were unconstitutional on the basis that they would tend to favor or aid religion. A concurring opinion by Justice Harry Blackmun in that case declared that "our cases have prohibited government endorsement of religion, its sponsorship, and active involvement in religion, whether or not citizens were coerced to conform."[14] Even more clearly, a whole series of cases in the 1970s and 1980s ruled against a number of programs aimed at assistance to religiously based elementary and secondary schools. In one such case the court majority declared: "Although Establishment Clause jurisprudence is characterized by few absolutes, the Clause does absolutely prohibit government-financed or government-sponsored indoctrination into the beliefs of a particular religious faith."[15] But the neutrality or equal treatment principle has recently been invoked in a significant number of cases, including ones that have allowed religious student clubs to use on-campus state university facilities, required a school district to rent its facilities to a church to show a religious film, required a state to fund the religious education of a blind student, and most recently, overturned an earlier decision and permitted public school teachers to provide remedial instruction in religiously based schools.[16]

Meanwhile, Congress entered the argument on the side of the equal treatment principle when it enacted the charitable choice provision of the 1996 act restructuring the welfare system. Charitable choice is Section 104 of the 1996 act.[17] It provides that if a state utilizes private sector agencies to deliver social services under the act, it may not exclude faith-based agencies, and then the provision goes on to protect the religious integrity of faith-based agencies that cooperate with states in providing welfare services. The principle is that of equal treatment or neutrality: the act does not mandate that a state must make use of religiously based agencies, and it surely does not seek to favor them over secularly based agencies. Rather, it says that faith-based agencies may not be excluded or treated worse than secular agencies—they are to be neither favored nor disfavored. In 1998 Congress passed and sent to the president a bill that would expand the charitable choice approach to include the $500 million community services block grant program.

Meanwhile, strict separationist groups, such as Americans United for the Separation of Church and State, have attacked charitable choice as a violation of the First Amendment. "It allows," it has written, "pervasively sectarian organizations, such as churches and other houses of worship, to receive government aid without watering down their religiosity one iota."[18] It goes on to threaten lawsuits and ends by quoting its executive director, Barry Lynn, as saying, "This is a critical issue, and we will not let it go unaddressed. Nothing less than the integrity of the wall of separation between church and state is at risk."[19] The editor of the *Texas Atheist* has described charitable choice as "a power-grabbing raid on the national treasury."[20]

There is no doubt that the political system is in the midst of a struggle between two competing visions of the religious freedom clauses of the First Amendment.

### The Crucial Importance of the Neutrality vs. No-Aid-to-Religion Struggle

The struggle between the neutrality and the no-aid-to-religion principles is not a struggle over arcane legal issues that may intrigue constitutional law experts but have no practical, public policy consequences. Rather, this clash of principles carries with it momentous, concrete societal and public policy consequences. All of society—all of us—will be deeply affected by its outcome. There are three especially important consequences that will flow from the outcome of this struggle that I wish to highlight.

First, there is the issue of the secularization of American society. Some have noted that the United States, as measured by the religious beliefs and practices of the American people as a whole, is one of the most religious countries on earth, yet as measured by the importance of the role religion plays in the public life of our nation, it is one of the most secular countries on earth. Religion is near the center of the lives of many ordinary citizens, but it has been marginalized among the leading cultural institutions of society—the nation's major universities, publishing houses, newspapers, television networks, and film companies. There are exceptions, but for the most part major cultural institutions such as these and their leaders write, act, and speak as though religion has nothing of significance to say to them and their concerns. Stephen Carter has referred to this, in the context of politics, as religion as a hobby. "The legal culture that guards the public square still seems most comfortable thinking of religion as a hobby, something done in privacy, something that mature, public-spirited adults do not use as the basis for politics."[21]

Going back to the example of Professor Bishop and the University of Alabama, I do not think that this should be thought of as an example of simple religious hostility. The university's position, rather, was rooted in a worldview that simply places religion—and Christianity in particular—outside the proper scope of the university. The appeals court decision reflected such a perspective when it stated: "The University has not suggested that Dr. Bishop cannot hold his particular [religious] views . . . ; nor could it so prohibit him. The University has simply said that he may not discuss his religious beliefs or opinions under the guise of University courses."[22] In the court's view, it was not being antireligious. It was only saying that religious beliefs simply have no place in a university classroom; to bring them in is to slip in something that does not belong in an academic course. But this trivializes and marginalizes religion. It is all right as long as it is sealed off in the private area of one's life, but if it starts seriously to influence one's academic work or politics or business . . . well, that is dragging in something that does not belong. But many Christians—especially from the Catholic, evangelical, and African American wings of American Christianity—are insisting with increasing vigor that their faith speaks volumes about racial discrimination, poverty, education, war and peace, health care, sexual orientation, abortion, and a host of other public issues.

There are many factors at play in the secularization of the public life of the nation. It would be too simple to draw a direct cause-and-effect line from the strict separationist, no-aid-to-religion interpretations of the First Amendment to the secularization of our republic. But the beliefs and assumptions of the no-aid-to-religion position certainly contribute to the marginalization of religion in the public sphere, since it holds that religion must largely be kept out of public institutions and that religiously based educational, health, and social service organizations may not share in governmental recognition and support in the same way their secular counterparts do.

To the extent this position wins in its struggle with the neutrality position, government and its policies will be weighing in on the side of the further marginalization of religion. To the extent the equal treatment or neutrality principle wins, government and its policies will weigh in on the side of freeing religion to play a robust role in the public sphere. Religion will not be privileged over nonreligious systems of belief, but it will gain new freedom to contribute to the public life of the nation.

A second consequence of the neutrality principle winning in its struggle with the no-aid-to-religion principle would be to make it easier for public policy to address pressing educational, social, and health problems in our society in an effective, creative manner. The evidence is slowly accumulating that faith-based programs are dealing with persistent social problems more effectively than private secularly based or government programs.

Teen Challenge is a case in point. Teen Challenge is a Christian organization that works to get and keep young people off drugs. A study commissioned by the National Institute of Drug Abuse found that 95 percent of former heroin addicts were abstaining from the use of heroin seven years after completing Teen Challenge's program.[23] In contrast, among persons who had completed drug addiction programs at Public Health Service hospitals, only 26 percent were found to be drug-free after six years.

Similarly, a study has shown that ex-offenders who had participated actively in Prison Fellowship Ministries Bible studies while incarcerated had lower recidivism rates than ex-offenders who had not done so.[24]

There is a mountain of evidence that there is a huge disparity between the quality of education children receive in inner-city Catholic and public schools. A Rand Corporation study, for example, found that low-income Catholic schoolchildren averaged more than 150 points higher on the Scholastic Aptitude Test. Another study found that only 48 percent of the public high-school students in New York City graduate in four years, while 98 to 99 percent of the students in Catholic high school do so.[25]

One can only guess at the extent to which our society has been plagued by such social ills as drug abuse, teenage pregnancies, high dropout rates, and criminal recidivism because of strict separationist, no-aid-to-religion interpretations of the First Amendment that discourage full partnerships between government and faith-based agencies.

A third and final point I would like to make in regard to the public policy consequences of the no-aid-to-religion versus neutrality struggle is related to the second consequence just noted. It is that the poor in our society will be especially hurt if the no-aid-to-religion position wins this struggle.

When the strict separationist, no-aid-to-religion principle is used to deny all government funds for religiously based schools and health and social service agencies—or grants them only under highly restrictive conditions—we need to be clear about who is being hurt the most. It is not the wealthy or middle-income families. They may be inconvenienced by having to pay more to purchase a house in a school district that provides their children with a solid education in a safe environment or by having to pay tuition for an education in a religious school in addition to paying their school taxes. There is an injustice or unfairness here, but no tragedy. But for the poor and low-income families, the results are often truly tragic. Such families do not have the option to move into desirable school districts, to send their children to nonpublic schools, or to pay for needed social or health services. They often face the prospect of sending their children to unsafe schools, where the religious values of the home are ignored and the flame of learning is squelched by stifling bureaucracies, crowded classrooms, burned-out teachers, and poor equipment. The poor have no choice but to make use of the social and health services provided by government agencies or by private agencies the strict separationist principle would deem to be sufficiently religion-free, even when those agencies are ineffective and lack any religious commitment.

For all of us, and especially for the poor, the neutrality or equal treatment principle holds the promise of greater freedom—a freedom marked by all Americans being able to live out their deepest beliefs in all areas of life, without the government favoring or disfavoring any particular system of belief, whether that system of belief be rooted in religion or secularism, Christianity or Judaism, Catholicism or Protestantism. It is my hope that this principle will win out in its struggle with the opposing no-aid-to-religion principle.

# 14

# ABORTION AND THE CULTURE OF DEATH

## RICHARD D. LAND

Deuteronomy 30:15–19 reads as follows:

> I set before you today life and prosperity, death and destruction. For I command you today to love the LORD your God, to walk in his ways, and to keep his commands, decrees and laws; then you will live and increase, and the LORD your God will bless you in the land you are entering to possess. But if your heart turns away and you are not obedient, and if you are drawn away to bow down to other gods and worship them, I declare to you this day that you will certainly be destroyed. . . . This day I call heaven and earth as witnesses against you that I have set before you life and death, blessings and curses. Now choose life, so that you and your children may live. (NIV)

Over the last twenty-five years, our nation has far too often chosen not life and blessing but death and cursing. In 1973 the infamous *Roe v. Wade* decision of the U.S. Supreme Court ushered in abortion on demand nationwide. Doing so made abortion a far more divisive issue—the most divi-

Richard D. Land (Ph.D., Oxford University) is President and CEO of the Ethics and Religious Liberty Commission of the Southern Baptist Convention.

sive issue in our nation's history other than race—than it otherwise would have been. If the Supreme Court had not taken the unprecedented step of striking down the existing restrictions on abortion in all fifty states, it is likely that the people would have reached a rough sort of political equilibrium that genuinely reflected American public opinion in its diversity. There would have been severe restrictions on abortion in most states, with a liberalization in abortion policy in states like New York and California, where in 1970 and 1971 the first cracks in the dike of abortion laws began to occur. But the court, through a remarkably raw use of judicial power, struck down all the existing abortion statutes in the nation. We went from about four hundred thousand legal abortions each year to about 1.5 million within one year and throughout most of the years since.

As horrible and terrible as it is in itself, the abortion issue was always the thin edge of a much larger issue and a much larger debate. Is human life of intrinsic value? Is human life unique? Is human life sacred? Some of us have always understood where this debate was going, and have become more and more aware of it with each passing year. For each year our legal system and some of our ethicists and philosophers have embraced the logical consequences of the reasoning underlying *Roe v. Wade* in decisions affecting other areas of life. There is loose in the West a culture of death, as it has been so aptly named by Pope John Paul II, in which death is increasingly perceived as a cure for all manner of human problems and challenges. We are witnessing an inexorable march of death from the womb to the delivery room, to the nursery, to the nursing home, to the intensive care unit, and to every station in between. At all points where there is any weakness, any abnormality, any illness, or any lack of productivity, human life is under increasing assault.

Our nation leads the world in the number of its young women who receive abortions each year. Even though the rate has dropped slightly in recent years, we are still number one in terms of the number of our teenage girls who get pregnant and who have abortions. We have seen at least thirty-six million babies killed since 1973. Approximately one out of every three children conceived in the United States since 1973 has had his or her life extinguished prior to birth. That's one-third of an entire generation.

I can remember having arguments with my friends and colleagues— some of whom were actually seminary student colleagues—back in the early 1970s over abortion. I heard them say things to me like "Well, Richard, we'll never get control of welfare unless we have abortion." That's certainly a chillingly utilitarian moral argument. Others would say, "If we could just have abortion on demand, we could do away with child abuse. Every child would be a wanted child and there would no longer be any child abuse." That fond hope has been dashed, hasn't it? We have witnessed a 700 percent increase in serious child abuse in the last twenty-five years in our nation, serious child abuse being defined as abuse significant enough to require the treatment of a physician. We should not be surprised. If we give a mother the absolute right of life and death over a child up until the point when it is, in its entirety, expelled from the mother's body, how do we then convince the mother that this baby is now a complete and full human being with the same rights and protections under the law that the mother has? It has evidently been a difficult sell. And let's not forget the men who participate in both abortion and abuse.

Now death has escaped from the womb into the nursery. In the infamous Baby Doe case of 1982, there was a baby boy born on Palm Sunday, known to our legal system as Baby Doe. He was a Down's syndrome baby, which meant that he was going to experience at least moderate mental retardation. His parents were told by their doctor that he also had a significant problem with his digestive system, which was present but not fully functional. He needed a rather simple operation that would attach his swallowing mechanism to his digestive system.

But the doctor went on to say that there was another "treatment" available. The parents could refuse to give their permission for the operation, making it impossible for him to have any form of nutrition or hydration. The doctor argued that this decision was their right as parents, given the mental retardation of the boy. They were free to decide to let their boy die if he did not meet their expectations. And that is what they decided to do. The baby was put back in the nursery with a sign on his bassinet that he was to receive no nutrition or hydration because he could not ingest it.

For four days, Baby Doe cried. Some of the nurses asked to be assigned to other duties because they could not stand to hear the constant crying of the starving child. Finally, one of them contacted the authorities, and the situation went rapidly up the legal ladder to the attorney general of Indiana and finally the state Supreme Court. The attorney general, much to his credit, argued that even a condemned criminal has a right to a stay of execution while his case is being adjudicated in the courts, and that the court ought to order that the little boy should receive the operation and nourishment until the legal issues could be settled.

Then the press found out about it, and fifty couples immediately came forward with the offer to adopt Baby Doe if the parents would allow them to do so. They refused. The Indiana Supreme Court sided with the parents, and as the attorney general was preparing to fly to Washington to plead Baby Doe's case before the U.S. Supreme Court, he died from dehydration and malnutrition.

Baby Doe's ordeal is over; ours continues. Because the Supreme Court of the United States ultimately did consider the case, and after due consideration, sided with the parents. Baby Doe ought to be the poster boy for the spurious "quality of life" argument. That's where it leads.

And now we have seen an inexorable march from the nursery to the nursing home. I went to a civic club meeting recently in Nashville and heard the head of the ethics department of one of our major hospitals say that we are going to have to rethink the way we do medicine in the United States. We can no longer afford to keep people alive beyond their natural life span, and we have got to quit spending all our money on bypass surgery and kidney dialysis and heart transplants. We need to reach the same level of efficiency that they have attained in Holland, including use of euthanasia, as is the law in that nation. This was being openly proposed and people were nodding their heads. Do they know that if we embrace euthanasia with Holland's enthusiasm, we will end up "euthanizing" a quarter of a million people each year? Do they know that even the Dutch admit that less than half of those being euthanized in Holland do so in a manner that is genuinely and fully voluntary?

Just a few years ago, in the Nancy Cruzan case, our courts defined the giving of nutrition and hydration—a feeding tube—as an extraordinary medical procedure, akin to adrenaline shots to the heart, the use of heart-lung machines, and all manner of cutting-edge emergency care. For the first time, the simple delivery of water and food to an unconscious patient was defined as an extraordinary medical treatment that could be with-held or withdrawn. When it was withdrawn, Nancy Cruzan died a slow and painful death. Euthanasia enthusiasts rapidly argued that ending her life with a lethal injection would have been more humane.

It's not an accident that Jewish civilization was the only society in the Mediterranean basin that did not routinely practice infanticide and did not practice abortion when medically advanced enough to do so. While the Hippocratic Oath was a product of ancient Greece, we need to remem-ber that in its own context it was considered impossibly idealistic. Will and Ariel Durant tell us that ninety-nine out of every one hundred girl babies after the first girl baby born in Roman families were either killed at birth or abandoned to die of exposure or to be picked up by the human vultures who would then raise them for a life of slavery—the life of one-third of the Roman population. Infanticide and abortion were both rou-tine in the Roman Empire. They were routine in every society except that of the Jewish people. The reason was that God had made it clear to his people that human life begins at conception and that any form of murder violates God's will. On the basis of texts such as Psalm 139, Jeremiah 1:5, and Psalm 51, as well as the overall structure of biblical moral thought, the Jewish people did not practice abortion, and Orthodox Jews do not do so to this day.

The early Christian witness was similarly clear, both in word and deed. Both abortion and infanticide were condemned in early Christian writ-ings, and when Christianity triumphed in the Roman Empire in the fourth and fifth centuries, infanticide and abortion were outlawed. This remained the case throughout the medieval period and into the Reformation. Both Luther and Calvin condemned abortion in the clearest terms. This remained the universal witness of the church and its leaders through Dietrich Bonhoeffer, who said in his *Ethics* that the killing of "nascent" human life in the womb was murder. He used the term "murder." There was no alternative view of any consequence until the great modern heresy of the last half of the twentieth century in which large segments of the church decided to stand in judgment of Scripture and pick and choose which parts they would accept and which they would not.

Where do we go from here? We can be encouraged by the drop in the abortion and teen pregnancy rates, and by the clear evidence that abstinence-based programs are making a difference. But we continue to be in the midst of a struggle for hearts and minds. We have won several aspects of the abortion debate. Most Americans are far more uncomfortable with abortion on demand than they were fifteen or twenty years ago. In fact, only about 4 percent of doctors will perform abortions. There are whole states where one cannot get an abortion simply because there are no abortion doctors or abortion facilities. When President Clinton lifted the ban on abortions at U.S. military facilities in Europe, they could not find a single physician in the armed services medical corps to perform the abortions. They actually had to contract with European physicians and nurses for abortion services. This was no right-wing conspiracy but instead simply reflected the moral convictions of our military medical corps.

Seventy-five percent of Americans think abortion is wrong if it is done solely to select the sex of a baby. Seventy-five percent think abortion is wrong if performed on a minor without notification of at least one parent. And 75 percent think abortion is wrong if a wife is having an abortion of her husband's child without at least notifying him.

The pro-choice argument that a woman has the right to do whatever she wants with her own body is also losing steam as we learn more about fetal development. Of course, it was always erroneous to make this argument about abortion, because when a woman authorizes the killing of her unborn child, she is not dealing with a part of her own body. Roughly half the babies are male, which means they have male sex chromosomes. I don't know of any woman's body that has male sex chromosomes. Babies have their own hearts. I don't know of any woman's body that has two hearts. These babies always have a different genetic code. They often have a different blood type. And besides, we do not give either women or men absolute right to do what they want with their bodies. With rare exceptions, for example, prostitution is outlawed. For that matter, murder is something we do with our bodies, and we are not free to do that. Paul Ramsay, my mentor and a great Princeton ethicist, once told me that dramatic gains in the science of fetology were going to reshape the abortion debate. He said, "Anyone who argues that we are not dealing with human life must be out of his or her wits."

Where does the pro-choice/pro-abortion/culture of death argument lead us? One sign is the recent appointment of Peter Singer to become professor of bioethics at the same (formerly Presbyterian) university where Paul Ramsay once taught. Singer has a clear and simple principle to apply to all moral debates, and that is the pleasure principle. In order to increase the total sum of planetary pleasure we should bring into the world more beings capable of experiencing pleasure, increase the pleasure of already existing beings, or remove from existence what he calls "miserable beings." He says that many of our moral intuitions and beliefs are formed for selfish reasons or are based on outdated religious traditions. On abortion, Singer's view is that the life of a fetus is of no greater value than the life of a nonhuman animal at a similar level of rationality, self-consciousness, or capacity to feel, and should not be viewed as having a different moral status from that of any other mammal. He then goes on to argue that it must be admitted that these considerations apply to newborn babies as well as to fetuses. The killing of newly born babies is not the killing of full human beings because they cannot fend for themselves, feed themselves, or live independently. So here we have a key ethicist at a major American university making the moral case both for abortion and infanticide.

Once we abandon the doctrine of the sanctity of human life, we can get on with the future. And if you want to know what the future might just look like, look back. Look back not just to Rome but to Germany in the 1920s, 1930s, and early 1940s. Germany practiced what Singer only writes about— the "euthanizing" of those it considered "useless eaters" or "lives unworthy of life," a practice that began not under Hitler but eleven years before he took power. Hitler's greatly expanded version of this activity was called the T-4 program, and it ultimately took the lives of over one hundred thousand "defective" German men, women, and children. Many of the doctors who made the "selections" of who should live and who should be gassed or starved to death later shifted their operation to such places as Auschwitz and Treblinka, where they did the same thing on a much larger scale.

There is a culture and philosophy of death loose among us, and it is not something *like* what happened in Germany. It *is* just what happened in Germany. Germany was perhaps the most sophisticated nation in the world. But in a time of cultural crisis, that nation turned its back on the God of their fathers and embraced the paganism and death-dealing ideology of Adolf Hitler and the Nazi party. We are today in a struggle for America's soul. If we win this struggle, we will once again clearly be a nation that stands for justice, truth, and the value of human life. If not, we will become a fully pagan nation.

# 15

# JUST PEACEMAKING

## A New Paradigm for Our New World

## GLEN H. STASSEN

I believe something new and tremendously important is happening in our world at the turning of the century and the millennium. It is providing an enormous opportunity to practice Jesus' commands on peacemaking in a way more effective than we have imagined. Most people don't notice what is happening because we're still thinking of the Cold War and the need to make peace with the Soviet Union. But things are very new now. An interdisciplinary team of twenty-three of the most qualified Christian ethicists and international relations experts have been working for five years to create a new paradigm for understanding our world after the Cold War. We have published our consensus just peacemaking theory in *Just Peacemaking: Ten Practices for Abolishing War* (Pilgrim Press, 1998). I want to begin explaining the ten practices of just peacemaking by telling the story of the fall of the Berlin Wall in East Germany—the symbol of the end of the Cold War and the beginning of the new era after the Cold War.

Glen H. Stassen (Ph.D., Duke University) is Lewis B. Smedes Professor of Christian Ethics at Fuller Theological Seminary.

In 1987 fifteen students came with me to West and East Germany to study peacemaking. We saw that prisonlike wall with the guards armed with rifles to shoot anyone who dared try to escape. We watched army draftees repairing the wall, with armed officers watching them, ready to shoot them if they tried to escape, and ready to shoot us if we came too close. We saw the barren stretch of land where all growth had been killed so the guards in the guard towers would see anyone trying to escape and could shoot them. We knew many people trying to escape did get shot to death.

We knew that Eric Honecker, the ruler of East Germany, was one of the most iron-willed dictators of all the Eastern bloc. He had kept himself in power by the brutality of his state security police. When students camped out in Tiananmen Square in China to ask nonviolently for human rights and democratic reforms, the Chinese government brought in army units from the country who could not speak the language that the students spoke, and had them massacre the students. After Tiananmen Square, Eric Honecker invited Chinese government leaders to East Germany so he could celebrate their "victory" and praise them in public for having the wisdom to do the right thing. The chances for change in East Germany looked poor.

But I also knew Andreas Zumach. He came to the United States as a part of Action Reconciliation, a Christian organization in West Germany that sent young volunteers to countries Germany fought against during World War II, and to Israel. It was an action of atonement and reconciliation. Andreas went to California to help César Chávez campaign for the human rights of farm workers. He learned the strategies of nonviolent direct action. When he returned to Germany, he traveled regularly to Poland and East Germany to teach the strategies and methods of nonviolent direct action.

But how could you do nonviolent direct action in East Germany, where it was illegal to hold any public meeting or to carry out any demonstration? People met in a Protestant church for an evening worship service and then walked across the bridge to the Catholic church to hold the second half of the worship service. Crossing the bridge symbolized their Christian unity. They walked with candles. The state security police roared up on their motorcycles: "You know it is illegal to demonstrate in East Germany! What do you think you are doing?" They answered: "We are just going to church." Going to church was not against the law, and the police backed off. The practice spread to other cities, and soon hundreds of thousands were marching, carrying candles, from church to church.

The people met in the churches to plan their strategies: it was the only place meetings were allowed. They studied the writings of Martin Luther King. I saw the German translations of King in the churches. They prayed that the demonstrations would be nonviolent. And they marched.

Then came the time when they were planning a massive march of two hundred thousand people in Leipzig. Honecker was furious. He ordered the army there to shoot the marchers. The hospitals were ordered to prepare for the slaughter. Pastors were to go to the hospitals to prepare to minister to victims of the massacre. But the chief of the state security police went to Leipzig and ordered the troops not to shoot; he countermanded the brutal order of Eric Honecker at the risk of his own life. And the march proceeded, without violence. It was named the time of "the turning," a turning from violence to nonviolence. It was led by the people, meeting in churches, studying the writings of Martin Luther King, praying that their commitment to nonviolent direct action would hold, and praying that there would be no violence.

The East German Baptists invited me to come back to East Germany for two weeks in November of 1989—during the time when the marching was going on—to speak and teach in seven different cities on peacemaking methods. I flew to West Berlin and stayed overnight in the Dietrich Bonhoeffer house Thursday night before entering East Berlin the next morning. That evening, at 10:00 P.M., suddenly Burkhardt Scheffler, my friend who was the director of the Bonhoeffer house, yelled upstairs, "Glen, come down in a hurry!" There on television they were announcing that the wall was opening the very next morning! It was the end of East Germany as a prison, walled off from the West. It was the end of the dictatorship of the communist party. It was a revolution in which the government changed, the constitution was rewritten, the role of the churches changed, the economic system changed, and East Germany would no longer be separated from West Germany.

It was unbelievable. My hostess in one city told me at breakfast how she lay in bed before getting up, working to orient herself to the meaning of this sudden change in the reality of her world. Then she got up, read the paper—it told of more sudden, unbelievable changes—and she was disoriented all over again. She'd had that experience each day for a week. She and others told me to pray for the people of Czechoslovakia, because it would be very hard to do the same thing there.

On Sunday morning in Bitterfeld, I preached in the Baptist church. It was packed. Then in the afternoon we went to the big cathedral in the city square. Thousands were there. Several spoke. Then we all went outside to the city square. There was an open microphone; anyone could speak who wanted to. People told of their joy and of their fears and of the injustices. And then they concluded by singing "We Shall Overcome" in English! They had been studying the strategies of nonviolent direct action so much that they had even learned the freedom songs in English. Do you feel it? The brutality of the dictator for decades. The discipline and prayers of the people. Singing "We Shall Overcome." And they were overcoming. They had brought about a total revolution by the methods of nonviolent direct action, and not a single person was killed. I was moved as if by an outside force, by the power of the Holy Spirit, in spite of my usual shyness, up to the stage and the microphone. The song was to be the conclusion, but they knew who I was since I was one of the speakers in the cathedral, so they stayed to hear what I would say. I said three sentences: "I was deeply engaged in the U.S. civil rights movement. You have done in East Germany what we were working to do in our civil rights movement by the strategies of nonviolence. I am very deeply moved, and deeply, deeply grateful for what you have done." They gave me by far the biggest and longest applause that I have ever received. Maybe there's a lesson there: it was the shortest speech I have ever given. But also they had felt so isolated in their struggle, and together we felt the connection and the mutual recognition of the amazing thing that had been wrought.

What they did was seen on television by people throughout Eastern Europe. The nonviolent direct action campaigns spread, and the dictatorships fell, first in Poland, then in East Germany, then in Czechoslovakia and throughout Eastern Europe. People in South Africa saw it on television too, and they brought about the change that I thought could not happen without enormous bloodshed. They toppled apartheid. And in the Philippines the people toppled the dictator Marcos by nonviolent action. And it spread in many countries in Latin America.

It dawned on me that nonviolent direct action is not only a practice in our civil rights movement, but it is spreading around the world, and in many places is replacing the bloodshed of revolution. In many of these countries it has replaced civil war with nonviolent change. It has abolished wars that would otherwise have killed thousands or millions. It is a new practice, a new discipline of the people, that we take with us into the next millennium. It comes from the Sermon on the Mount, with its emphasis on taking transforming initiatives to confront hostility between us and our enemies, and to seek to transform the relationship into one of peace, love, and justice. Gandhi was greatly impressed by the Sermon on the Mount. Martin Luther King writes in his "Pilgrimage to Nonviolence" of his loyalty to the Sermon on the Mount, but not knowing how to follow it until he learned of Gandhi's method of nonviolent direct action, and then the fusion of the two produced a bright flash of light for him.

And I realized there is another new practice. It is the struggle for human rights. It is closely related to Jesus' emphasis in the Sermon on the Mount on righteousness or justice that delivers the oppressed and the outcasts and restores them to community. In East Germany the churches drafted a small book on justice, peace, and the integrity of creation. It included a section called "More Justice in East Germany," listing their demands for change toward justice and human rights. They circulated the draft through the congregations of the various denominations and then brought all the suggestions together to reach a consensus document, which they sent back to the churches for ratification. It was the one and only way the people of East Germany could meet together and develop their common understanding of what must change. One day on the autobahn, traveling to the next city, we heard on the radio the new leader of East Germany addressing the parliament for two hours. He listed the changes they were instituting as of that day. They were the same list of changes that the churches had demanded! I was so moved at what the churches' work for human rights had brought about that I wept.

The struggle for human rights turned East Germany into a democracy. The same process has been working throughout Latin America and in Korea, Taiwan, and now Indonesia, and we hope for Burma. Michelle Tooley tells the story of women struggling for justice and human rights in Guatemala. Before they gathered together in groups to support each other, women thought that only men could participate in the struggle for human rights. "They believed women acted only in the home as they cared for the children, cooked, and cleaned. . . . Women felt powerless to act outside the home, in the public sphere." The keys to being transformed from fatalistic silence to finding their voice were not only that the cup of endurance ran over and that they realized that oppression depends on the conspiracy of silence, but their joining together in community and support groups, and finding support from allies.[1] When they joined with each other and organized, they were able to accomplish remarkable change that the men had not been able to accomplish against long-standing historical, systemic, and violent suppression. And here, too, the struggle for human rights created the beginnings of democracy.

The result is that democracy is spreading to Latin America, Eastern Europe, Asia, and Africa. And here is the astounding fact: No democracy has fought another democracy in all of the twentieth century. As we support the struggle for human rights by joining with others in groups like Witness for Peace, Amnesty International, and Bread for the World, we spread human rights and democracy. And the result is to abolish wars and create regions of peace. Western Europe, once the originator of two world wars, is not going to originate another one. Germany is not going to fight France again. The same may be true of Latin America, and surely is true of North America. We really are abolishing war where once it was endemic and enormously destructive. The challenge is to help it spread to areas like Russia, China, Africa, and Asia, where it is just beginning to catch hold.

The evidence is not that democracies do no evil or that they have no problems or that they never support war, as the United States did for several years in Nicaragua until the pro-democracy grassroots citizens' and church groups persuaded Congress to halt the funding for the contra war. The evidence is simply that democracies do not themselves make war against each other. It is not a claim of perfection, but it is a remarkable fact, and it abolishes war as it spreads.

The struggle for human rights and democracy is a new practice, a new discipline of the people to bring about peaceful change and prevent war. It has developed in the last half of this century. It is a new thing that we take with us into the next millennium.

And a third new practice: cooperative conflict resolution. Just as Jesus taught that when there is hostility between us and our brothers or sisters, we must go, talk with them, and seek to be reconciled to them, so theorists and practitioners have created a new practice in our time, conflict resolution (chapter 3 in *Just Peacemaking*). Leaders of the marches in East Germany had obeyed Jesus' command; they had been talking with the hated chief of the state security police, explaining their commitment to nonviolence and explaining that the government must be nonviolent also or it would surely lose the support of all the people. That is part of the practice of conflict resolution. It is the embodiment of Jesus' command that when there is hostility between you and another, you must go and seek to be reconciled. Former president Jimmy Carter practiced the new skills of conflict resolution in achieving the Camp David Accord, making peace between Egypt and Israel. We were praying in our church that week for peace in the Middle East. Carter more recently brought his conflict resolution skills to Haiti as the bombers were about to take off to begin a violent invasion. His practice of conflict resolution abolished that war. And he did similarly in North Korea when we were in a hot dispute over their nuclear program. Senator George Mitchell was sent by President Clinton to Northern Ireland, and he led a process of conflict resolution that now, remarkably, seems to have brought the possibility of peace in that deep and long violent struggle. Who would have believed it? Conflict resolution is now being taught in many schools, where it is decreasing violence dramatically. And sometimes it occurs to youth and to ordinary people like you and me: if we can practice conflict resolution here, why can't governments do the same and avoid war? And so we praise presidents when they make peace in the Middle East or help make it in Ireland. And when presidents make war, although initially we rally behind our troops, later, as we think about it, we are less likely to praise presidents who made war rather than peace.

I believe God has brought about dramatic changes in the last half of the twentieth century, new strategies of peacemaking that really are abolishing wars in many places, new strategies that are going with us into the next millennium. Twenty-three of the best Christian ethicists and international relations scholars have reached a similar conclusion. Working together for five years, we have identified ten new practices that are in fact abolishing wars. We call the consensus that we have reached the just peacemaking theory. It is a new paradigm for ethics and a road map and how-to manual for us as we enter the next century and the new millennium. Following this road map, we believe we can abolish wars that otherwise will kill millions of people and create unbelievable misery. We can spread the zones of peace to new areas.

The ten practices can be remembered by an acronym: D.C. GUERNICA. (The District of Columbia and Guernica have been symbols of war and violence; we hope they may become symbols of peace.)

Democracy, human rights, religious liberty

Cooperative forces

Grassroots groups

UN and international organizations

Economic and sustainable development

Reduce offensive weapons and weapons trade

Nonviolent direct action

Independent initiatives

Conflict resolution

Acknowledge responsibility, repent, forgive

When I had finished lecturing at the Baptist Seminary in East Germany, Siegfried Rosenmann presented me with a going-away present: a hunk of the Berlin Wall bigger than my large hand. And he said to us, "Everything is new!" This hunk of the wall is my symbol that everything is new in our world. We need a new paradigm of peacemaking practices to make sense of God's call to responsibility and effectiveness in this new world that we have been given. Let me name, more briefly, the other practices that are new in our world and that are abolishing wars.

## Acknowledge Responsibility, Repent, Forgive

In the Sermon on the Mount, Jesus commanded us to take the log out of our own eye and told us that as we forgive those who sin against us, we will be forgiven. But for centuries it has been agreed that governments would never apologize to other governments. It would be a sign of weakness and beneath their dignity, and it would lose them political support at home. A new reality in our world began when Dietrich Bonhoeffer wrote a confession on behalf of Germany. Churches in Germany later issued their own confessions of sin during the Hitler period. They were criticized, but they prepared the way: political leaders do not like to lead unless someone prepares the ground so they have assurance people will follow them. Chancellor Willy Brandt went to Poland and presented a wreath at the memorial in the Warsaw ghetto to those who were killed by the Nazis. He kneeled and offered repentance. Then in the Bundestag, the German parliament, President Karl Friedrich von Weizsäcker presented a remarkably eloquent and specific confession of German guilt during the time of the Nazis. He received strong affirmation; the school in Germersheim, where I spent my last sabbatical, is named after him, and that is true in many towns. Since then, Germany has worked out repentance, forgiveness, and reconciliation with Poland, Israel, and Czechoslovakia.

President Bush made public apology for the Japanese internment camps during World War II, and Congress finally voted reparations payments to families of those interned. President Clinton traveled to Africa and apologized for what the U.S. had done and what it had failed to do. During the visit of South Korean president Kim Dae Jung to Japan October 5–8, 1998, Emperor Akihito and Prime Minister Keizo Obuchin expressed "deep sorrow" and "deep remorse" over Japan's aggression against Korea earlier this century, and its colonial rule over Korea. Kim accepted the apology, saying "the weight of Japan's words was different" from the vague apology of 1995. "It clarified whom they were talking to, and this time expressed regret and apology." He told the Japanese parliament that Japan and Korea have had a fifteen-hundred-year relationship marred only "for a short time by tragedy. . . . We should not overvalue this sad period, and we look toward the future and a strong relationship." A Korean businessman commented: "Past is past. Since they apologized in writing this time, I don't see why we shouldn't accept their apology and allow the emperor to visit." In fact, Kim did invite him to visit. I have seen graphic displays of the torture of Korean people by the Japanese government at the Korean national monument. The hostility has been deep and long-lasting, and only acknowledgment of responsibility and repentance like this can begin to lance the boil and bring peace. Now it is happening. It is a new practice for governments to learn. Churches can teach it and practice it.

## Foster Just and Sustainable Economic Development

In the Sermon on the Mount, Jesus emphasizes a delivering justice that delivers the poor and the outcasts from their powerlessness and restores them to community. That is the meaning of the word that has been translated "righteousness," and which Jesus emphasizes five times in the Sermon on the Mount, in addition to his emphasis on almsgiving,

giving to the one who begs, and not hoarding our money but investing it in God's kingdom and righteousness. Jesus taught in Aramaic and quoted the Bible in Hebrew. The word that is translated "righteousness," *tsedaqah* in Hebrew, means delivering justice that restores the powerless to community.

Countries often make war when they experience serious economic downturns. Iraq got vicious when its economy was going down, because the price for oil was down, because its neighbors, including Kuwait and Saudi Arabia, were selling more than the quota they had agreed to. Serbia was the poorest part of Yugoslavia and was being deserted by the other parts that had the wealth. In Northern Ireland the Catholics were being economically deprived. In Indonesia, when the economy plummeted, violent riots against the Chinese Christians followed, and the danger is still great.

My former student invited me to Uganda, where I saw the Uganda Rural Development Project. There Musheshe and his group help farmers do a kind of composting, double digging, and using of local seeds to achieve two growth seasons a year and thus improve their lives significantly. They begin with what farmers want to improve in their lives, including clean water, latrines that don't spread disease but kill flies, and homes with ventilation and more healthful conditions. Church groups in the United States provide key support for the Uganda Rural Development Project. One Sunday, Christians in Pasadena went on the CROP walk to raise money to help Church World Service or their own denominations' hunger and disaster relief program to foster just and sustainable economic development in many needy nations. Some join Bread for the World and push the government to support just and sustainable economic development too.

### Strengthen the United Nations and International Networks for Cooperation and Human Rights

Jesus commanded us to love our enemies. Loving enemies in our world does not mean just having a sentimental feeling but understanding and affirming their valid interests, even while you disagree with their invalid interests. To do that in our world, nations need to be members together in organizations where they regularly talk and work together to solve problems. We have recently seen how the United Nations and NATO have stopped war in Bosnia, Croatia, and Kosovo, getting relief to 250,000 homeless people in Kosovo driven out of their homes by Serbian attacks.

In February 1998, President Clinton, Secretary of State Madeleine Albright, and other administration leaders went to Ohio State University to speak to the nation, explaining why we must bomb Iraq. At the very time they were speaking, Fuller Theological Seminary faculty were gathering for the installation lecture of theology professor Miroslav Volf on the social meaning of reconciliation in Paul's letters. The clash between the two addresses was very much in the minds of many of us. Just prior to the lecture, Professor James McClendon asked me if I could write a letter for Fuller faculty. On the way into the lecture, I saw President Richard Mouw and asked what he thought of the idea of a letter. He said, "If you do it, I have three points I would like to see in the letter." As you can imagine, those three points got in the letter. Other faculty encouraged the idea. After the lecture, I had just forty-five minutes to write the letter, proof it, and Xerox it before the faculty luncheon. I could write it quickly because I had been working on our just peacemaking theory. The twenty-three authors of *Just Peacemaking: Ten Practices for Abolishing War* want church members to know just peacemaking theory so they can respond to crises and opportunities in pertinent ways, too. The Fuller faculty knew the president would be listening to hear how Americans responded to his advocacy of bombing, and we needed to respond quickly.

The theme of our letter was "bombing can wait, but initiatives to save lives can't." We urged initiatives to make peace, incentives for Iraq to allow the inspections to resume, and support for United Nations General Secretary Kofi Annan to travel to Iraq and try to work out a resumption of inspections. Almost every faculty member and top administration member of Fuller Seminary signed the statement, and we faxed it off to the White House and the media. It got significant attention and praise, and the White House saw that our statement—the one organized evangelical statement—aligned closely with the statements of the African Methodist Episcopal church leaders, the Roman Catholic bishops, the National Council of Churches, and other church leaders. They invited us to the White House for a briefing, and they changed their tune, supporting the UN General Secretary in his trip to Iraq. As you know, it got the inspections resumed and the palaces inspected without all the killing.

The United Nations and other regional organizations also provide enormously needed services for world health, for children's needs, and for sustainable economic development.

At the time of this writing, the United States is the largest debtor to the UN. The stalemate over paying our debts is causing the UN not to be able to do crucial peacemaking work. It is creating severe deprivation for millions of people. It is creating situations where the U.S. is likely to have to intervene with U.S. military forces at a cost many times greater than the debt we are not paying.

## Work with Emerging Cooperative Forces and Transnational Linkages in the International System

Another way that nations seek to be reconciled and do the practical work of understanding each others' valid interests is the rapidly growing web of transnational linkages. It is symbolized for me by the fact that among the fifteen students in the Ph.D. seminar in Christian ethics that I am currently teaching at Fuller Theological Seminary, there are students from nine different nations—where worldwide Christian missions has been doing its work. One of those students, Emily Choge from Kenya, has been living in our home. She is regularly on e-mail with her friends back home in Kenya. Parush Parushev, who with his family used to live in our home, also regularly uses e-mail, not only with his friends back in Bulgaria but also with Christians in other European countries, the U.S., and all over the world.

In *Just Peacemaking*, historian of international relations Paul Schroeder observes that there has been

> a dramatic increase in the volume, density, and speed of international exchanges, communications, and transactions of all kinds, and the increasing integration of these exchanges into organized, complex international, supranational, and transnational networks, corporations, and other institutions. This has now developed to such a degree that the domestic economics, politics, and culture of individual states cannot be isolated from them or do without them. Along with this has gone an equally startling increase in the number, scope, durability, and effectiveness of international organizations of all kinds, both governmental and non-governmental, which both modern governments and non-governmental groups must pay attention to and use for their particular purposes. . . .

> This is not just theory; it is happening. The continued existence and success of organizations like NATO, the European Union, the UN, and many others go a long way to make it demonstrable fact. To argue that voluntary associations for peace cannot work better today than in the past seems to me a bit like arguing that manned heavier-than-air flight is not possible for the same reasons it was impossible before 1903.

> Yet of course none of this will happen, or has happened, automatically. If the system can and does work for good as I claim, where it does and to the extent it does, it is because people, leaders and followers, make it do so. All these useful societal trends and potentially valuable peacemaking and peacekeeping organizations and developments can readily be corrupted for wrong purposes, or defeated, or overwhelmed by new challenges, or so stultified and confined that they become useless for meeting the emerging problems of peace today and in the future. This makes just peacemaking into a task for action—a process in which ordinary citizens individually and

in groups work to sustain, criticize, goad, influence, reform, and lead the many kinds of voluntary associations, governmental and private, which can contribute to transcending the contradictions and managing and overcoming the conflicts of an anarchic international society. In other words, it means exploiting, encouraging, and strengthening the concrete world trends that enable cooperation to fly—the decline in the utility of war; the priority of trade and the economy over war, the strength of international exchanges, communications, transactions, and networks, and the gradual ascendancy in the world of liberal representative democracy and a mixture of welfare-state and laissez-faire market economy. Citizens, intermediate associations, and governments should act so as to strengthen these trends and the voluntary associations that they make possible.[2]

Another new reality in our world is the realization that war does not pay because of the enormously destructive new kinds of weapons. If you make war with another nation, that nation or its international supporters will have such enormous destructive power that making war is suicide. The exception that proves the rule is Serbia. In the old communist Yugoslavia, the Yugoslavian army was almost all made up of Serbians. So when the country split up, Serbia had almost all the offensive weapons. So they thought they could get away with making war. We can enhance the force of the reality that war does not pay by *reducing offensive weapons and weapons trade* so that no nation has an offensive preponderance, and by international pressure against aggression.

This fits what Jesus taught in Matthew 5:38–48. It is usually translated "do not resist evil," but in fact it means "do not be in violent and revengeful resistance by evil means." Clarence Jordan, Walter Wink, and I have shown this elsewhere, based on the Greek grammar of Matthew 5:39. Paul understood that correctly and taught it that way in Romans 12:18–21.

One effective practice to reduce the spread of offensive weapons is to prod nations to turn from dictatorships to democracies that respect human rights. Then their rulers do not need so many weapons to keep their people suppressed. And they are less threatening to their neighbors, so their neighbors need fewer weapons. The other practices of just peacemaking also make war less likely, so they need fewer weapons to defend themselves. And the International Monetary Fund, one of the transnational forces mentioned above, is pressuring nations not to waste their budgets on weapons. The result of all these kinds of prodding and peacemaking practices is that developing countries do not waste so much of their money that they desperately need for their human needs on buying imported weapons. In 1995, arms imports by developing countries were cut to $15 billion, just one-quarter of the $60 billion that it was seven years earlier. That saved $45 billion per year for human needs and debt repayment, while also decreasing the number of wars.[3]

Congress, surprisingly, has been voting that our taxpayer money should subsidize the spread of violent weapons to dictators, who often end up using the weapons against our own troops, as in Somalia and Iraq. U.S. arms exports in 1995 totaled an estimated $12 billion. Of that sum, $7.6 billion was paid by taxpayer subsidies—more than one-half of all exports. And another half billion of taxpayer money was spent lobbying Congress and other countries to promote this subsidizing of the spread of U.S. weapons to governments who often turn them on their own people and on U.S. troops. And then the manufacturers skim off half of a tenth of a percent and give it to the members of Congress who voted for this $8 billion subsidy.[4]

A causative factor of the arms trade is large contributions of money to political candidates from weapons manufacturers.[5] When the United States exports billions' worth of weapons a year, weapons manufacturers can contribute millions to politicians—a major factor for political campaigns but a small investment for manufacturers as a percentage of their huge profits. The Center for Defense Information presented this table from data of the Federal Election Commission:

### Selected Military Contractor Political Action Committee Contributions to 1994 Congressional Campaigns

| | |
|---|---|
| General Electric | $328,300 |
| Lockheed | $315,891 |
| Martin Marietta | $285,160 |
| General Dynamics | $258,263 |
| Textron | $243,460 |
| Boeing | $173,745 |
| Northrop | $164,068 |
| Rockwell | $160,020 |
| McDonnell Douglas | $153,200 |
| Loral Systems | $144,400 |

To correct this distortion of the decision-making process to determine how our tax money is spent, we have to curtail contributions from political action committees of arms manufacturers and from all sources, and place limits on campaign spending, including soft as well as hard money. Until the power of money to corrupt governmental decision-making processes is curtailed, it will be hard to make the process peaceable.

If we learned that in the World Series, or in Monday night football, some of the teams were paying $3 million to the referees to influence their calls, we would be outraged. But that is what is happening in Congress. And the members of Congress are influenced by the $3 million not just on a ball game but on life-and-death matters—and on "calls" regarding basic economic justice, like how our taxpayer money should be spent. Increasing numbers of us are saying, "No more. We won't stand for this corruption of our nation and its democratic processes." We are demanding an end to soft money donations. We pushed the majority of the House to pass it in 1998, and we pushed the majority of the Senate to vote for it. But in spite of bipartisan majority support of the McCain-Feingold campaign spending reform bill in the nation and in Congress, the congressional leadership team opposed it and killed it. The people overwhelmingly want it, though, and we will be back. It may become a key issue in the 2000 presidential election campaign.

Another just peacemaking practice is the practice of *independent initiatives*. This deserves more space than I have here. Instead of waiting for slow negotiations about arms reductions, a nation announces that it will initiate a specific and verifiable reduction of a kind of weapon or of a kind of hostile and threatening practice. It invites the other nation to initiate a similar kind of reduction and promises more reductions if the other nation reciprocates. Later, the reductions can be put in an official and mutual agreement. A dramatic case in point was the reduction of nuclear weapons by the U.S.S.R., the United States, and NATO. The break came with "the Zero Solution": NATO and Gorbachev agreed to destroy all medium-range and shorter-range nuclear weapons. Then Presidents Reagan and Bush negotiated START I and START II. And President Bush announced that negotiations were too slow; the U.S. would remove all nuclear missiles from its ships at sea. The Soviet Union then announced it would do likewise. And each took yet other initiatives, upping each other's bid to make the world safer and less costly. The result was to reduce the combined nuclear warheads of the United States and the former Soviet Union from 47,000 to 15,500. Agreements have been reached to ban the production of chemical and biological weapons and to destroy their stockpiles. The Comprehensive Test Ban Treaty will impede the development of new types of nuclear weapons if finally approved by the Senate. Russia and the U.S. no longer aim their nuclear missiles at each other. These dramatic reductions in offensive weapons increase our security significantly.

Jesus taught the Sermon on the Mount to his group of disciples as well as to the crowds. Just peacemaking requires *grassroots groups, church peacemaker groups, and voluntary associations* to strengthen support for the practices of just peacemaking, and to teach them to others. With every practice above, there are blocking forces that seek to prevent peacemaking practices. Governments are like jalopies that can't quite get started; they need a shove from a group of people to get them over the hill. We need people who will form small groups in churches with a mission to support the peacemaking that Jesus called us to. We need people who will join Amnesty International, Witness for Peace, Bread for the World, Peace Action, UN-USA, the campaign against land mines, and on and on. We need people who will teach cooperative conflict resolution to children and youth. We need missionaries and world alliances of Christians, and seminaries that encourage international students, thus strengthening transnational linkages. We need groups that will encourage governments to acknowledge their own responsibility for conflict and injustice, and repent and forgive. We need to practice just peacemaking within our own churches and our own denominations. The encouraging truth is that in fact small groups of peacemakers are emerging in churches and outside of churches all over the world. The story of the fall of the wall in East Germany is just one chapter in that spreading story. I pray that it will spread all the more, and that we may abolish many wars, if not war completely.

### Conclusion: A Call for Us

We need another paradigm for ethics in addition to pacifism and the just war theory. When pacifism and the just war theory dominate the debate about war, the question narrows to whether it is okay to make war or not. What falls out of the debate is whether or not we should take peacemaking initiatives to prevent war. Jesus did not focus on when it is okay to make war but on peacemaking initiatives that he commanded us to take. We need a third paradigm, a just peacemaking theory. We twenty-three who worked for five years have reached a consensus that these are the practices that must be tried before war is made.

Ever since World War II, we have lived under a gigantic and life-threatening cloud. Youth have not known whether they really had a future. People saw that war can kill us all.

Many responded by developing these ten new practices of peacemaking. They are not mere ideals; they are actual practices, each of which has abolished some wars. Every time they abolish a particular war, they prevent unimaginable misery, pain, death, destruction, hatred, and impoverishment. Christine Pohl and Ben Donley have helped us imagine and feel the plight of refugees from war. Saving the life of just one child is worth it. Together these practices save the lives of millions of children. They are gaining strength, being effective, and together they can abolish wars in whole regions of the world. And they can spread. Working together, they have abolished war in Western Europe, in North America, maybe in Latin America, and they may be spreading to Eastern Europe, Africa, and Asia.

War does not pay, and it is not legitimate. Maybe we really are turning a millennium.

It is a call for us to notice what's happening in our world. It is a call for us to strengthen these forces. The new paradigm of just peacemaking is a road map, an instruction manual for how and where to add our bodies and our minds and our prayers to God's purpose for all humankind—that we beat our swords into plowshares and be at peace.

A vivid image in my mind is the picture on the front of the *New York Times* the day of the funeral of Chief Justice Warren Burger. The picture showed ten men, his friends, of his generation, carrying his casket up the steps into the Supreme Court. My ninety-one-year-old father was carrying the front of the casket up the steps, in spite of his badly lame knee. No one of those men was strong enough to carry that casket. But each of them working together had the strength. No one of the ten practices of just peacemaking can abolish all war. But working together they are weaving a web of peace; they are changing international expectations. War is no longer normal; it is an aberration that should be prevented or stopped. I really want to envision these ten practices spreading and together having the strength to bury the casket of war.

This is not a prediction that we will have no wars. I am a realist; I know sin. Each of these practices of peacemaking has forces that try to block it. And as one who started out in nuclear physics, I know something of the destructive power of the fifteen thousand nuclear weapons still possessed by the U.S. and Russia. As the son of a captain in the Navy during World War II, and the teacher and friend of veterans of the Vietnam War, I have just a sense of the destructive forces of war. I have experienced some of the hatred and violence that lead to war. They are still with us. But I also know the empirical data. I know we are abolishing many wars and creating regions of peace that can spread. This is an empirical pointing to what works in reality.

And I know the call of our Lord Jesus Christ to be peacemakers. It is like New Testament eschatology: Jesus told us no one knows the times or the seasons. We are not to spend our time speculating and predicting. We are to be ready. And to be ready means to be doing the teachings of Jesus. The teachings of Jesus call for peacemaking. The Book of Revelation teaches that it may seem as if the evil beasts rule the world, but

> God is the real Ruler; God is judging the Powers that seem to be ruling for now, and that are causing wars. God will redeem the followers of the Lamb; therefore, do not lose hope; follow the teachings of the Lamb. The followers of the Lamb do the deeds Jesus teaches. The same point is repeated again and again in varieties of phrasing—so often that one wonders how people could miss it: The followers of the Lamb are those who do the deeds

Jesus teaches, who do God's will, keep God's word, keep God's command-
ments, hold faithful to the testimony of Jesus, do the teachings of Jesus,
follow God's teachings as given through Jesus, obey God's commands (Revelation 2:2; 2:23; 2:19; 2:26; 3:8, 10; 9:20–21; 12:17; 14:4; 14:12; 16:11; 20:12–13;
22:11).

The Book of Revelation does not teach that we should avoid taking peacemaking initiatives because God will do everything; it teaches that we should
take the peacemaking initiatives that Jesus teaches.[6]

I am not just concerned with *whether* we will be politically engaged. I
am concerned with *what* we will be engaged *for:* the peacemaking that
Jesus commands, or the power of the beasts.

Christian Wolf, who taught Christian ethics and Old Testament in the
East German Baptist Theological Seminary, admonished people not to
speculate about when or whether the wall would ever come down. That
would only lead to a sense of detached speculation and powerlessness.
Instead, we should be preparing for the time when the wall would come
down. That is also the best way we can participate in the forces that will
eventually bring it down. This is very much like the teachings of the New
Testament. Our job is not to speculate about the end; our calling is to do
the teachings of Jesus, to live as participants in the coming of the reign
of God, with its salvation, presence of God, justice, and peace. We are
called by Jesus not to be speculators but to be peacemakers.

# NOTES

**Chapter 1: *The Evangelical Kaleidoscope***

1. Harvey Cox, "The Warring Visions of the Religious Right," *Atlantic,* November 1995, 62.

2. Timothy Smith, "The Evangelical Kaleidoscope and the Call to Christian Unity," *Christian Scholars Review* 15 (1986): 125–140.

3. Quoted in James D. Hunter, *Evangelicalism: The Coming Generation* (Chicago: University of Chicago Press, 1987), ix. The very impressive work of, for instance, evangelical historians, philosophers, and political scientists has since demolished the stereotypes Mencken so enjoyed promoting.

4. Michael Weisskopf, "Energized by Pulpit or Passion, the Public Is Calling," *Washington Post,* February 1, 1993, 1.

5. The most comprehensive recent studies are John C. Green et al., *Religion and the Culture Wars: Dispatches from the Front* (Lanham, Md.: Rowman and Littlefield, 1996); Mark J. Rozell and Clyde Wilicox, eds., *God at the Grass Roots: The Christian Right in the 1994 Elections* (Lanham, Md.: Rowman and Littlefield, 1995); and Duane M. Oldfield, *The Right and the Righteous: The Christian Right Confronts the Republican Party* (Lanham, Md.: Rowman and Littlefield, 1996).

6. Quoted in George M. Marsden, *Fundamentalism and American Culture: The Shaping of Twentieth-Century Evangelicalism 1870–1925* (New York: Oxford University Press, 1980), 188.

7. See *U.S. News and World Report* (May 4, 1998) cover story on the influential ministry of Dr. James Dobson to see just how disappointed and displeased he and many of his followers are with current Republican party leadership.

8. See Joel A. Carpenter, *Revive Us Again: The Reawakening of American Fundamentalism* (New York: Oxford University Press, 1997), espe-

cially chapter 5, "A Window on the World," for an illuminating description of how their eschatology led to a pessimistic view of human progress. According to fundamentalists, "terrible times were descending upon the world, and the progression of evil was quickening. Only Christ's second coming could redeem and restore humanity and the creation" (90).

9. Winthrop Hudson, *American Protestantism* (Chicago: University of Chicago Press, 1961), 128.

10. George Marsden, *Reforming Fundamentalism: Fuller Seminary and the New Evangelicalism* (Grand Rapids, Mich.: Eerdmans, 1987), 4.

11. Quoted in Robert D. Linder, "The Resurgence of Evangelical Social Concern," in *The Evangelicals: What They Believe, Who They Are, Where They Are Changing*, ed. David Wells and John Woodbridge (New York: Abingdon, 1975),198.

12. Walter Rauschenbusch, *A Theology for the Social Gospel* (1917; reprint, New York: Abingdon, n.d.), 5.

13. Ibid., 50. "Sin is essentially selfishness. That definition is more in harmony with the social gospel than with any individualistic type of religion."

14. Ibid., 31.

15. Ibid., 117.

16. Quoted in Craig M. Gay, "When Evangelicals Take Capitalism Seriously," *Christian Scholars Review* 21 (June 1992): 348.

17. Ibid., 349.

18. Ibid., 350.

19. Carl F. H. Henry, *The Uneasy Conscience of Modern Fundamentalism* (Grand Rapids, Mich.: Eerdmans, 1947), 17.

20. Ibid., 32.

21. Ibid., 45.

22. Carl F. H. Henry, "The Uneasy Conscience Revisited" (paper presented at the fortieth anniversary of the founding of Fuller Theological Seminary, Pasadena, California, November 3, 1987), 5. For an interesting critique of Carl Henry's view of the state, see Nicholas Wolterstorff, "Contemporary Christian Views of the State: Some Major Issues," *Christian Scholars Review* 3 (1974): 319–322.

23. Jim Wallis, "Revolt on Evangelical Frontiers: A Response," *Christianity Today,* June 21, 1974, 20–21.

24. Jim Wallis, "Post American Christianity," *Post American* 1 (fall 1971): 2.

25. *Chicago Sun-Times*, December 1, 1973.

26. Ronald J. Sider, ed., *The Chicago Declaration* (Carol Stream, Ill.: Creation House, 1974), 1.

27. Ibid.

28. Ronald J. Sider, *Rich Christians in an Age of Hunger* (Downers Grove, Ill.: InterVarsity Press, 1977). A twentieth-anniversary revision was published by Word in 1997.

29. See especially Richard J. Mouw, *Politics and the Biblical Drama* (Grand Rapids, Mich.: Eerdmans, 1976); Robert K. Johnston, *Evangelicals at an Impasse* (Atlanta: John Knox, 1979), particularly chapter 4; and John Howard Yoder, *The Politics of Jesus* (Grand Rapids, Mich.: Eerdmans, 1972).

30. *Time,* August 5, 1974.

31. John R. W. Stott, ed., *Making Christ Known: Historic Mission Documents from the Lausanne Movement, 1974–1989* (Grand Rapids, Mich.: Eerdmans, 1997), 24.

32. Edward Dobson recounted this story at a conference sponsored by the Ethics and Public Policy Center in Washington on "The New Religious Right: Assessing the Past, Scouting the Future," in November 1990. He further observed: "The Religious New Right was a disenfranchised movement, a countercultural movement not accepted by any of the cultural elites or the mainstream. When President Reagan embraced the evangelicals, leaders like Jerry Falwell assumed that this legitimized a movement that had been demeaned, ignored, and branded as 'double-knit, Appalachian, pew-jumping, holy-roller, anachronistic, white-socks,' and all that. Once we got into the White House, we thought 'we are now legitimate because we are now equal partners.' But we never were. Many put on 100 per cent wool suits and became politicized by the activist process but, as a consequence, lost some of their impact." See Michael Cromartie, ed., *No Longer Exiles: The Religious New Right in American Politics* (Washington, D.C.: Ethics and Public Policy Center, 1993), 53.

33. Daniel Bell, "The Dispossessed," in *The Radical Right*, ed. Daniel Bell (Garden City, N.Y.: Anchor, 1964), 2.

34. Joseph Gusfield, *Symbolic Crusade: Status Politics and the American Temperance Movement* (Urbana: University of Illinois Press, 1963).

35. Steve Bruce, *The Rise and Fall of the New Christian Right* (Oxford: Clarendon, 1988), 49.

36. Nathan Glazer, "Toward a New Concordat?" *This World* (summer 1982): 113.

37. Quoted in Oldfield, *The Right and the Righteous,* 55.

38. Glazer, "Toward a New Concordat?" 112.

39. Bruce, *Rise and Fall,* 22.

40. Of course, the liberalization of our cultural mores did not begin in the 1960s. For a brilliant analysis of this, see Rochelle Gurstein, *The Repeal of Reticence: A History of America's Cultural and Legal Struggles over Free Speech, Obscenity, Sexual Liberation, and Modern Art* (New York: Hill and Wang, 1996). She offers a fascinating history of the arguments for and

against the forces that altered public discourse between the late nineteenth century, when they first appeared, and the 1960s, when new controversies erupted about mass culture, avant-garde art, and sexual liberation. She shows how the "party of exposure" successfully opened American public life to matters that had once been hidden away in private and looks at the unexpected consequences of their victory over the "party of reticence."

41. Bruce, *Rise and Fall,* 31.

42. Quoted in ibid., 68.

43. Christopher Lasch, *The Revolt of the Elites and the Betrayal of Democracy* (New York: Norton, 1995), 215.

44. Quoted in *U.S. News and World Report,* April 24, 1995, 39.

45. See, for instance, "The Power of James Dobson," *U.S. News and World Report,* May 4, 1998; "For God's Sake," *U.S. News and World Report,* April 24, 1995; "The Right Hand of God," *Time,* May 15, 1995; "Pat Robertson's God, Inc.," *Esquire,* November 1994; and "Life beyond God," *The New York Times Magazine,* October 16, 1994.

46. Peter Beinart, "Battle for the 'Burbs," *The New Republic,* October 19, 1998, 25–29.

47. Ibid., 27.

48. Irving Kristol, "Conservative Christians: Into the Fray," *Wall Street Journal,* December 22, 1995.

49. John Murray Cuddihy, *No Offense: Civil Religion and Protestant Taste* (New York: Seabury, 1978), 201.

50. Richard J. Mouw, "Evangelical Ethics in the Time of God's Patience: Recovering Some Neglected Themes" (paper presented at the inaugural conference for the Alonzo McDonald professorship in evangelical theological studies, Harvard Divinity School, February 13–14, 1998), 8–9.

51. Ralph Reed, *Active Faith: How Christians Are Changing the Soul of American Politics* (New York: Free Press, 1996), 262–263. Reed expressed the hope that when future historians look back at the Christian Coalition they will reflect on a movement that "had an uncommon commitment to caring for those in need, loving those who attacked us, and displaying the love, dignity, and decency that are the hallmarks of an active faith" (281).

52. Mark A. Noll, *Adding Cross to Crown: The Political Significance of Christ's Passion* (Grand Rapids, Mich.: Baker, 1996), 18.

53. Ibid., 32.

54. See especially Timothy Smith, *Revivalism and Social Reform: American Protestantism on the Eve of the Civil War* (1957; reprint, Baltimore: John Hopkins University Press, 1980); Donald Dayton, *Discovering an Evangelical Heritage* (New York: Harper and Row, 1976); Garth Lean, *God's Politician: William Wilberforce's Struggle* (London: Darton, Longman, and Todd, 1980); Ernest Marshall Howse, *Saints in Politics: The Clapham Sect*

(London: Unwin, 1974); and J. Wesley Bready, *England: Before and after Wesley* (London: Hodder and Stoughton, 1939).

55. Grant Wacker, "Uneasy in Zion: Evangelicals in Postmodern Society," in *Evangelicalism and Modern America*, ed. George Marsden (Grand Rapids, Mich.: Eerdmans, 1984), 26.

56. Alexis de Tocqueville, *Democracy in America* (New York: Vintage, 1945), 135.

57. Richard John Neuhaus, "The Christian and the Church," in *Transforming the World,* ed. James M. Boice (Portland: Multnomah, 1988), 120.

58. Max Weber, "Politics as Vocation," in *From Max Weber: Essays in Sociology*, ed. H. H. Gerth and C. Wright Mills (New York: Oxford University Press, 1958), 128.

59. Reinhold Niebuhr, *The Children of Light and the Children of Darkness* (New York: Scribner's, 1944), 118.

## Chapter 2: *From Despair to Mission*

1. Pope John Paul II, *Evangelium Vitae* (New York: Random House, 1995), 46.

2. Among other accounts of this sentiment, see "Unity Is Elusive as Religious Right Ponders 2000 Vote," *New York Times,* March 7, 1999, sec. A1.

3. Quoted in Gerald R. McDermott, "What Jonathan Edwards Can Teach Us about Politics," *Christianity Today,* July 18, 1994, 33.

4. It should be noted that the interpretation of what Jesus meant by the kingdom/reign of God is notoriously controversial. For one recent survey of scholarly opinion that takes the position I take here, see C. C. Caragounis, "Kingdom of God/Heaven," in *Dictionary of Jesus and the Gospels,* ed. Joel B. Green et al. (Downers Grove, Ill.: InterVarsity Press, 1992), 417–430.

5. The Reformed tradition, at least in its current presentation by such thinkers as James Skillen, is most helpful in unpacking the concepts of "sphere sovereignty" and "structural pluralism," in which various spheres of human life all function under divine authority but none is permitted to become the totalitarian ordering authority in human affairs. See Skillen, *Recharging the American Experiment* (Grand Rapids, Mich.: Baker, 1994), especially part 2.

6. A term I borrow from Stephen C. Mott's excellent book, *Biblical Ethics and Social Change* (New York: Oxford University Press, 1982), chapter 7.

7. Pope Leo XIII, *Rerum Novarum* (1891), 30, quoted in *Readings in Christian Ethics,* ed. J. Philip Wogaman and Douglas M. Strong (Louisville: Westminster John Knox, 1996), 281.

## Chapter 5: *Religion and the American Democracy*

1. Alan Wolfe, *One Nation after All* (New York: Penguin, 1998), 51.

2. Ibid., 63.
3. Ibid., 70.
4. Stephen Carter, *Civility* (New York: Harper, 1998), 224.
5. E. T. Dionne, *Why Americans Hate Politics* (New York: Touchstone, 1992).

## Chapter 6: *Toward an Evangelical Political Philosophy*

1. Mark Noll, *The Scandal of the Evangelical Mind* (Grand Rapids, Mich.: Eerdmans, 1994).
2. For example, *Recharging the American Experiment* (Grand Rapids, Mich.: Baker, 1995).
3. See my *Completely Pro-Life* (Downers Grove, Ill.: InterVarsity Press, 1987).
4. Ralph Reed, *Active Faith: How Christians Are Changing the Soul of American Politics* (New York: Free Press, 1996), 23.
5. See John Courtney Murray, *We Hold These Truths* (New York: Sheed and Ward, 1986); and J. Budziszewski, *Written on the Heart: The Case for Natural Law* (Downers Grove, Ill.: InterVarsity Press, 1997).
6. See, for example, my "Toward a Biblical Perspective on Equality," *Interpretation* (April–June 1989): 156–169, where I work toward a biblical paradigm on "economic equality." It is obvious that developing a canonical biblical paradigm on any issue involves many different steps: detailed exegesis of all relevant biblical passage, a hermeneutical understanding of the relationship between the Old and New Testaments, etc. Disagreement can arise at any point.
7. See my further comments on this in my "A Plea for More Radical Conservatives and More Conserving Radicals," *Transformation* (January–March 1987): 11–16.
8. This is not to argue for universalism (i.e., the salvation of every person).
9. In principle one would need to examine every relevant biblical passage using appropriate exegetical tools, understand the trajectory of biblical revelation on that issue, and then formulate a comprehensive canonical paradigm in each specific area. To develop each such paradigm requires a lifetime of exacting scholarship. Here I can only sketch in the briefest fashion what I believe would be the result of that kind of task. Undoubtedly, of course, my understanding is only partial. Wherever better exegesis and more faithful integration of all canonical material requires modification of the following brief parts, I eagerly agree to change them.
10. See an extended treatment of this issue in Stephen Mott and Ronald J. Sider, "Economic Justice: A Biblical Paradigm," in *Toward a Just and Caring Society,* ed. David P. Gushee (Grand Rapids, Mich.: Baker, 1999), 15–45.

**Chapter 8:** *Evangelicals and Politics in the Third World*

1. Rubem César Fernandes, *Censo Institucional Evangélico CIN 1992: Primeiros Comentários* (Rio de Janeiro: ISER, 1992).

2. David Stoll, "'Jesus Is Lord of Guatemala': Evangelical Reform in a Death-Squad State," in *Accounting for Fundamentalisms,* ed. M. Marty and R. Scott Appleby (Chicago: University of Chicago Press, 1994), 99–123.

3. Daniel Levine and David Stoll, "Bridging the Gap between Empowerment and Power in Latin America," in *Transnational Religion and Fading States,* ed. Susanne Hoeber Rudolph and James Piscatori (Boulder, Colo.: Westview, 1997), 63–103.

4. James Grenfell, "The Participation of Protestants in Politics in Guatemala" (master's thesis, Oxford University, 1995).

5. Daniela Helmsdorff, "Participacíon Política Evangélica en Colombia," *Historia Crítica,* January–June 1996, 79–84.

6. Timothy Paul Longman, "Christianity and Democratisation in Rwanda: Assessing Church Responses to Political Crisis in the 1990s," in *The Christian Churches and the Democratisation of Africa,* ed. Paul Gifford (Leiden: Brill, 1995), 187–204.

7. Roger Bowen, "Rwanda: Missionary Reflections on a Catastrophe," *Anvil* 13 no. 1 (1996): 33–44.

8. Gordon White, "Civil Society, Democratization and Development (II): Two Country Cases," *Democratization* 2 no. 2 (summer 1995) 56–84.

9. *Africa Confidential,* February 14, 1997.

10. Donald Chanda, ed., *Democracy in Zambia: Key Speeches of President Chiluba 1991/92* (Lusaka: Africa Press Trust, n.d.), 78.

11. Paul Gifford, "Chiluba's Christian Nation: The Churches in Zambian Politics" (paper presented at the African Studies Association of the U.K., Bristol, September 1996), 4.

12. Ibid., 15.

13. Quoted in David Throup, "'Render unto Caesar the Things That Are Caesar's': The Politics of Church-State Conflict in Kenya, 1978–1990," in *Religion and Politics in East Africa,* ed. Holger Bengt Hansen and Michael Twaddle (London: James Currey, 1995), 146.

14. G. P. Benson, "Ideological Politics versus Biblical Hermeneutics: Kenya's Protestant Churches and the Nyayo State," in *Religion and Politics in East Africa,* ed. Holger Bengt Hansen and Michael Twaddle (London: James Currey, 1995), 185.

15. Throup, "'Render unto Caesar,'" 160.

16. David Gitari, *In Season and Out of Season: Sermons to a Nation* (Carlisle: Regnum, 1996), 108.

17. Ibid., 109.

18. Ibid., 112.

19. Ibid., 118.
20. Ibid., 114.

**Chapter 9:** *Christian Faith and Educational Policy*

1. Judith Rich Harris, *The Nurture Assumption* (New York: Free Press, 1998).

2. Lamar Alexander, introduction to *Time for Results: The Governors' 1991 Report on Education* (Washington, D.C.: National Governors Association, 1986).

3. B. K. Eakman, "It's about Mental Health, Stupid," *Education Week,* October 20, 1993, 40.

4. Ibid., 43.

5. E. D. Hirsch, *The Schools We Need . . . and Why We Don't Have Them* (New York: Doubleday, 1996).

6. Jay P. Greene, "Civic Values in Public and Private Schools," in *Learning from School Choice* (Washington, D.C.: Brookings Institution Press, 1998), 96–98.

**Chapter 10:** *The Divorce Epidemic*

1. The author gratefully acknowledges the research assistance of Jessica Pritchett.

2. For a discussion of the constitutive dimension of marriage and divorce law, see Milton C. Regan, Jr., "Postmodern Family Law: Toward a New Model of Status," in *Promises to Keep,* ed. David Popenoe et al. (Lanham, Md.: Rowman and Littlefield, 1996).

3. American Bar Association, *Guide to Family Law* (New York: Random House, 1996), 21. Interestingly, after a sad chapter on the decision to divorce, this guide says, "Perhaps if before marriage, prospective husbands and wives spent more time exploring issues they will have to deal with during marriage, the divorce rate would be lower" (p. 62). Yet they do not suggest any legal reforms to that end, as we will do here.

4. Reported in Michael McManus, "Florida Passes Nation's Most Sweeping Reform of Marriage Law." Cited May 16, 1998, in http://www.smartmarriages.com/mcmanvsflorida.html.

5. Ann Scott Tyson, "States Put Speed Bumps in Divorce Path," *Christian Science Monitor,* September 10, 1996. See also Pia Nordlinger, "The Anti-Divorce Revolution," *Weekly Standard,* March 2, 1998, 26.

6. News release from office of Rep. Jessie Dalman, "Proposal to Abolish No-Fault Divorce," House Republican Communication Services, Lansing, Michigan, February 14, 1996.

7. Will Sentell, *Kansas City Star.* Cited March 12, 1998, in http://archives.his.com/smartmarriages/smartmarriages.9803/0024.html. To receive the

money, couples would also have to certify that they had never had a child.

8. Carl E. Schneider, "The Law and the Stability of Marriage: The Family as a Social Institution," in Popenoe, *Promises to Keep,* 196.

9. Quoted in Nordlinger, "Anti-Divorce Revolution," 27.

10. See Michael J. McManus, *Marriage Savers,* 2d ed. (Grand Rapids, Mich.: Zondervan, 1998), chapter 7.

11. Regan, "Postmodern Family Law," 166.

12. Sylvia Ann Hewlett and Cornel West, *The War against Parents* (New York: Houghton Mifflin, 1998), 242.

13. Ibid., chapter 9.

14. For a discussion of some of the starkly different approaches that go by the name of "pro-family" politics, see David P. Gushee, "Family Values?" *Prism* 3, no. 4 (May–June 1996): 15–17.

15. For the concept of marriage as a status relationship, see Regan, "Postmodern Family Law," 157–171.

16. Among the most common fault grounds that appear in state laws are adultery, physical and mental cruelty, attempted murder, desertion, habitual drunkenness, use of addictive drugs, insanity, impotence, and infection of one's spouse with a venereal disease. See American Bar Association, *Guide to Family Law,* 68–69.

17. For this analysis, see Mary Ann Glendon, *Abortion and Divorce in Western Law* (Cambridge: Harvard University Press, 1987), 65.

18. Ibid., 79–80.

19. Ibid., 66.

20. Barbara DaFoe Whitehead, *The Divorce Culture* (New York: Knopf, 1997).

21. Thomas Morgan, George Washington University law professor, quoted in Amitai Etzioni, "How to Make Marriage Matter," *Time,* September 6, 1993, 76.

22. Bryce J. Christensen, "Taking Stock: Assessing Twenty Years of 'No Fault' Divorce," *The Family in America* 5, no. 9 (September 1991): 3.

23. Ibid., 4.

24. See Lenore J. Weitzman, *The Divorce Revolution: The Unexpected Social and Economic Consequences for Women and Children in America* (New York: Free Press, 1985). Weitzman's dramatic findings have been modified by later research, though the negative economic impact of divorce on women and children is a settled matter in current scholarship. For an authoritative recent analysis, see Council of Economic Advisory, *1998 Economic Report of the President* (Washington, D.C.: Government Printing Office, 1998), chapters 3 and 4. Accessed at http//www.access.gpo.gov/eop.

25. See Barbara DaFoe Whitehead, "The Divorce Trap," *New York Times,* January 13, 1997.

26. Daniel Sitarz, *Divorce Yourself: The National No-Fault Divorce Kit,* 3d ed. (Carbondale, Ill.: Nova, 1994), 312.

27. Amy Black, "For the Sake of the Children: Reconstructing American Divorce Policy," *Crossroads Monograph Series on Faith and Public Policy* 1, no. 2 (1995), 40.

28. For the text of the Georgia bill, see http://www2.state.ga.us/legis/1997-98/leg/fulltext/hb1472.htm.

29. Nordlinger, "Anti-Divorce Revolution," 26.

30. William A. Galston, "The Reinstitutionalization of Marriage: Political Theory and Public Policy," in Popenoe, *Promises to Keep,* 285–286.

31. Glendon, *Abortion and Divorce,* 77–78.

32. Schneider, "The Law and the Stability of Marriage," 202.

33. Glendon, *Abortion and Divorce,* 74.

34. Elizabeth S. Scott, "Rational Decisionmaking about Marriage and Divorce," *Virginia Law Review* 76 (1990), quoted in Schneider, "The Law and the Stability of Marriage," 200–201.

35. For a list of covenant marriage precursors, see http://www.divorce reform.org/wv.html anchor 1282489.

36. Etzioni, "How to Make Marriage Matter," *Time,* September 6, 1993, 76. For another early article, see Christopher Wolfe, "The Marriage of Your Choice," *First Things* 50 (February 1995): 37–41.

37. David Boaz, "Private Marriage," http://www.divorcereform.org/lea.html.

38. As reported by Religion News Service, November 11, 1997.

39. Galston, "Reinstitutionalization of Marriage," 285–287.

40. Perhaps the best recent works documenting these consequences are Judith Wallerstein and Sandra Blakeslee, *Second Chances: Men, Women, and Children a Decade after Divorce* (Boston: Houghton Mifflin, 1996); David B. Larson, et al., *The Costly Consequences of Divorce: Assessing the Clinical, Economic, and Public Health Impact of Marital Disruption in the United States* (Rockville, Md.: National Institute for HealthCare Research, n.d.); Paul R. Amato and Alan Booth, *A Generation at Risk: Growing Up in an Era of Family Upheaval* (Cambridge: Harvard University Press, 1998).

41. See Amato and Booth, *A Generation at Risk,* 220.

42. See Wallerstein and Blakeslee, *Second Chances.* For a powerful glimpse at an all-too-typical young couple who are both children of divorce, see Tamara Jones, "The Commitment," *Washington Post Magazine,* May 10, 1998, 8–13, 21–26.

43. See William A. Galston, "Divorce American Style," *The Public Interest* (summer 1996): 14.

44. Black, "For the Sake of the Children," 40.

45. Galston, "Reinstitutionalization of Marriage," 286.

46. For complete text of the 1998 law, see http://www.leg.state.fl.us/session/1998/house/bills/billtext/html/billtext/hb1019e1.html.

47. Quoted by Schneider, "The Law and the Stability of Marriage," 206–207.

48. The best available statement calling for just such a partnership is "Marriage in America: A Report to the Nation," authored by the Council on Families in America. See Popenoe, *Promises to Keep,* 293–318.

## Chapter 11: *Welfare Reform's Challenge to the Evangelical Church*

1. The program in Anne Arundel County, Maryland, is called the Community-Directed Assistance Program. It is a state pilot program, started before federal welfare reform. For a description and evaluation, see Amy L. Sherman, *Fruitful Collaboration between Government and Christian Social Ministries: Lessons from Virginia and Maryland,* Policy Papers from the Religious Social Sector Project (Washington, D.C.: Center for Public Justice, January 1998). The speech included above is a synthesis based on a presentation by a program representative to a church committee, discussions with program staff, and published information about the program.

2. Amy L. Sherman, *Establishing a Church-Based Welfare-to-Work Mentoring Ministry: A Practical "How-To" Manual* (New York: Center for Civic Innovation at the Manhattan Institute, 1999.) A helpful compilation of the verses is found in Ronald J. Sider, ed., *Cry Justice: The Bible Speaks on Hunger and Poverty* (Downers Grove, Ill.: InterVarsity Press, 1980).

3. See Marvin Olasky, *The Tragedy of American Compassion* (Washington, D.C.: Regnery Gateway, 1992); and Marvin Olasky, "Beyond the Stingy Welfare State," *Stewardship Journal* 1, no. 1 (winter 1991): 41–54.

4. John Perkins with Jo Kadlecek, *Resurrecting Hope* (Ventura, Calif.: Regal, 1995), 24.

5. On the CCDA and this strategy, see John M. Perkins, ed., *Restoring At-Risk Communities: Doing It Together and Doing It Right* (Grand Rapids, Mich.: Baker, 1995).

6. See, e.g., Donald Dayton, *Discovering an Evangelical Heritage* (New York: Harper and Row, 1976); Norris Magnuson, *Salvation in the Slums: Evangelical Social Work, 1865–1920* (Grand Rapids, Mich.: Baker, 1990); and Olasky, *Tragedy of American Compassion.* Of course the Christian tradition more broadly has always included a strong social component. For an illuminating treatment of the earliest centuries, see Rodney Stark, *The Rise of Christianity* (San Francisco: HarperSanFrancisco, 1997).

7. David O. Moberg, *The Great Reversal: Evangelism and Social Concern,* rev. ed. (Philadelphia: Lippincott, 1977).

8. Sherman, *Establishing a Church-Based Welfare-to-Work Mentoring Ministry,* 5; see also Amy L. Sherman, *Restorers of Hope: Reaching the Poor in Your Community with Church-Based Ministries That Work* (Wheaton, Ill.:

Crossway, 1997); Perkins, *Restoring At-Risk Communities*; John M. Perkins, *Beyond Charity: The Call to Christian Community Development* (Grand Rapids, Mich.: Baker, 1993); and Virgil Gulker with Kevin Perrotta, *Help Is Just around the Corner: How Love Inc. Mobilizes Care for the Needy* (Lake Mary, Fla.: Creation House, 1988).

9. Sherman, *Establishing a Church-Based Welfare-to-Work Mentoring Ministry*, 6.

10. Amy L. Sherman, "A Call for Church Welfare Reform," *Christianity Today*, October 6, 1997, 46–50.

11. For a biblically grounded perspective defining government's responsibilities as both constructive and limited, see Luis E. Lugo, *Equal Partners: The Welfare Responsibility of Governments and Churches* (Washington, D.C.: Center for Public Justice, 1998); Luis E. Lugo, "Caesar's Coin and the Politics of the Kingdom: A Pluralist Perspective," in *Caesar's Coin Revisited: Christians and the Limits of Government,* ed. Michael Cromartie (Washington, D.C.: Ethics and Public Policy Center/Grand Rapids, Mich.: Eerdmans, 1996), 1–22; James W. Skillen, *Recharging the American Experiment: Principled Pluralism for Genuine Civic Community* (Grand Rapids, Mich.: Baker, 1994); Paul Marshall, *Thine Is the Kingdom: A Biblical Perspective on the Nature of Government and Politics Today* (Grand Rapids, Mich.: Eerdmans, 1986); and Bernard Zylstra, "The Bible, Justice, and the State," in *Confessing Christ and Doing Politics,* ed. James W. Skillen (Washington, D.C.: Association for Public Justice Education Fund, 1982), 39–53.

12. On the welfare content of government's responsibility to do justice, see especially Lugo, *Equal Partners;* and John D. Mason, "Biblical Teaching and the Objectives of Welfare Policy in the United States," and Stephen Charles Mott, "Foundations of the Welfare Responsibility of the Government," both in *Welfare in America: Christian Perspectives on a Policy in Crisis,* ed. Stanley W. Carlson-Thies and James W. Skillen (Grand Rapids, Mich.: Eerdmans, 1996).

13. Kirk Fordice, "Welfare That Works: Faith and Families," *Policy Insights* 710 (November 1995): 1.

14. For an extensive and insightful examination of the program as a cooperative effort between government and the churches, see Amy L. Sherman, *Mississippi's Faith and Families Congregational Mentoring Program* (Washington, D.C.: Center for Public Justice, January 1998).

15. Cf. Stanley W. Carlson-Thies, "[On a Charity Tax Credit:] There Is No Substitute for Government's Special Role in Fighting Poverty," *Policy Review* 87 (January–February 1998): 40–41.

16. Quoted in Mott, "Foundations," 194.

17. Welfare Responsibility Project, "A New Vision for Welfare Reform: An Essay in Draft," reprinted in Carlson-Thies and Skillen, *Welfare in America,* 577.

18. Ibid., 578.

19. This pluralist or enabling idea of government is rooted in the Catholic tradition of subsidiary and the Calvinist or Kuyperian tradition of sphere sovereignty. See Lugo, *Equal Partners,* and James W. Skillen and Rockne M. McCarthy, eds., *Political Order and the Plural Structure of Society* (Atlanta: Scholars, 1991). The idea was pushed into the public policy arena especially by Peter L. Berger and Richard John Neuhaus, *To Empower People* (1977), reprinted in Berger and Neuhaus, *To Empower People: From State to Civil Society,* ed. Michael Novak (Washington, D.C.: AEI Press, 1996).

20. See, e.g., U.S. General Accounting Office, *Welfare Reform: States Are Restructuring Programs to Reduce Welfare Dependence,* GAO/HEHS-98-109 (Washington, D.C.: GAO, June 1998).

21. See, e.g., Sherman, *Fruitful Collaboration*; Sherman, *Restorers of Hope;* Government Affairs Department of the American Public Welfare Association, *State Human Service Mentoring Programs* (Washington, D.C.: APWA, October 1997); Jessica Yates, "Partnership with the Faith Community in Welfare Reform" (March 1998), posted at www.welfareinfo.org/faith.htm.

22. Stephen V. Monsma, *When Sacred and Secular Mix: Religious Nonprofit Organizations and Public Money* (Lanham, Md.: Rowman and Littlefield, 1996).

23. The point is emphasized by Monsma, *When Sacred and Secular Mix.* For details of typical regulations, see Carl H. Esbeck, *The Regulation of Religious Organizations as Recipients of Governmental Assistance* (Washington, D.C.: Center for Public Justice, 1996).

24. For a detailed explanation of the provision, see *A Guide to Charitable Choice: The Rules of Section 104 of the 1996 Federal Welfare Law Governing State Cooperation with Faith-Based Social-Service Providers* (Washington, D.C.: Center for Public Justice/Annandale, Va.: Center for Law and Religious Freedom of the Christian Legal Society, January 1997). On the significance of the provision, see Stanley W. Carlson-Thies, "Faith-Based Institutions Cooperating with Public Welfare: The Promise of the Charitable Choice Provision," in *Welfare Reform and Faith-Based Organizations,* ed. Derek H. Davis and Barry Hankins (Waco, Tex.: Dawson Institute of Church-State Studies, 1999). For a quick introduction to the provision and to the controversy over it, see Stanley W. Carlson-Thies and Melissa Rogers, "Charitable Choice: Two Views," *Sojourners* 27, no. 4 (July–August 1998): 28–30.

### Chapter 12: *Refugees*

1. Elie Wiesel, "Longing for Home," in *The Longing for Home,* ed. Leroy S. Rouner (Notre Dame: University of Notre Dame Press, 1996), 19.

2. U.S. Committee for Refugees, *World Refugee Survey 1998* (Washington, D.C.: Immigration and Refugee Services of America, 1998), 4–6. Precise counts on the numbers of refugees and internally displaced persons at any moment are extremely difficult to come by.

3. Myron Weiner and Rainer Munz, "Migrants, Refugees, and Foreign Policy: Prevention and Intervention Strategies," *Third World Quarterly* 18, no. 1 (March 1997): 44–45.

4. Gil Loescher, *Beyond Charity: International Cooperation and the Global Refugee Crisis* (New York: Oxford University Press, 1993), 91.

5. United Nations High Commissioner for Refugees, *The State of the World's Refugees 1997–98: A Humanitarian Agenda* (New York: Oxford University Press, 1997), 1.

6. Ibid., 31.

7. Ibid., 25.

8. U.S. Policy Initiatives Related to Refugee Women, *Fact Sheet,* 1997 (Washington, D.C.: Bureau of Population, Refugees, and Migration, March 1997), 1.

9. See Elizabeth G. Ferris, *Beyond Borders: Refugees, Migrants, and Human Rights in the Post-Cold War Era* (Geneva: WCC Publications, 1993), xviii–xxiii.

10. Article I, 1951 UN convention relating to the Status of Refugees, on *Refworld* CD-Rom (Geneva: UNHCR, 1997), quoted in UNHCR, *State of the World's Refugees,* 51.

11. Loescher, *Beyond Charity,* 6.

12. Ibid., 151.

13. See UNHCR, *State of the World's Refugees,* 116–118.

14. Ibid., 52–53.

15. U.S. Committee for Refugees, *World Refugee Survey 1998,* 243.

16. Loescher, *Beyond Charity,* 131.

17. Ibid.

18. Article 33 of the Refugee Convention, quoted in Loescher, *Beyond Charity,* 143. See also UNHCR, *State of the World's Refugees,* 184.

19. See UNHCR, *State of the World's Refugees,* 86–89.

20. U.S. Committee for Refugees, *World Refugee Survey 1997* (Washington, D.C.: Immigration and Refugee Services of America, 1997), 54.

21. UNHCR, *State of the World's Refugees,* 64.

22. Loescher, *Beyond Charity,* 99.

23. Quoted in UNHCR, *State of the World's Refugees,* 204.

24. Ibid., 69.

25. Ibid., 48, 39–41.

26. Ibid., 80, 41.

27. USCR, *World Refugee Survey 1997,* 16.

28. Ibid., 27.

29. UNHCR, *State of the World's Refugees*, 147–148, 154.

30. Gil Loescher, "The International Refugee Regime: Stretched to the Limit?" *Journal of International Affairs* 47, no. 2 (winter 1994): 376–377.

31. Loescher, *Beyond Charity*, 39.

32. Gil Loescher and John A. Scanlan, *Calculated Kindness* (New York: Free Press, 1986), 209.

33. Quoted in John H. Leith, *John Calvin's Doctrine of the Christian Life* (Louisville: Westminster John Knox, 1989), 186; and John Calvin, *Commentary on a Harmony of the Evangelists, Matthew, Mark, and Luke*, 3 vols. (Grand Rapids, Mich.: Eerdmans, 1949), 3:61–62.

34. See an example of this argument in the fourth-century Christian writer Lactantius in *The Divine Institutes*, book 6, chapter 12, *Ante-Nicene Fathers*, vol. 7 (Grand Rapids, Mich.: Eerdmans, 1979) 176–177. For a fuller discussion of Christian hospitality, see Christine D. Pohl, *Making Room: Recovering Hospitality as a Christian Tradition* (Grand Rapids, Mich.: Eerdmans, 1999).

35. John Calvin, *Commentaries on the Epistles to Timothy, Titus and Philemon* (Grand Rapids, Mich.: Eerdmans, 1948), 79.

36. John Wesley, "On Visiting the Sick," sermon 98 in *The Works of John Wesley*, vol. 3: *Sermons 3:71–114* (Nashville: Abingdon, 1986), 387–388.

37. See Stephen C. Mott, *Biblical Ethics and Social Change* (New York: Oxford University Press, 1982), 49–53.

38. See UNHCR, *State of the World's Refugees*, 89.

39. Ibid., 85.

40. See Susan Martin and Andy Schoenholtz, "Fixing Temporary Protection in the United States," in USCR, *World Refugee Survey* 1998, 40–47.

## Chapter 13: *Where Church and State Intersect*

1. *Everson v. Board of Education*, 330 US at 18 (1947).

2. *Everson v. Board of Education*, at 16 (1947).

3. *Abington School District v. Schempp*, 374 US at 217 (1963). Emphasis added.

4 . Ibid., at 226.

5. *Everson v. Board of Education*, at 18 (1947).

6. *Mueller v. Allen*, 463 US at 404 (1983).

7. A. James Reichley, *Religion in American Public Life* (Washington, D.C.: Brookings, 1985), 165. Reichley's emphasis.

8. *Rosenberger v. Rector*, Court of Appeals for the Fourth Circuit, 18 F.3rd 281, 1994.

9. Ibid.

10. There is a potential for confusion in my use of the term "substantive neutrality" to describe this position. This concept is itself rooted in

a particular view of religion and its proper role in society and of government and its proper role in society. Thus "substantive neutrality" is itself not neutral in that it claims a certain, specified relationship that ought to prevail between religion and government. But I am convinced that the relationship that ought to exist between government and religion is one of neutrality, with neutrality defined as government pursuing policies that will not make it easier or harder for anyone to follow his or her religious beliefs or his or her nonreligious, secular beliefs. See Stephen V. Monsma, *Positive Neutrality* (Grand Rapids, Mich.: Baker, 1995); and Douglas Laycock, "Formal, Substantive, and Disaggregated Neutrality towards Religion," *DePaul Law Review* 39 (1990): 993–1018.

11. *Rosenberger v. Rector,* 515 US at 839 (1995).

12. Ibid., at 847.

13. Ibid., at 882.

14. *Lee v. Weisman,* 60 LW 4731 (1992).

15. *Grand Rapids School District v. Ball,* 473 US at 385 (1985). This decision was partially overturned in 1997 in *Felton v. Agostini.*

16. The cases are *Widmar v. Vincent,* 454 US 263 (1981); *Lamb's Chapel v. Center Moriches School District,* 508 US 398 (1993); *Witters v. Washington Department of Services for the Blind,* 474 US 481 (1986); *Agostini v. Felton,* 1997 US Lexis 4000.

17. On charitable choice, see *A Guide to Charitable Choice* (Washington, D.C.: Center for Public Justice/Annandale, Va.: Center for Law and Religious Freedom, 1997).

18. See Americans United for Separation of Church and State, "Why 'Charitable Choice' Is Wrong," and Barry Lynn, "The 'Charitable Choice' Charade," *Church and State* 51 (February 1998): 7–12.

19. Ibid., 12.

20. Howard Thompson, "Christian Agendas Underlying Issue," *Austin American-Statesman,* October 6, 1998, sec. A., p. 11.

21. Stephen L. Carter, *The Culture of Disbelief* (New York: Basic Books, 1993), 54.

22. *Bishop v. Aronov,* 926 F.2d 1076 (1991).

23. U.S. Department of Health, Education, and Welfare, Public Health Service, Alcohol, Drug Abuse, and Mental Health Administration, National Institute on Drug Abuse, "An Evaluation of the Teen Challenge Treatment Program" (Washington, D.C.: GPO, 1977), 10–11.

24. Bryon R. Johnson, David B. Larson, and Timothy C. Pitts, "Religious Programs, Institutional Adjustment, and Recidivism among Former Inmates in Prison Fellowship Programs," *Justice Quarterly* 14 (March 1997): 145–166.

25. See Richard Lacayo, "Parochial Politics," *Time,* September 23, 1996, 31–32. There are a host of studies demonstrating that poor and minority

students, especially, fare dramatically better in Catholic than in public schools. See, for example, Anthony S. Bryk, Valerie E. Lee, and Peter B. Holland, *Catholic Schools and the Common Good* (Cambridge: Harvard University Press, 1993); and James S. Coleman, Thomas Hoffer, and Sally Kilgore, *High School Achievement: Public, Catholic, and Private Schools Compared* (New York: Basic Books, 1982).

## Chapter 15: *Just Peacemaking*

1. Michelle Tooley, *Voices of the Voiceless: Women, Justice, and Human Rights in Guatemala* (Scottsdale, Pa.: Herald Press, 1997), 84, 89–91.

2. Glen Stassen, ed., *Just Peacemaking: Ten Practices for Abolishing War*, 138, 141.

3. Ibid., 165–167.

4. Ibid., 179.

5. Ibid., 169.

6. Ibid., 21.

# INDEX

Faith and Families program 173
Falwell, Jerry 22, 231 n. 32
family 37, 61, 64, 81, 87, 90, 91, 96, 134, 172
Family Research Council 23, 38, 95
fearfulness 74
First Amendment 32, 60, 91, 95, 141, 196–204
Focus on the Family 38
force, just use of 53–55
Ford, Gerald 97
Ford, John 77
Fordice, Kirk 173, 175
forgiveness 217–218
Forrest, Nathan Bedford 102
freedom 90
    and restraint 73
free exercise of religion. *See* First Amendment
Fuller Theological Seminary 19, 220, 221
fundamentalist-modernist controversy 17
fundamentalists 18–20, 24, 26
    pessimistic eschatology 230 n. 8

Gaebelein, Frank 21
Gallup, George 103
Galston, William 156, 161
Gandhi 94, 214
Garrison, William Lloyd 74
Gay, Craig 18
general revelation 82–83
genocide 113–115
George, Francis Cardinal 73
Gifford, Paul 119
Gitari, David 121, 122–124
Glazer, Nathan 23–24
Glendon, Mary Ann 157
globalization 105–106, 107
gnosticism 34
Good Samaritan 168, 170, 189
Gorbachev, Mikhail 224
government 47–48, 89
    limits 49
    role 19–20, 81, 92, 101, 171–175
    suspicions toward 171

Great Commission 40
"Great Reversal" 169
Greene, Jay 138–139
Grenfell, James 112
Grounds, Vernon 21
Guatemala 110, 111–112, 125, 188, 215
Guernica 217
Gurstein, Rochelle 231 n. 40
Gusfield, Joseph 23

Haiti 188, 216
Harris, Judith 133
Havel, Václav 62
"health and wealth" gospel 21
Helmsdorff, Daniela 113
Henry, Carl 19–20, 21
Hewlett, Sylvia Ann 151
Hines, Richard 99–100
Hippocratic Oath 208
Hirsch, E. D., Jr. 133, 137
Hitler, Adolf 210, 217–218
Hofstadter, Richard 22
Holocaust 210
Holy Spirit 35
homelessness 62
home schooling 132–133
homosexuality 31, 134
Honecker, Eric 212–213
hospitality 189, 192
Hudson, Winthrop 16
human dignity 87
human life
    consistent ethic 65, 67, 81, 93–94, 95
    sanctity 206, 210
human responsibility 47, 48
human rights 91, 114, 121, 185, 187, 191, 214–216, 219, 222
    abuses 187, 188
humility 84–85
hunger 62
Hutu 113–114

image of God 51, 87, 189
immigration 62, 182, 183
incentives, in public policy 146
indifference 72

United Nations High Commissioner on
	Refugees 180, 184, 185, 186,
	192
United States
	business interests and human
		rights violations 188
	moral leadership 192–193
	as Protestant nation 16
	refugee policy 187–194
	spiritual malaise 103
Universal Church of the Kingdom of
	God (Brazil) 110–111
University of Alabama 197–198, 200,
	202
University of Virginia 198–199, 200

values 30
	"imposing" 132, 140
Vietnam War 226
viewpoint discrimination 135
violence 62–63, 65
vision 64
Volf, Miroslav 220
voluntary associations 90, 224
volunteerism 170–171, 174
vouchers 138–140

Wacker, Grant 26
Walesa, Lech 62
wall of separation 195–196
Wallis, Jim 20–21
war 216–217, 222–223

*Washington Post* 16
Watergate 100
"We Hold These Truths" 96
Weber, Max 27
Weitzman, Lenore J. 237 n. 24
Weizsäcker, Karl Friedrich von 218
welfare 93, 165–178
Wesley, John 191
Wesleyans 80
West, Cornel 151
western civilization 32–33, 70
Whitehead, Barbara DaFoe 153
widows 190
Wiesel, Elie 179
Wilberforce, William 26, 169
Wink, Walter 222
Winthrop, John 27
Witness for Peace 215, 225
Wolf, Christian 227
Wolfe, Alan 73–75
women, justice for 31
work 88, 92–93
World Relief 184
World War II 226

Yugoslavia 219, 222

Zambia 115–120
Zionism 117
zoning 52
Zumach, Andreas 212